D1596587

TONGUE
SCREWS AND
TESTIMONIES

"I finished *Tongue Screws and Testimonies* with my heart strangely warmed. I was especially moved by observing three generations of writers engaged in the common task of re-interpreting for today the book that stands at the beginning of Mennonite literary and visual art. More than any scholarly essay, these provocative poems, narratives, and essays refresh and make relevant a book now in its fourth century of use."

—Ervin Beck, Editor, *Journal of the Center for Mennonite Writing* (www.mennonitewriting.org/journal)

"It matters how we think about violence perpetrated or accepted in faith. It matters what we make of the religious violence in our past or the past of those we love, have as neighbors, or hear of (supposedly) far away. Allowing artists to help us in this work is essential. So dive in—let this collection provoke you and make you squirm. Be amused. You may even jump up and shout 'Amen' a time or two."

—Nancy R. Heisey, dean, Eastern Mennonite University and author of a dissertation on Origen's *Exhortation to Martyrdom*

"Three-hundred-fifty years after its first publication in the Netherlands, the *Martyrs Mirror* still has the power to evoke awe, fear, inspiration and horror. This remarkable collection of poetry, stories, essays, and artwork is microcosm of contemporary Mennonite culture refracted through the prism of this powerful text. Original and creative, *Tongue Screws and Testimonies* is a witness to the collective memory and spirituality of a people. Read it to be informed, stirred, and possibly even provoked."

—John D. Roth, Professor of History, Goshen College

TONGUE SCREWS AND TESTIMONIES

POEMS, STORIES, AND ESSAYS INSPIRED BY THE MARTYRS MIRROR

EDITED BY KIRSTEN EVE BEACHY

FOREWORD BY JULIA SPICHER KASDORF

Herald Press
Scottdale, Pennsylvania
Waterloo, Ontario

Library of Congress Cataloging-in-Publication Data
Tongue screws and testimonies : poems, stories, and essays inspired by The martyrs mirror / edited by Kirsten Beachy.
   p. cm.
  Includes index.
  ISBN 978-0-8361-9519-4 (pbk. : alk. paper)
  1. Christian martyrs—Literary collections. 2. Anabaptists—Literary collections. 3. Mennonites—Literary collections. 4. Martyrdom in literature. 5. Braght, Thieleman J. van (Thieleman Janszoon), 1625-1664. Bloedig toneel. I. Beachy, Kirsten, 1979-
  PS509.C55T66 2010
  810.8'08382897—dc22

                                            2010029443

Scripture quotations marked NRSV are from the *New Revised Standard Version Bible*, copyright © 1989, by the Division of Christian Education of the National Council of the Churches of Christ in the USA and are used by permission. Scripture quotations marked KJV are quoted from the King James Version.

For the bulk of material in this volume, further copyright information is included in the "Credits" section on pages 301-5.

To an expanding family of writers and readers.

Contents

MEMORY

ENEMIES

HEIRS

Foreword

Farmers, cats, and writers don't like to take orders from anyone—nor do heretics and martyrs. The best fruits of an author's labor rarely come from heeding assignments or obligations, but instead grow from whatever grabs the imagination. Given the particular kinds of violence now afoot in the world, some writers have been drawn to the spectacle of martyrdom, its motivations and complicated legacies. This collection demonstrates that quite a few North Americans with various ties to the Anabaptist diaspora have also chosen to work with their own martyr memories.

I had no idea that such a quantity and range of imaginative writing on this topic existed—much of it already in print—last spring when Gerald Mast and the Mennonite Historical Society convened formal conversations at Goshen College and Bluffton University to seek new directions for scholarly and editorial work on *Martyrs Mirror*, the 17th century martyrology central to the identity of groups who trace their origins to the pacifist wing of the Anabaptist movement. Mast offered a brief bibliography of literary prose related to the big book, but talk moved in other directions: toward the feasibility of publishing a new translation or annotated edition, toward finding fresh approaches to history or gathering narratives of sacrifice since 1660.

During the Bluffton conversation I wondered aloud whether creative writing might also present a useful approach to this cultural artifact, and especially to the communal memories and identities it creates. Mast's enthusiasm for an anthology of contemporary writing in response to *Martyrs Mirror*, along with the support of Jeff Gundy, helped to launch this project that afternoon. But we are not the first Mennonites to recognize that literature can be a valuable form of cultural inquiry and knowledge.

John Ruth made a similar point in 1978 when he delivered the Menno Simons lectures at Bethel College, later published in a Herald Press booklet titled "Mennonite Identity and Literary Art." Apart from Canadian Rudy Wiebe and American Dallas Wiebe, no Mennonites had published with major mainstream presses then. Yet Ruth predicted the emergence of a Mennonite literature in

English and warned against the literary sensationalism and cultural assimilation he witnessed among other American subcultures. For instance, he pointed to Philip Roth, accused of being a "self-hating Jew" after *Portnoy's Complaint* was published in 1969. That novel deals with ethnic and religious identity and the psychic weight of history, even as Portnoy agonizes about his own sexual liberation. This can be no model for Mennonite literature, Ruth admonished.

> Shall I take my cue from the taste in current fictional protagonists? There he is, waiting impatiently in the wings for his Mennonite incarnation: the sentimentally conceived *schlemiel* of a thousand current novels, poised for his agonized quest of authentic being that will drive him through a series of colorful trysts with Mennonite coeds, conveniently sharing his eagerness to be disburdened of moribund inhibitions. Thus will they exorcise, if they are true to their best-selling precedents, the falsely ascetic, intolerable myth of the *Martyrs Mirror*, sequel by sequel outperforming their honest profanity and compulsive lubricity while they pursue an increasingly aimless war against hypocrisy.

> No. Mennonites don't need such evidence that we, too, can be packaged and sold in the market-place of literary sensation. We don't need the equivalent of an *Ebony* magazine to show us ourselves in expensive clothes and staggeringly over-powered automobiles, so that we can feel real, while hucksters persuade us, figuratively speaking, to buy hair-oil to straighten out our cultural kinks and make us normal Americans. The Mennonite writer has much more interesting possibilities than proving that he too can dissolve his covenant-identity in that kind of success. He can tell his story. (Ruth, 68)

His story, according to Ruth, lies in the collective memory of the faith community, retained in oral tradition or inscribed in *Martyrs Mirror*. The writer must be free to remember, to see and to "wrestle" with whatever she finds in these sources, Ruth argues, and every version of the authentic Mennonite story will be unique.

When I first read his booklet some years ago, I resisted Ruth's directives as any willful young writer might. But in this anthology we have the fulfillment of "Mennonite Identity and Literary Art." These writers have not exorcized "the falsely ascetic, intolerable myth of the *Martyrs Mirror*" from their minds or bodies by any means! Instead, martyrdom has inspired fine works of fiction, poetry, and essay—some earnest, some ironic and witty, and perhaps far from the tales of "covenant identity" that Ruth imagined in the 1970s. With a Mennonite memoir stubbornly stuck on the *New York Times* bestseller list this past summer and a Mennonite novel on the Canadian bestseller list for more than a year during 2004–2005, Mennonite stories have entered the literary mainstream. Many more are available through university and small presses.

Thanks go to John Ruth for anticipating this wave more than four decades ago. And thanks to Kirsten Eve Beachy, without whom the work of these authors from across the United States and Canada would not be gathered here. During the year it took her to collect and shape this manuscript, she made many wise decisions and showed kindness and diplomacy in her dealings with all. In short order, she formed an important contribution to Mennonite culture and a distinctive addition to North American literature. I also commend Amy Gingerich and those at Herald Press who embraced this project at a time when literary anthologies promise publishers only financial risk.

Tongue Screws and Testimonies suggests that although Mennonite authors may write about anything, a significant number of them have reckoned with distant memories of martyrdom. This collection, by no means univocal or narrowly didactic, proves that a heritage of dissent and persecution can be expansive and enabling. Readers will find reasons to revisit their own religious and cultural understandings among these pages. Many literary pleasures await here, and much speaks to current conversations about identity, memory, sacrifice, violence, forgiveness, and finally what in this blessed, broken world might inspire articulate resistance.

— *Julia Spicher Kasdorf*
Bellefonte, Pennsylvania
2010

Editor's Preface

Last July, Jeff Gundy asked if I'd like to edit an anthology of creative writing inspired by the *Martyrs Mirror*—a brainstorm by Gundy, Julia Spicher Kasdorf, and members of the Mennonite Historical Society. We sat on a log overlooking an isolated lake in the waters between Minnesota and Ontario, in the midst of a canoe trip/writing retreat with Wilderness Wind. We were probably slapping mosquitoes and ignoring the bits of ash in our hot drinks. It was one of the rare moments that week when the rain had stopped, but the air was chilly and we were bundled in most of the layers of clothing we'd brought. Knowing nothing about anthologies and only a little about Mennonite writers, I agreed. Today, in Virginia, the heat wave is unrelenting and I wish for rain. But the book is finished.

It has been, from start to finish, a community effort. Most of the works in this collection were recommended or submitted by other writers, and even the ones I discovered myself would have been impossible to find without the prior work of librarians, editors, and reviewers. The anthology has been a pretext for dozens of introductions and conversations with writers and historians. Snippets from some of those conversations appear in the occasional editor's notes.

The material in this collection has been selected with an eye to its aesthetic qualities, the strength of its insight about diverse communities' and individuals' connections with the *Martyrs Mirror,* and sheer readability. Some of it comes from established authors, some from members of the Anabaptist diaspora who simply have stories to tell. I've selected pieces with strong narrative elements, hoping that anywhere readers dip into the collection they'll find a good story or memorable image. With regret I laid aside several scholarly essays that provided great insight on the martyrs and their heirs, but did not fit within the scope of this book.

While I will not attempt to make pronouncements about the current state of Mennonite literature, I hope this collection will inspire future discussion to that end.[1] Here I wish only to emphasize that there is no single Mennonite

---

1   Various anthologies and critical collections provide perspective on this topic. For an excellent narrative on the rise of Mennonite writing in North America, see Ann Hostetler's afterword to her collection of Mennonite poetry, *A Capella* (Iowa City: University of Iowa

voice—we are many. In the arrangement of this anthology, I have tried not to limit our range or suppress dissonance, though I have chosen an order that creates a movement toward harmony in the resolution of each section of the book.

Disclaimers

This collection has room to grow. None of the pieces in this anthology explicitly plumbs the experience of minority groups in North America, though I know there are overlaps between the descendants of the Anabaptists and those of Asian, Latino, African American, and First Nations descent. I will continue to seek out ways the *Martyrs Mirror* has creative resonance in these communities. My initial efforts to find material from Europe and the burgeoning Mennonite Church in the southern hemisphere were also not promising, and I limited the scope of the collection to North America.

I also find myself unable in this book to do justice to the wealth of personal reflections authors shared from their first encounters with the *Martyrs Mirror*. And, for the sake of length and consistency, I've left out of this collection some excellent work inspired by the *Martyrs Mirror*.

The digital age offers a fine solution to these omissions; I invite readers to join me at www.martyrbook.com to see (or suggest) the pieces that got away, as well as corrections or amendments to the historical record, more thoughts from the authors in this book, links to the Mennoliterary world, a bibliography of resources, and updates about readings and events connected to the book.

Tongue Screws and Testimonies is a collection of literary work rather than a discipleship resource. As an editor, I have balanced sensitivity to the expectations of Herald Press's regular audience with an attempt to truly represent the material, particularly previously published work. In some cases, I worked with authors to minimize the use of language and images that might not be suitable for Sunday school and did not seem integral to the narrative. In others I let the language stand in respect for the literary nature of the material and as a reflection of the various perspectives we bring to a martyr heritage.

Press, 2003). Elsie K. Neufeld's anthology, *Half in the Sun* (Vancouver: Ronsdale Press, 2006) gathered writing from west coast Canadian Mennonite writers. John D. Roth and Ervin Beck collected critical analyses and surveys of Mennonite writing in the U.S. in *Migrant Muses* (Goshen, IN: Mennonite Historical Society, 1998). Hildi Froese Tiessen edited a collection of Canadian Mennonite writing for the Spring/Summer 1990 number of *The New Quarterly* as well as an anthology of short stories from Canadian Mennonite authors, *Liars and Rascals* (Waterloo, ON: University of Waterloo Press, 1989). Earlier efforts to trace the rise of Mennonite literature include Al Reimer's *Mennonite Literary Voices* (Newton, KS: Bethel College, 1993) and John L. Ruth's *Mennonite Identity and Literary Art* (Scottdale, PA: Herald Press, 1978).

On occasion, I inserted explanatory footnotes where I felt they were warranted for a broad audience, and these are preceded by "Ed." The other footnotes are as they originally appeared in the pieces.

A Note on Images

Readers familiar with the *Martyrs Mirror* will note the absence of Jan Luyken's astonishing detailed copper etchings in this book. Many of the poems, essays, and stories within this collection refer to or are inspired by his images. Luyken's works are true treasures, both as works of art and as artifacts of Anabaptist history, and are in part responsible for the wide distribution and perpetuation of the *Martyrs Mirror*. His celebrated image of Dirk Willems[2] has found a place in this book, for it inspired the pen and ink drawings by Ian Huebert that open each section of the anthology. Luyken's original can be viewed at the beginning of the "Water" section.

Visual texts are powerful. On a page, our eyes go first to pictures, then to words. Though the authors included in this collection are eloquent, wise, and witty, I wondered whether Luyken's compelling etchings might upstage their work. Without them, readers will have space to dwell on the mental images, to first feel in their hearts Sarah Klassen's description of Anneken Jans, then seek out the picture that inspired it: "See how the rope binds her/ to the jailer's wrist, the fibers twisted / rough as justice."

Only a writer can paint a rope as rough as justice.

This collection should be read as a companion to the *Martyrs Mirror*. It does not attempt to replace or explain that important book; instead, it reveals how individual authors have been shaped by it. The text and visuals of the *Martyrs Mirror*, including some images unavailable in current print editions, are available online and are linked from www.martyrbook.com. Even better, this book can be read alongside a print copy of the *Martyrs Mirror*. The Index of Martyrs and Witnesses cross-references the stories and images of martyrs within this anthology to the appropriate pages in the big book.

—Briery Branch, Virginia
July 1, 2010

---

2   Ed.: Dutch Anabaptist imprisoned and killed in 1569. He escaped from prison, but turned back to rescue his pursuer when the man fell through thin ice. He was returned to prison and later burned at the stake. For his act of selflessness, Dirk gets a lot of play in Mennonite churches and in this book. See the Index of Martyrs and Witnesses for further references.

Acknowledgments

This book was the brainchild of Jeff Gundy and Julia Spicher Kasdorf at an informal Mennonite Historical Society gathering to discuss initiatives related to the *Martyrs Mirror*. For entrusting me with their idea and for ongoing support and enlivening emails through the whole process, I owe them an enormous debt of gratitude. Thanks to Julia for sound advice and editing help with my poetry picks, and to Jeff for helping me plow across a stormy lake in the canoe on the Wilderness Wind writer's retreat, an apt metaphor for his support through the editing and publication process. I first wrote about martyrs in Kevin Oderman's creative nonfiction class at West Virginia University, in the essay which appears in this collection. Kevin, without you, without that essay, this book would not exist.

I'm also grateful to Michael King and J. Denny Weaver for helping me articulate a vision for the collection, to Ann Hostetler and Hildi Froese Tiessen for advice on anthologies and leads on Mennonite writers, to James Lowry, Stephanie Krehbiel, and Ervin Beck for thoughtful conversations and correspondence, and to several colleagues and mentors who shared coffee and advice: Vi Dutcher, Jay B. Landis, Nancy Heisey, and Mary Sprunger. Thanks to the folks at *Dreamseeker Magazine*, *Rhubarb*, the Mennonite Artists Project, and *The Center for Mennonite Writing Journal* for spreading the call for submissions. Thanks are due to the staff at Herald Press, particularly to Amy Gingerich for believing in the book; Josh Byler for help navigating permissions; Byron Rempel-Burkholder for editorial assistance; and attentive proofreaders and designers. Thanks to the Shenandoah Valley Inkslingers for a year of discussions of martyrs and writers, notably Andrew Jenner and Jessica Penner for their comments on several prose pieces; to colleagues at Eastern Mennonite University's Kairos Place for writing support, especially Vi Dutcher and Ray Gingerich; to the staff at EMU's Menno Simons Historical library, particularly Lois Bowman and Cathy Baugh; to Jeff Bach and other conference organizers for the *Martyrs Mirror* conference at Elizabethtown College's Young Center for Anabaptist and Pietist Studies for the invitation to present and further shape my thoughts around this collection. I'm indebted to

Joe Springer at the Goshen Historical Library for his help with fact checking and advice on standardization and to Shawn Snider for website assistance. Dad, for telling me the martyr stories; Mom, for the story-telling gene; big sister Elizabeth for being a model of faithful writing. And to my husband, Jason Alderfer, for your unstinting support, *thanks.*

This book would not exist without the many writers who so generously shared and submitted their work for the collection. Thank you all for entrusting me with your work, for waived and reduced permissions fees, patience with obsessive editing, stimulating conversation, and insightful observations. It is a pleasure to be part of this writing community.

Introduction

The heirs of the Anabaptists are diverse, and only special circumstances formally bring together the many branches of the tree of those who claim literal or spiritual descent from the early Anabaptists. Acts of service draw these groups together: stitching quilts and raising money for the material relief efforts of Mennonite Central Committee or raising hammers with Mennonite Disaster Service to rebuild after hurricanes. Here in the Shenandoah Valley of Virginia, the old songbook *Harmonia Sacra* unites people who wouldn't otherwise meet in church for monthly singings. And recently, at a *Martyrs Mirror* conference at the Church of the Brethren's Elizabethtown College, black hats, bonnets, bare arms, and bobbed hair mingled freely. Together we probed the history of the book, marveled over lovingly preserved copies of early editions, and discussed the ways the stories continue to live today. We might differ in practice and theology, but we can't forget the stories we share.

Jesus knew this power of stories, their ability to seize the heart and the gut as well as the intellect. Who can forget the widowed woman in his parable, lighting her lamp and searching for that lost and desperately needed coin? We continue to be troubled by the man who sold everything for a single shining pearl, and the elder son who did everything right but missed out on the party. The critics of Jesus' time panned him—in fact, they crucified him. They couldn't tolerate his unorthodoxy—a Samaritan as a model of ethical behavior? A welcome for prodigals? His metaphors made listeners uncomfortable—easier for a rich man to pass through the eye of a needle than to enter the kingdom of heaven?—but at the same time they made them laugh. Later the stories found their way into print in the biographies and memoirs that make up the Gospels. These fragments of narrative capture reflections of Christ, the Word incarnate.

Theileman J. van Braght understood the power of stories, too. He collected accounts of martyrdom by word of mouth, from scraps of smuggled paper and out of court records and built them into a tome of his faith, the *Mirror of the Martyrs*, published in Dutch in 1660. In his book, he traces Anabaptist martyrs back through early Christian martyrs all the way to Christ, who was to van Braght the original Anabaptist martyr. (Several essays early in this anthology provide a more thorough history of the *Martyrs Mirror:* "Me and the Martyrs" and "Family Things.")

In "Writing Like a Mennonite," Julia Spicher Kasdorf cites this etymological fact from Dana Gioia: in its original form, the word *martyr* means simply "witness." Kasdorf enlarges: "It is a matter of consequence that the word *witness* means not only 'to see' but also 'to speak.' To write like a martyr means, not to choose death, but to choose to bear life-giving witness." Martyrs are witnesses, storytellers. It was for their stories that the martyrs died.

Today, heirs of the Anabaptists are part of a growing literary scene. It's no surprise that in their work they return to the *Martyrs Mirror*, the first great literary effort of early Anabaptists. In their writing, we see how the *Martyrs Mirror* continues to inspire and disturb the descendants of Anabaptists. It's a gruesome book, with scenes of torture and murder delineated in minute detail in both the written accounts and the etchings by Jan Luyken. It's also a testament to faith and steadfastness, to a profound spirit of dissent that counts the cost (tongue screws, thumbscrews, burning iron, drowning, the sword) as little. Along with the descriptions of torture, van Braght recorded dialogues from court records; letters from the martyrs to husbands, wives, and children; confessions of faith; and lectures against worldliness.

Should We or Shouldn't We?

What happens when we take creative approaches to a venerated text like the *Martyrs Mirror*? While early Anabaptists eschewed the cathedrals, saints, and icons of High Church tradition, we developed sacred traditions of our own. In church, we tend to treat our martyrs with the same reverence as other groups treat their saints.[1] One member of the Mennonite Artist Project demonstrated this book's place in our sacred hierarchy when she noted that questioning the martyrs' stances "feels worse than doubting the Bible itself." In a recent letter,[2] James Lowry explained some misgivings about creative writing about the *Martyrs Mirror*:

> I believe that the *Martyrs' Mirror*[3] is a gift from the past . . . [which]
> ought to be respected as a more or less integrated whole, a unique world

---

1   Nancy Heisey first pointed this out to me. See also Ian Huebert's comments on iconoclasm in the Artist Statement, page 289.
2   March 18, 2010, cited with permission.
3   The use of the apostrophe in the title is preferred by Lowry, but is otherwise left out in this collection.

of ideas, of Christian ideals, of a recovery of the New Testament church. I believe that we should set aside the standpoint of present fads and ideologies and allow the *Martyrs' Mirror* to speak to us. This has not been done by some present-day writers, who read their own contemporary ideas back onto the martyrs—ideas which might be very strange, even antagonistic to the martyrs themselves.

Many writers in this collection do indeed read contemporary ideas back onto the martyrs—sometimes questioning, adding creative twists, even making light of the stories. The original martyrs, transported to Scottdale, Pennsylvania, and given a functioning knowledge of English, would likely be as surprised by this book as by the descendants who claim them.

And on the postmodern side, why should we spend time on a narrative that is not, after all, so uncommon? Anabaptists are not the only people who have been oppressed, not the only religious martyrs. Foxe's *Book of Martyrs* predates the *Martyrs Mirror* by a century. Mennonites tend to be essentialist; we take pride in our traditions and habits and forget that we are not the only people who rinse and reuse Ziploc bags.[4] Past suffering is not a necessary ingredient for a current commitment to peace, service, and the way of Christ, and dwelling on these stories may alienate readers who aren't blood descendants of this particular tradition.

It turns out, though, beyond all questions of *should* or *should not* that we can't help writing about the martyrs, whether we were born into the tradition, adopted into it, or live in exile from it. Their stories are compelling, and they are, by whichever route, about *our* people. Long before I sent out a call for submissions for this anthology, Mennonite, MennoNot,[5] and Amish writers were engaging the martyrs. When I entered the Menno Simons Historical Library at Eastern Mennonite University, I found their poems, stories, and essays waiting for me. It's our responsibility to recognize how these martyr stories shape us, and it's our privilege to continue to shape them.

Poet Audrey Poetker-Thiessen asks what has become the central question of this collection: *Out of so many martyrs, how do we live?*

---

4 Credit to Stephanie Krehbiel for this trenchant observation.
5 Those with connections to the Mennonite tradition who find themselves a little inside or a little outside the leftmost margins of the community; also the title of an alternative publication edited by Sheri Hostetler in the late '90s and early 2000s.

The Story of a Mennonite Writer

What does it mean to come out of many martyrs? Our connections to the martyr history are as diverse as our backgrounds. A composite biography of this
anthology's community of writers would read something like this:

I was born in a Mennonite peasant village in southern Manitoba, in Lancaster
County, in Alaska—not Mennonite, but surrounded by them in Elkhart County;
I was born to conservative Mennonite farmers, Old Order Amish, Mennonite hip-
pies; my mother, father, grandparents escaped atrocities in Russia; I can trace my
father's side back to the generation before the immigrant from the Palatinate; I have
a rich family tradition that I will not describe on this form because the question was
"what is your connection to Anabaptist traditions?" and we were something else.

Our church was Evangelical Mennonite Church, Mennonite Brethren,
Church of the Brethren, Amish Mennonite, kind of untraditional. I attended
Mennonite high school, public schools in Winnipeg, Jamaica, Kansas, and Sas-
katchewan, Mennonite college, seminary, a state graduate school. I worked for
Mennonite missions, Mennonite Central Committee, a Mennonite historical
society, was a surfer, a radio personality, live in an intentional community.
I've encountered Japanese history, Turkic Muslims in Northwest China, First
Nations peoples, Lutherans; I lived or traveled in Tanzania, Somalia, Zambia,
Salzburg, Holland, Switzerland, El Salvador. I'm a Mennonite/Amish/United
Methodist pastor, a professor, an editor, a student, a stay-at-home mom.

I learned about the *Martyrs Mirror* by osmosis, when I read it in my grandmother's basement, from my Amish neighbors, when I begged my mother to
read it to me, in graduate school, seeking out the mother-book. It thrilled me
to the core, it was too horrible to speak of, it challenged me, it humbled me, it
made me proud. I was intrigued by the radical women, the revenge fantasies,
the transmission of historical trauma, the implicit question: "Could you do it?"

Writers Approach the *Martyrs Mirror*

As I collected material for this anthology, I expected to find descriptions of torture and steadfastness, writers struggling with inherited wounds, and insights
into the more human aspects of self-sacrifice. All this is present, but some surprising threads emerged as well. I did not expect to encounter so many stories
of children. I didn't expect to see a theme of Anabaptists, from Menno Simons
himself to poet Todd Davis, taking refuge in the natural world, in gardens. I
did not expect the gift of laughter to visit so often or so freely.

Tongue Screws and Testimonies is arranged in segments that explore common images: book, fire, water, wounds, tongue, memory, enemies, and heirs. Each segment includes a mix of genres and tones; some pieces depict the martyrs and some their heirs. Within these works, writers take on the *Martyrs Mirror* from a variety of overlapping approaches, four of which are described below.

1. Retellings: Making the *Martyrs Mirror* Accessible

The tradition of retelling the stories from the *Martyrs Mirror* in sermons and Sunday school materials is widely established. Retellings have been published in books by authors like Dave and Neta Jackson,[6] James Lowry,[7] and Joseph Stoll.[8] Robert S. Oyer and John S. Krieder wrote one such collection to accompany and help interpret a traveling exhibit of Jan Luyken's plates mounted in 1990.[9] Others, like Myron Augsburger[10] and Cindy Snider,[11] have extended the retellings to make novels of the tales of the martyrs. Through the work of these authors and others, audiences may approach the stories without broaching a daunting book of more than 1150 pages. These authors also provide helpful tips for understanding the cultural context of the stories. Like the Jewish tradition of *midrash*, imaginative retellings of the *Martyrs Mirror* allow readers to empathize with characters. Many of the poems, stories, and essays in this collection include retellings within them, but they generally interweave these tales with additional historical sources, personal history, and imagination. For straight retellings, I refer readers to the collections mentioned above.

2. Aesthetic Approaches: Art in the *Martyrs Mirror*

The authors in this collection are clearly concerned with the craft of creating precise images and impressions with words. They may invite readers to enter directly into the sensory experience of a martyr in her last moments or to view a painting by Jan van Eyck or an etching by Jan Luyken. Some have inspired other artists in cross-genre collaborations, as when Brent Weaver composed three organ solos based on poems from Sarah Klassen's *Singing at the Fire* sequence.[12]

---

6 *On Fire for Christ* (Scottdale, PA: Herald Press, 1989).
7 *In the Whale's Belly and Other Martyr Stories* (Harrisonburg, VA: Christian Light Publications, 1981).
8 *The Drummer's Wife and other stories from the Martyrs' Mirror* (Aylmer, ON: Pathway Publishing, 1968).
9 *The Mirror of the Martyrs* (Intercourse, PA: Good Books, 1990).
10 *Pilgrim Aflame* (Scottdale, PA: Herald Press, 1967).
11 *Finding Anna Bee* (Scottdale, PA: Herald Press, 2007), children's novel.
12 Commissioned by Shirley Sprunger King and available with other works on the

The deaths of martyrs are brutal, difficult to render lyrically. Rudy Wiebe's stonemason discusses the challenge of shaping the ugly physical reality of martyrdom:

> Sometimes, when I'm at work splitting or polishing stone, trying to shape it exactly into what it needs to be, I see my scarred hands and tools chipping away forever at what already exists: our immovable past. Which surrounds Janneken and me like an immense plain of irreducible stone. Hand, hammer, chisel, stone and the years of our life, we keep on trying to split and shape them right; so they will fit.
>
> Fit into what? How? If you could remember perfectly, could you shape a horror the way you work a stone? Shape it for what? To build what?

And yet, this collection is full of images of aching beauty, a testament to the skill of these artists.

3. Cultural Icon: the *Martyrs Mirror* as Symbol of Identity

The *Martyrs Mirror* appears in some literary works almost in passing, as shorthand for the stories and the tradition they represent. In these pieces, the book serves as a vessel for cultural foibles and failings as well as theological and ethical commitments. These works demonstrate how the stories are inextricably linked to our identities.

4. Seeking Meaning: Grappling with the *Martyrs Mirror*

Some writers in the Anabaptist tradition overtly grapple with the narratives and lessons of the *Martyrs Mirror* in their own essays and poems, or put their fictional characters in situations where they, too, must interrogate the martyr narrative. What do the stories of the martyrs mean to us today, particularly given the difference between our situations and theirs? Writers use the stories to critique their communal narratives and also to critique broader society.

Reading About Communal Narratives

When Stephanie Krehbiel published her essay "Staying Alive: How Martyrdom Made Me a Warrior" in *Mennonite Life* in 2006, she received copious response

---

recording *Singing at the Fire: Voices of Anabaptist Martyrs* (Scottdale, PA: Herald Press, 1998).

from community members who engaged her description of the ways the martyr stories oppressed her in the wake of 9/11. Krehbiel and others involved in the discussion[13] demonstrated how Mennonites may be inclined to read creative work that addresses a communal narrative, and provided hints about how to most fruitfully do so.

Krehbiel's essay did what good stories do: it inspired response and started half a dozen conversations. Yet even as they grappled fruitfully with the martyr history, some respondents oversimplified Krehbiel's personal essay, with one even framing her piece as an "argument against the martyrs." They missed the difference between argument and shared experience and overlooked the many layers of storytelling. Out of conversations with Krehbiel and others, I submit a few suggestions for readers who want to take seriously literary responses to their communal experience:

1. *Read closely for multiple meanings.* This is almost too simple to say, but a reminder may be in order. Understand that poets and literary essayists are interested in describing portions of a journey; they aren't necessarily arguing a thesis. When reading fiction, realize that authors and characters don't always agree. Flannery O'Connor routinely created grotesque, wrong-headed characters to explore themes that arose from her strong Catholic convictions.

2. *Expect personal narratives to differ from the communal narrative, and don't be too quick to dismiss or normalize them.* Krehbiel notes that "on the occasions when we encounter difficult stories, we respond with either 'dismissive irritation' . . . or by making whatever interpretive stretch is needed to render the difficult stories the least challenging to our worldview."[14]

3. *Read with an awareness of any positions of privilege you may unwittingly hold within the community.* It was hard, Krehbiel admits, to not think of the discussion surrounding her essay in terms of age and gender. If stories of wounds don't ring true, perhaps it's because the reader is not in a position to be wounded.

4. *Tell your own stories.* Gerald Mast and Robert Kreider both opened their responses with stories of personal encounters with the *Martyrs Mirror*

---

13   Essays by Robert Kreider, Gerald Mast, Joseph Liechty, Jesse Nathan, and Hannah Kehr in *Mennonite Life,* Spring 2007. http://www.bethelks.edu/mennonitelife.
14   Krehbiel's second essay, "Joiner, Agent, Storyteller," *Mennonite Life,* Fall 2007.

to show how their own experiences contributed to their stances. Mast said, "I think that our own personal histories shape our response to any text or conversation. . . . the conversation in *Mennonite Life* models at least one way to be up front about our own personal investments in the discussion."

5. *Believe that sacred stories are strong enough to welcome examination and carry enough layers of meaning to remain relevant.*

The poems, essays, and stories collected in this anthology speak to the *Martyrs Mirror* as it is received by contemporary readers. Only a few of the writers in my collection claim to be scholars of the book. Some have read it cover to cover; others have avoided it intentionally. In their work, they speak back to individual stories, to an ethos, to Bible school, to images viewed in horrified fascination as children, to snatches from sermons. Their responses are a fragmented, incomplete, but honest and highly personal reflection of the incarnate *Martyrs Mirror.*

BOOK

Views from a Pond:
Dirk the Manual
Ian Huebert

AUDREY POETKER-THIESSEN[1]

who is *this coming from the wilderness*
leaning on her love?

meaning in the beginning
it was a thought
thought hard
almost a vision

there is a light up ahead

    like a door
    or a bridge
    or a fit word
    or a yoke that fits

    or unites a common
    memory out of foxfire

    (we know in part
    we see in part
    an unsafe journey
    but a sure arrival)

not a star but a light anyway

---

1   This excerpts the opening, "a." of a much longer, untitled poem.

we have reached light
    have not reached day
    follow foxfire
    find graveyards

death cannot celebrate thee
the grave cannot praise thee
out of so many martyrs
how do we live

the book
on the shelf is large heavy hard
to hold to turn pages
like a large stone it weighs me down
each crisp page flips to my touch
oh the woodcut pictures[2]
racks screams faces screwed up in pain
fires burning people
their gaze heavenward
help never came
instead leering searing faces of executioners
and the captions about martyrs of my faith
the horror bores a hole in my stomach
I clamp the book shut
screams inside

---

2   Ed: Historian Joe Springer notes that Jan Luykens' images were actually etched on
    copper plates.

Me and the Martyrs

The *Martyrs Mirror* crowns the pile of genealogical charts, family histories, and half-written manuscripts in our tiny office. The book details torments endured by Anabaptists and their predecessors all the way back to Christ—burnings, drownings, and more creative torture. Which surprises you more: that the *Martyrs Mirror* came to Jason and me as a wedding present or that we put it on our gift registry along with the *Moosewood Cookbook*? Jason's aunt bought it for us. Maybe she got it at a discount through her library connections; if so, we're proud of her. That thrift proves we're Mennonite: When a Mennonite dies, someone else has to find a use for the empty egg cartons, the drawers crowded with re-straightened twist-ties. I can't throw out food; sour milk waits at the back of my fridge because I hope to bake it into something, sometime. Our people saw long years of suffering. Generations later, we're still stocking up, just in case there's another round of persecution, another bloody theater.

That's the full name of the book by Thieleman J. van Braght: *The Bloody Theater or Martyrs Mirror of the Defenseless Christians: Who Baptized Only Upon Confession of Faith, and Who Suffered and Died for the Testimony of Jesus, Their Savior, From the Time of Christ to the Year A.D. 1660*. First published in Dutch, it is as heavy as a library dictionary. We usually keep it on the living room bookshelf. If I need a break or Jason's head hurts from telecommuting, we brew some tea and read the letters and court records, pore over the pictures. We might open the book to a vivid engraving by Jan Luyken, like the print of Ursel van Essen. She hangs by her bound wrists from a post, naked toes dangling a foot above the ground, back bared, while a man flails her with bundles of branches, one in each hand. In the background, a dozen men in fine hats watch. Van Braght, with painstaking attention to detail, explains that before Ursel's 1570 imprisonment, she was so "tender of body" that "she had to turn her stockings inside out, and put them on and wear them thus, because she could not bear the seams of the stockings inside on her limbs." Tender-bodied Ursel endured the scourging twice and the rack repeatedly, refusing to renounce her faith. Reading, we must be careful not to spill our tea on the pages.

~

Who were these Anabaptists? Who am I? It's taken me years to straighten out the story of these radicals who tried to reform the Reformation and as a result were despised by both Catholics and Protestants: When Martin Luther nailed his ninety-five theses to the door of Wittenberg Church in 1517, priests and laity across Europe joined him in questioning the Roman Catholic Church. While Luther was content to reform the state church, some radicals wanted to depart entirely from state-sponsored religion and return to what they believed were the practices of the original church. Anabaptism began, some say, in Zurich when Conrad Grebel baptized George Blaurock. Others place the beginning two years later, with Michael Sattler's Schleitheim Confession, which delineated key beliefs: baptism of repentant adults, renunciation of the sword, and separation from the world. Thieleman J. van Braght of the *Martyrs Mirror* traces Anabaptism directly to Christ through various incarnations of the "true" church, whose members were often vigorously persecuted. The authorities imprisoned Grebel for life; he managed to escape. He soon died of the plague, and so is not listed with van Braght's martyrs. Sattler's trial and letters, however, hold a prominent place in the *Martyrs Mirror,* for his persecutors cut out his tongue, tore him repeatedly with red hot tongs, and then burned him to ashes. A few days afterward, they burned his wife; she, too, refused to recant. The rebaptized Blaurock also ended in flames. Persecution only encouraged the spread of Anabaptism. The Anabaptists who survived the ideological purges fled to Alsace, the Netherlands, Moravia, and the Palatinate.

In the Netherlands and northern Germany, Menno Simons emerged as a leader. In spite of a bounty on his head (full pardon for murderers plus 100 Carolus guilders), Menno lived to die of old age. His followers took, or were given, his name. The Amish developed from the Swiss Mennonite tradition; the groups that fled to Moravia became Hutterites. Other denominations have been called Anabaptists for their approach to baptism, but are not directly linked to the traditions of the *Martyrs Mirror.*

Today the descendants of the Anabaptists range from Amish groups who farm with draft horses and pray in German dialects, to members of Hutterite communities who keep their possessions in common, to modern Mennonite congregations who sing choruses glowing on the wall in Powerpoint projections. Jason and I drive an hour each week to attend a house church where communion is a potluck, volunteers sign up on a clipboard to give sermons, activism and wisdom are primary concerns, and almost as many John Denver songs are known by heart as our beloved four-part hymns. I wear blue jeans but feel instant kinship when I pass an Amish buggy on the road. There is a deep though tenuous connection between us, in our blood, in our combined relatedness to the martyrs.

Modern Mennonites avoid war but like to send food and blankets to war-torn countries. When gruesome battle images appear on our televisions, we turn them off. My fascination with the bloody martyrs is out of vogue. The *Martyrs Mirror* was once considered the perfect wedding gift, but I got odd looks from folks when I asked for one. It's okay to use small excerpts in Sunday school materials, or to study the book if you're a scholar, but it's rather suspect to read it at leisure.

It's fine, however, to want to know your origins, so I can write it off as interest in my heritage. Jason has a keen taste for genealogy. Sometimes I turn from my desk to catch him surfing Amish genealogical databases instead of grooming email servers and firewalls. His exploration started during our engagement, as a search to see whether we were related. It turns out we're sixth cousins and share many forebears. We collect their stories.

The best-known story of an ancestor we share—a story I shall return to— is the tale of Jacob Hostetler and the Indian raid. In the classic version of this story by William F. Hochstetler,[1] Jacob and his wife arrived in Philadelphia on the ship *Harle* in 1736, made their way to what is now Berks County, Pennsylvania, and carved a farm out of the forest. The raid occurred twenty years later, during the French and Indian War. The family refused to defend themselves. The attackers captured Jacob and two of his sons but murdered the mother and two other children. Multiple accounts of the raid exist: blood ensures a history will be handed down.

I recognized the Hostetler story as one my father had told my sister and me when we were little girls. Mom read us fairy tales and the Bible and *Heidi*, but

---

1   Introduction to Harvey Hostetler, *Descendants of Barbara Hochstedler and Christian Stutzman* (Berlin, OH: Gospel Book Store, 1998), first printed in 1938. Commonly known as "The Stutzman Book." William F. Hochstetler's introduction, "History of the Hochstetler Family," first appeared in 1912 in Harvey Hostetler's *Descendants of Jacob Hochstetler,* commonly known as "The Hoschstetler Book."

Dad told us our history. We didn't have the *Martyrs Mirror*, but he made sure we knew about Maeyken Wens of Antwerp, who refused to renounce her beliefs and was burnt in 1573. They clamped her tongue with a specially fitted screw to prevent her from singing hymns or preaching heresies. Her son stood on a bench at the back of the crowd, but the sight overcame him and he fainted. Afterwards, he sifted the ashes and, finding no trace of her body, kept the screw. A century later, as van Braght compiled the stories, he knew of this souvenir. Perhaps he even saw it; perhaps he held it in his hand. I thought my father had seen it, too. He held out his hand, empty, and we imagined the cruel screw nesting inside.

I was a child among Virginia Mennonites whose old women covered their heads in church and let me sit under their quilts at Homemaker's Fellowship. When I was ten, we moved to small-town southern Indiana. My Amish fifth cousins farmed the surrounding hills, but we did not visit them. The local Mennonites wore blue jeans and Indian prints and were granola-making, talkative coffee addicts. They baptized me in the midst of my awkward adolescence, burning with embarrassment as the water dripped from my head onto my green suede skirt, as everyone who could reach into the circle laid their hands upon my shoulders, my back, my arms, even my feet.

Over the years, our Sunday school materials and church bulletins featured one engraving from the *Martyrs Mirror* that didn't portray immediate gore. In the foreground, Dirk Willems, in broad-brimmed hat and billowing frock coat, kneels on the ice of a frozen river, his hands outstretched to a man struggling in open water. There's urgency in Willems' stance: he has been running, but this final reach must be careful. The arms of the drowning man stretch toward his arms; the white space where they almost meet is full of tension.

We learned that Dirk Willems, condemned for his beliefs, escaping across a frozen river, turned back to rescue his pursuer. Afterwards, he was taken into custody, tried, and burned on another blustery day, a day too windy for the fire to burn properly; he died a lingering death, calling out to God again and again. These horrors did not distress me. They seemed necessary, inevitable as the closing of white space between the arms of rescuer and supplicant. My ancestors could not cast off their beliefs.

Perhaps because of this steadfastness, schisms are not uncommon among Anabaptists. It is so important to be right, to be the true church, that our communities splinter to protect the pure from contamination. It's surprising I haven't split off from the church myself. Instead, I've embedded myself in a small church, a sprout from the tree of the Mennonites, that accepts doctrine-wary dreamers. If someone tried to shun me, I wouldn't go.

The distance between me and the martyrs is a comfortable one. I can imagine them from afar like classical heroes. I don't know whether any of the martyrs in the book are my ancestors—we moved and lost so much, left generations behind on the journey across the Atlantic, lost too many stories in the translation from German to English. We have no souvenirs to hold. There is a wide, white space between us. If I pursue them and they turn back to close the gap and grasp my hands, what will I do?

The Amish and Mennonite settlers in Pennsylvania valued the stories as I do. The Mennonites in Ephrata somehow found the resources to print a full German translation of the original Dutch. Printing started in 1748. When complete, the tome of more than 1,500 pages measured 15 by 10 by 5 inches, at that time the largest book printed in Colonial America. It's likely that our Hostetler ancestors in Berks County, Pennsylvania, saw the book or heard the stories before the Indian raid of 1757. Perhaps the histories strengthened Jacob's decision not to defend his family against their attackers. I return to their story, curious about Jacob Hostetler's unfortunate wife, whom William F. Hochstetler suggests was named Anna Lorentz. It's not clear whether she was born in the Amish community or married into it, but she agreed to sail with Jacob on the *Harle*. Perhaps they sought to put a greater distance between themselves and the threat of torture, or perhaps they were inspired by the feats of their ancestors to seek new hardships.

In the story, the peaches are ripe: autumn. The family hosted an apple schnitzing at their home. Anna may have been a jolly woman, glad to host the community young folk, or she may have wanted help slicing her apples. What I do know is that after everyone went home, late at night, a party of Delaware Indians arrived. They weren't stopping by to slice apples.

The Delawares hoped to harry settlers off land that had once been theirs. They came at night in small parties to the fringes of settlements, killing or capturing the inhabitants of one house and leaving the neighbors alone, slipping away before sunrise. Our family stories mostly ignore the fact that three French scouts joined in the raid on the Hostetler family.

The Hostetlers barricaded themselves in the house. The oldest boys reached for their hunting rifles, but Jacob commanded them to put down the guns. I try to imagine Anna Lorentz that night. Did she approve, fold her hands in her lap, and trust God? Did she remember the martyrs' witnesses and give her husband a gimlet eye to remind him of his faith? Or did she plead with him to use the guns? Was the refusal to bear arms a shared decision or his first display of authority after years of following orders?

When the Delawares set the house afire, the family fled to the cellar, hoping to last until dawn. With barrels of apple cider they quenched the sparks that fell among them, but soon they feared for their lives. At sunrise the attackers dispersed. But one Delaware lingered behind to gather peaches. He saw the family slipping out the cellar window and called his companions back. There was no need to hurry. Anna, a woman of considerable girth, had stuck fast in the window, and the family stopped to help. I don't know whether they got her out of the window or if the Indians stabbed her as she struggled there. They killed her without honor, with a knife.

William F. Hochstetler says the use of a knife suggests a particular grudge against Anna; she may have had earlier contact with her attackers. One story attempts to explain the raid: years before the massacre, she'd turned away a party of Indians who came begging at her door. Jason shakes his head over this; it's less verifiable than the other facts, he says, which appear in various letters and news accounts of the time. And even if Anna had turned away some Indians, I see no direct link to the attack. We might as well say they stabbed her because she scolded the attackers, harangued the one who lingered to steal peaches. Maybe Anna liked peaches. It could have been her own tree, planted with the pit of a peach brought from the Lorentz homestead in the Old World where she was born.

But the knife story isn't the only hint that my ancestress was not a pleasant woman. Hochstetler records a Michael Hostetler who immigrated with the Hostetlers but turned back. A single line suggests that he was Jacob's brother and that he left because of the way Anna treated him. What if this woman I'm trying to claim as a family martyr was actually a bitch? What about the other martyrs far back in history: were they the outspoken ones, the obstinate ones, the ones with too much temper to lay low? The *Martyrs Mirror* contains the letters that Maeyken Wens, she of the tongue screw, sent to her husband, a local mason and an Anabaptist pastor. Why was she imprisoned and burned while he escaped censure? Are we surviving Anabaptists calm and quiet as a result of unnatural selection?

There's a final tradition about Anna. Months later, Jacob escaped from the Indians and wandered for days, certain that he had lost his way. Hopeless and starving, he stumbled on the maggoty remains of a possum and ate ravenously. He fell asleep, and in his dreams Anna appeared, telling him he was going in the right direction. Did he dream her young and supple or wreathed in blood and flame, or both? Did she speak as a saint or an angel, or was it a tongue-lashing?—"Get up, you fool, press on!"

Jason catches me up on his latest reading. According to Virgil Miller,[2] Jacob's wife has been mistakenly named. A Moravian Hostetler immigrant, not our Amish Hostetler, sailed on the *Harle* in 1736 and married a woman named Anna Lorentz. Our Jacob actually sailed in 1738 on the *Charming Nancy*, married to a woman who was probably named Anna. The family record is corrupt; no one remembers Jacob's wife's name. For my ancestress, there is no Lorentz peach orchard to dream of, gazing East. She has no family name at all. On the plus side, the mistreated brother-in-law goes with the Moravian crew. Maybe my ancestress wasn't so bad after all, or maybe her reputation tainted Anna Lorentz's story. In the end, all I can say for certain is that she died horribly.

The more I hear, the more empty-handed I feel. This new book lists her as Anna Burki, question mark. Anna the hostess: round and apple-cheeked; overtaken by events; dying tragically and returning as an angel in a dream. Or Anna, sharp-tongued devotee of the way of peace: unsparing of opinions to family and strangers; urging them to take a bath and convert before she hands out peach fritters; dying as she must, a sarcastic saint. Or Anna the harridan: frustrated, bitter, fat on sorrow. She didn't know when she married this Amish man that he would prefer the terrors of the frontier to the religious prejudice of her homeland, that he would ask her to plunder their stores for anyone who asked, to give up her safety for a dream of peace in a hard new land.

And now, learning more history, I find that the very name Anabaptist is questionable, that the word means *re-baptizer*, and was abhorrent to my forebears. They didn't consider themselves rebaptized—it was their first baptism; infant baptism didn't count. They had no wish to be executed as Anabaptists, but they kept arguing the point. Pages of the *Martyrs Mirror* are devoted to the court arguments of my righteous, contentious predecessors. The authorities were generally unconvinced. All that blood and fire for a technicality.

Who are we then? The Mennonites and Amish broke themselves into dozens

---

2   Virgil Miller, *Both Sides of the Ocean: Amish Mennonites from Switzerland to America* (Morgantown, PA: Masthof Press, 2002).

of subgroups and conferences with different names, all over fine points. Pick a name, any name: Old Order Amish, Conservative Mennonite, Swartzentruber Amish, Evangelical Mennonite Church, Mennonite Brethren, Old German Baptist Brethren, Mennonite Church USA, Beachy Amish Mennonite. And that's just a sample from the United States. I won't venture into Canada, let alone the rest of the world—and there are more of us outside than inside this country. Van Braght calls us simply Christians, or the brethren, which is problematic today, as an associated group, the Dunkers, still goes by the name Brethren. Brethren is a problem for me, anyway, because I am a woman—what of Ursel, Maeyken Wens, my no-name ancestress, and all the others?

Thieleman J. van Braght may have forgiven his enemies, but he kept good records of his people's wrongs, down to the last confiscated guilder. Did he write the *Mirror* so that the martyrs' children and great-grandchildren might also have the opportunity to forgive? Or to remind those of us in quieter generations that our piety lacks proof? Jason and I are not the only ones who have welcomed this dubious reminder over the years—more than three centuries past its first publication, the book is still in print. Ours is the twenty-fourth printing of the second English edition.

In North America today, we can baptize any way we want to. We can refuse war, become conscientious objectors by filling out a form. We tend to get richer than makes us comfortable, because we believe in good work. We try to compensate for our easy lives with personal sacrifice, go out of our way to seek hardship. Al Kiem once told me the story of an Amish farmer who made a fortune on grain during the Second World War. The man was so distressed by the weight of his money that he gave it all away to a Mennonite relief organization, to be free of it as quickly as possible. Those of us who are more a part of the world quiet our consciences by collecting school supplies to send to children in Third World countries, sending work teams to hurricane-flattened neighborhoods, raising our children overseas where we hand out canned meat to refugees.

For all of my sheltered childhood, I am still a product of this time, this culture, my liberal arts education. There are few churches that I can enter without leaving parts of myself outside. But I love the four-part hymns I grew up singing, and I believe in the way of peace, though I don't often speak of my baptism. What of my spiritual ancestors, the ones in tongue screws, the ones hung in cages, the ones stretched on the rack because they couldn't stop talking about it? Should I be ashamed of their fanaticism, or should I be ashamed of my own small faith? In the shadow of their fiery acts of renunciation, my ambitions for good seem small and dim, my beliefs wavering and insufficient. And yet I nourish them.

Even at a Mennonite college, it was difficult to be completely myself: I found friends among the artsy types who couldn't care less about the martyrs, the activists who saw faith as an obstacle to freedom, and the wholesome, bread-baking folk who shared my love for our heritage but might have been troubled by my take on the Gospels. I hid pieces of myself. I found comrades and mentors to nourish the different pieces of my soul, but few could be part of all my worlds. It's an old story: I was lonely.

There's a story about loneliness that's also a story about the Hostetler name. You might hear it in Switzerland, if you asked an old-timer. In the middle of the fourteenth century, the plague decimated the villages of Europe and wiped out two hamlets in the region of Schwarzenburg. The ghost villages Aekenmatt and Hostetten stood close together, but a deep ravine and a rushing stream separated their dead. If you were the young woman standing at the edge on the Aekenmatt side, you would have seen one light shining in one house on the other side. And when the last man left in Hostetten looked across and saw your single lantern, he would have known that he was not quite alone, yet. He crosses the ravine, clasps your hand, and you bury your dead. Where you go, you become known as the family from Hostetten, the Hostetlers.

When Jason found his way to my heart, with his willingness to join me in the lonely regions of life, I felt my light doubled. Here was a farm boy immersed in technology, equally excited by genealogy and string theory, who grew up loving Jesus and wary of church authority, who argues the way of peace and chose his own baptism as a child, who feels the call of the land and a simple life, yet longs to be engaged in the world of the mind. I felt complete.

For our first anniversary, Jason and I skipped the romantic weekend getaway and purchased a water buffalo through Heifer Project, which distributes animals and training to those in need. I feel the glare of Thieleman J. van Braght upon my back. "Is that all?" he asks. "Is that the best you can give? A water buffalo? While you sit home in comfort!"

We arrived at my parents' for Christmas to find my father's present for us: another water buffalo. He shares our ancestors, after all. It is through him I first heard the stories, inherited the sense of obligation. How big must the herd be, how empty our pockets, our houses, how much flesh must we flay from our bones before we feel we've expiated the ease of our lives?

~

Today, sifting through the *Martyrs Mirror,* I find a tiny souvenir. It's a tenuous connection, like all these links I try to make with history, but the name fits. I find it in a list appended to the German edition of the *Martyrs Mirror*, published in Ephrata before the French and Indian War. It's a list of martyrs from the Tower Book of Berne. On the 28th of May, 1538, two women were executed for their faith. One, I read, was a woman from Hoestetten. Jason has taught me how to run my finger lightly across a printed page and feel the ink of the letters, and I do it now. The word stands up in barely perceptible relief from the page: Hoestetten. It is an object in its own right, separate from the paper, placed on this page of copy after copy of this book by generations of people who don't want me to forget. I could almost scoop it up, almost hold it in my hand.

Gap

At the Rockvale Outlets next to a patchwork quilt of color-coordinated socks, you cut me off in line to request directions to a restaurant where you might find some Amish or at least Mennonites. You—hoisted up by shopping bags from Mikasa, Hugo Boss, and Donna Karan—ask the cashier what it's like to live among them. Do the buggies get in the way? You're in my way of picking up a quick pair of cheap Gap jeans before I drive home in my husband's bull of a car. Me, a cheerleader in a short pleated skirt, voted most energetic of my senior class, who has never buried my blond, sometimes dyed copper, hair under a prayer covering. I watch *Star Trek*, own two cell phones, you ignorant urban schmuck. I drank Chianti and danced to "Blue Moon" as a tattoo of a dove peeked out the shoulder of my sleeveless wedding dress. And this is how some Mennonites cut our bangs short, sassy from an issue of *Celebrities Hairstyle*. I want to offer you a Pennsylvania Dutch obscenity or something else of the Mennonite experience you're not looking for—a conversation about the Reformation, how Jacob Ammann led a schism over shunning, or the impact of reading *Martyrs Mirror* on a child. But the Amish Farm Museum across the street only offers carriage rides through the covered bridge until five, and the cashier just finished writing directions to the Good & Plenty Restaurant. Tonight you'll feast on creamed corn and Shoofly pie while I microwave my TV dinner into rubbery, stir-fried oblivion.

Joanne Epp

Greater Danger[1]

Oh! be careful in this matter says the preacher.
He means: don't forget the martyrs, their contentment
with pursuing the good and true.
He means: beauty is a trap; let it go.

O corroding and cankering luxury
to own two pairs of shoes,
to drink tea in restaurants,
to play the organ in church.

The wearing of clothes from foreign countries
is impossible to avoid these days.

Would he mourn us, their descendants, as lost?
How we eat and drink *without the least necessity*
(and yet, is necessity all?
There is no need for gardens, for paintings.
But there is.)

*They ate bread to satisfy their hunger, and drank water to quench
their thirst; more they had not* and more they could not ask
but I do, I ask for red late-summer tomatoes,
winter-blue shadows on white walls
and the choir singing Bach,

---

1   Lines in italics are quotations from the "Author's Preface" to the *Martyrs Mirror*.

and I don't want to turn with him
away from the tangible world, from
a body of clay, a heavy load of the soul.
O, he says, *that we were free from it.*
The preacher writes *Of the Greater Danger there is at this time,*
than in the bloody and distressing times of the Martyrs.
He means: beauty is a sinister attraction.

O, that Satan would show himself, as he really is.

A Bonfire of Books

Boys should not cry. But Simon could not help himself. He burrowed deeper into the rugs that lay in the corner of the deserted weaver's shop and shook with sobs. Here no one could hear him crying, so what did it matter?

But suddenly someone spoke, "Simon, lad, what is wrong here?"

The boy recognized the voice at once, but he could not understand how the minister had entered the shop without being heard.

"Come, boy, 'twill do no good to weep so long, though I daresay a good cry will make you feel better." The minister, Bouwen Lubberts, bent down and placed a kind hand on the boy's shoulder.

Young Simon turned up his tearstained face, "Have you heard from prison today?"

"I thought 'twas likely you were crying about your father. Yes, I have a letter for you that he wrote. That is why I came." Bouwen Lubberts handed a piece of paper to the boy. Simon reached eagerly for it.

"Can you read it yourself, Simon, or shall I read it aloud to you?" the minister asked.

"Read it to me, will you?" replied the boy, his tears forgotten. "I read so slowly, and I can hardly wait."

Before he began reading, the Anabaptist minister looked out the windows to see that no one else was within hearing distance. Then he read in a low but clear voice,

> May God through His great mercy be with my son, Simon, that he may grow up virtuously, in order to obtain eternal salvation through His beloved Son, Jesus Christ.
>
> My child and dear son, listen to my advice, how I began and am now about to finish my life. In my youth I was proud, puffed-up, drunken, selfish, and deceitful. I wanted only what pleased my flesh, an easy life. I was greedy, and what I did in secret is too shameful to mention.
>
> But my dear child, I searched the Scriptures and found that my life

deserved eternal death. Everlasting woe was hanging over me, and the fiery pool which burns with brimstone and pitch was prepared for me.

When I thought about this, I became alarmed. Which would be better, to live an easy life here for a little while and to expect the ever-lasting pains of hell, or to suffer here a little and enjoy eternal happiness? I looked in the Word of God for the answer.

The letter was a long one and the minister read on and on. Simon listened closely to each word.

My dear son and beloved child, this is my testament to you. I want you to read it often and compare it with the Scriptures, so that you may live a holy life. Mark well, my son, what I write. Many will appear in the garb of good teachers, saying they have medicine for your sick soul. But the ones that will profit you are those who have the truth. Listen to them.

You cannot understand this so long as you are carnally-minded, so long as you do not become the fool and enemy of the world. Out of a faithful father's heart I have left you this, when about to depart from this world, and to die for the Word of the Lord.

May the Lord grant you to take it to heart and to act according to it. Then you can be eternally saved. Farewell.—Your Father, Joriaen Simons

The man and the boy sat in silence for some time. At last the minister spoke, "You miss your father, don't you?"

The boy nodded.

"I know it is hard, but it is not in vain. Your father is in prison for the true faith, and he must not deny it."

"Don't you think. . . ? Might he not. . . ?" the boy faltered.

"No, I don't think he can escape. When they captured your father, they searched the house and found boxes and boxes of books. That made them bitter. Now that they have caught the book seller, they are taking no chances."

"But how did the bailiff know Father and Clement[1] were Anabaptists?" asked the boy.

"That I can't tell you, Simon. Perhaps someone told him who was bringing Menno Simons' books into Haarlem. And Pieter van Zouteland is a clever bailiff."

---

1   Clement Dirks.

"I wish we still lived in Friesland! Everything has gone wrong since we came to Haarlem," asserted the boy.

"But Simon, this may be God's will. Many souls have been saved through the work of your father, and all Haarlem talks about our faith. I think many people are thinking."

The boy did not say anything, but Bouwen could almost read his thoughts— *That may all be true, but I still want my father.*

"Your father is not unhappy in prison," said the minister. "He sent word that Clement and he spend much time singing and rejoicing. I remember his exact words: 'I have many hours in which I never once think of it that I am prisoner, such is the joy which the Lord gives me.' "

Darkness settled upon the city, and Bouwen Lubberts bade goodbye to the boy. He walked home in the April night, sorrow in his heart for Simon, but with joy when he thought how God was working in Haarlem.

Three weeks passed. On another April evening, men and women from all over Haarlem hurried mysteriously toward Schoudts Street. Word had spread that a meeting was to be held there, not secretly as Anabaptist meetings were usually held, but in the street.

The crowd gathered, but there was tenseness in the air. Would the bailiff come galloping down upon them at any moment? Bouwen Lubberts stood up boldly to preach.

"The fires of the Gospel are burning mightily in Haarlem these days," he began. "Many souls are turning from sin and deception to the faith of the Bible. We are still being persecuted, but we have many friends in the city. We hope and pray that they will become more than friends, yea, brethren with us in the saving faith of Jesus Christ.

"Persecution has not ceased, this we all know. For tomorrow two of our brethren are sentenced to be strangled and burnt. They have lain in the prison at St. John's Gate for a month, but they are not discouraged. The thought of death does not frighten them. They have written a hymn in prison, explaining the main points of our faith. We owe these two brethren much for their labor and love in the Lord's vineyard here in Haarlem. Joriaen and Clement have been our teachers in the faith, and we will miss them. But their deaths will not be a defeat. God can turn it into a triumph, and I think He will."

The meeting closed without incident, and the people of Haarlem went home to their beds, wondering what the morrow would disclose.

Among the throngs of people that filled the streets of Haarlem the next day was a frightened boy, Simon, the little son of prisoner Joriaen Simons. He had been comforted somewhat by his father's friends, but there was still much he could not understand.

The prisoners were led forth. A cry of pity swept the crowd. It was a shame that strong young men, both talented weavers, should thus die. A few women at the front began to weep openly.

"Weep not for us," called out Joriaen Simons. "Weep instead for your sins, and repent truly."

The prisoners were brought to the stake where they would be tied, back to back. They fell to their knees and lifted up their hands in prayer. The crowd grew silent as the words of their prayer could be heard, earnestly commending their souls into the hands of God.

They were strangled and then burnt. The audience watched in sullen silence.

No sooner had the fires died down than the bailiff called for the attention of the people, "These two men have now been executed as rebaptized heretics and disturbers of the common peace. One was guilty of selling and distributing many false books, and the other of reading and teaching from them."

The bailiff's voice took on a note of triumph, "We have been fortunate to seize a large quantity of these false books. It is proper that on the site where these heretics were burnt, their books should also be burnt." He motioned to the servants, "Cart them forth, please."

Box after box full of books were brought out from the city hall and dumped upon the ashes. The smoke began to rise around the edges of the books, and soon a yellow flame broke out.

The crowd had stood silently while the two martyrs were burnt. But now the people began to move about restlessly and to cry out in anger. A bold person slipped between the guards and began to fling the books out of the fire. Like a madman he threw the books in all directions.

Before the guards could remove him, the crowd surged forward, and with a shout they pushed the guards almost into the fire. The bailiff and the judges scattered and ran for shelter as the mob bore down upon them.

Quickly the people grabbed the books from the flames and passed them around till almost everyone had a copy. Bouwen Lubberts and many of the brethren were in the crowd, and quietly watched as the books were picked up.

"Thank God," said the minister fervently. "Today the truth is not quenched as the lords intended, but it is being spread all through Haarlem as never before!"

Only a few of the books had been burned. The rest had been distributed much better and more effectively than Joriaen Simons had ever been able to do in life.

A lad walked home alone toward the weaver's shop. He clutched in one hand the letter his father had written from prison. In the other hand he held a booklet, its edges browned by the flames of his father's funeral pyre.

JULIA SPICHER KASDORF

Mennonites

We keep our quilts in closets and do not dance.
We hoe thistles along fence rows for fear
we may not be perfect as our Heavenly Father.
We clean up his disasters. No one has to
call; we just show up in the wake of tornadoes
with hammers, after floods with buckets.
Like Jesus, the servant, we wash each other's feet
twice a year and eat the Lord's Supper,
afraid of sins hidden so deep in our organs
they could damn us unawares,
swallowing this bread, his body, this juice.
Growing up, we love the engravings in *Martyrs Mirror*:
men drowned like cats in burlap sacks,
the Catholic inquisitors,
the woman who handed a pear to her son,
her tongue screwed to the roof of her mouth[1]
to keep her from singing hymns while she burned.
We love Catherine the Great and the rich tracts
she gave us in the Ukraine, bright green winter wheat,
the Cossacks who torched it, and Stalin,
who starved our cousins while wheat rotted
in granaries. We must love our enemies.
We must forgive as our sins are forgiven,

---

1   Ed: Maeyken Boosers. Kasdorf notes in retrospect that the actual mechanism of a
     tongue screw is more like a clamp. The image of tongues screwed to cheeks, jaws,
     etc., is a common misperception by readers of the *Martyrs Mirror*, to judge from
     similar errors in numerous submissions to this collection (including my own essay).
     Most of these have been corrected.

our great-uncle tells us, showing the chain
and ball in a cage whittled from one block of wood
while he was in prison for refusing to shoulder
a gun. He shows the clipping from 1916:
Mennonites are German milksops, too yellow to fight.
We love those Nazi soldiers who, like Moses,
led the last cattle cars rocking out of the Ukraine,
crammed with our parents—children then—
learning the names of Kansas, Saskatchewan, Paraguay.
This is why we cannot leave the beliefs
or what else would we be? why we eat
'til we're drunk on shoofly and moon pies and borscht.
We do not drink; we sing. Unaccompanied on Sundays,
those hymns in four parts, our voices lift with such force
that we lift, as chaff lifts toward God.

OMG!! Geleijn Cornelus Is Hott!!

For J. S.

You probably won't understand—no one does—but this is what it's like:

You're at Sunday dinner, only a couple of hours since your baptism, and already you're irritated that Grandma Ediger doesn't know you well enough to get you something useful, a new iPod say, or, at the very least, a gift card to Hollister. You're proud of the fact that you didn't succumb to Grandma's bribes when you were twelve, when she offered you her anniversary silver in exchange for your baptism and membership into the church; no, you liked to play by your own rules, like the time you wore all black to your sister's wedding because, as you said, someone had to if the bride didn't. But that was three years ago and you're more mature now, more *world-wise*, as you often tell Staci, more aware of the nuances of faith. But still, the *Martyrs Mirror* for a baptism present? It's something Grandma Ediger would like, not you. The book, in a library binding of puke brown with gold printing, is heavy enough to be deadly.

Your mother reads the disgust in your eyes. "Be thankful," she says, putting her hand on your arm. "She means well."

You push away your plate of half-eaten pot roast and rush to Grandma's chair like a little girl. "Thank you," you tell her, "thank you so much for the book. It means a lot to me."

Grandma Ediger gives you a dry kiss on the cheek. She smells like vanilla lotion and bacon grease. "That book was your great-great-grandfather's," she says. "Look for your reflection in it."

You didn't even know you had a double great grandfather.

The new boy is named Jesús, from Guatemala, and he's your age. He's shorter than you by at least three inches, but what he lacks in stature he makes up for in muscle. He wears his shirts as tight as the sausage casings around Uncle Andy's pork, and sometimes you can see his nipples, little bumps that remind you of chocolate chips.

His short, black hair is gelled nicely in the front, making little spikes that he doesn't ruin with Dekalb or Pioneer caps. He doesn't care much for football or basketball, which you find refreshing, nor does he seem interested in NASCAR, hunting, or fishing. He is, essentially, the antithesis of every guy you've ever known, and you discover that you like him despite the names he's called.

The book sits for a week on the desk in your room, catching your eye only after you pick up a Diet Coke can and see that it has left a water ring on the cover. The stain encircles part of the book's title, the two *r*'s and part of the *o* in *Mirror*, the rest of the *o* being squeezed like the soft fat around Grandma Ediger's girdle. You think *Martyrs Mirror* a funny name to call a book: martyr you sort of get, but not mirror. The pages don't reflect anything, contrary to what Grandma thinks, but you open it anyway and look at the pictures.

You call Jesús and he meets you at the DQ. You order a Dilly bar, and he gets a banana split. He pays, and you smile.

"Do you like it here?" you ask.

"Yes," he says. "It's safe."

"Safe?"

"Guatemala City is not safe," he tells you. He's got whipped cream on his nose.

"Everyone thinks you're Mexican," you say.

Jesús shrugs. "No shame. Mexicans are good."

"You know what they call you?"

"I have a name?"

"Burrito Boy," you say. "Can you believe that?"

He smiles and says, "Is that an American super-hero?"

Your best friend Staci, who got a hundred dollar gift card to Hollister for her baptism present and who, Sunday after church, is going on the hour drive to the mall, makes fun of your gift.

"It's just so lame," she says, "so typical *old-person*. My mom, for her birthday, once got a bunch of letters that her grandpa had written to her grandma. And she cried! Oh my God, I was so embarrassed. I mean, who cries over old letters? Give me a break! I gave her lipstick, but she never wears it."

"Tell me about it," you say.

"Old people are clueless."

"Mom said she means well."

"Parents always say that," Staci says, snapping your compact shut. "Well?"

"Beautiful," you say. "As usual."

Staci smiles. "That Mexican, Jesús, you like him?"

"He's from Guatemala."

"Whatever—they all talk Spanish. You like him?"

"He has Mayan blood in his veins."

"Whatever. You like him?"

"Yes," you say, "yes I do."

Staci giggles. "They're calling you a wetback lover."

At night you thumb through the book while lying in bed. The text is dull, like your history book mashed with a Bible, but the pictures are kind of cool. The engravings of the martyrs are gory, sure, yet you find them strangely alluring and moodily glamorous, like the models in the *Vogue,* which is opened across your Bible on the floor. No one appears to be in pain, not really, as if both martyrs and persecutors are actors in a play and are, off stage, actually BFF who desperately drink liters of bottled water between scenes. You turn the pages. There's a stubborn man with a smirk on his face refusing to bow to the wafer, and his friends are trying to pull him down into submission.[1] There's a shirtless guy, a student, according to the caption, pushing away a crucifix while his persecutors pour hot oil on his head.[2] You like his ripped abs, but his shoulders are slouched—a real turn-off. There's a man named Dirk helping another man from a hole in the ice. There's a woman being thrown into a fire, a woman being drowned, a woman being buried alive. There's a man having his tongue clamped.[3] All this for Jesus, you think, and you wonder if you'd be able to do

---

1   Simon de Kramer.

2   Algerius of Padua.

3   Anneken Hendriks, Maria of Monjou, Anneken van den Hove, and John Bret.

that, to put your life on the line for some great cause. But, honestly, what good would it do? Look where it got them: they're dead now, reduced to pictures in a book. No, you think, you couldn't do that, you'd cave in a heartbeat. You want to live—thank God we're past that.

You turn the page and see a picture of a man hanging by his thumb from a beam in a room. A weight is tied to his foot to make it painful. His persecutors are playing cards—Rook? Dutch Blitz?—and seem like pretty nice guys. But you can't stop staring at Geleijn the martyr, your Dutch Jesús, at his six pack, his toned arms, his sculpted chest. You text Staci:

—*OMG Stac!*
—*Wat?*
—*U hav 2 c dis!*
—*Wat?*
—*Geleijn is so hott!!!*
—*?? Who's Geleijn?*
—*Tell U 2moro!*

You close your iPhone, turn out the light, and think about Jesús, imagine his dark hands on your hips, his chest against yours, his breath in your ear. You hear him whisper, "Te amo, Rachel, te amo. Beso me mi amor."

The next day you lug your book to the cafeteria and show Staci the engraving of Geleijn the martyr.

"That's disturbing," Staci says. "Your grandma's a sick puppy."

"But look at him!"

"How do you even say his name?"

"Galen, maybe?" you say. "I don't know, but look at his six pack."

"He's pretty ripped!"

"And look at his arms!"

"His pecs look rock-hard," Staci says. "He's got to be a lifter."

"He's probably just a farmer," you say, but you don't finish because there's a commotion near the vending machines and suddenly it seems like every guy in school has materialized in the cafeteria. Somebody upturns a table and you catch a glimpse of Jesús lying on the floor covering his head with his arms.

You shut your book and Staci tries to pull you back into your seat, but you're the stronger one. You push your way through the boys and see Alex Johnson kicking Jesús in his gut. Jesús looks like a curled-up pill bug, and you know that he could kick Alex Johnson's sorry ass all the way to Kansas City if he could only stand up. You know it's wrong, but you do it anyway—whack

Alex on his head with your baptism present. He falls, and you hit him again, this time on his face. You hear a crunch, then see blood splattered on your Converse. The boys howl like rabid animals and the football coach grabs your arm to keep you from hitting Alex a third time.

"Someone like you shouldn't be fighting," he says.

"But Jesús never did anything to those jerks."

"There's two sides to every story," Coach says. "I'll let you explain that to Mr. Anders."

You're about to speak, but you say nothing because idiot Coach wouldn't get it.

"That's a good girl," Coach says. "You just keep your pretty mouth shut and leave the fighting to boys." He drags you to the principal's office. Your book is stained with blood from Alex's nose.

"If you'd only spent a little more time with the *Mirror* and your Bible and not those worldly magazines of yours, you wouldn't be in this mess," Grandma Ediger says.

"Mother," your mom says.

"Who'd stand up for Jesús if I didn't?" you say. "He didn't deserve that."

"You have to watch out for boys like him," Grandma says. "It's best not to get involved."

"Mother," your mom says. "That's enough."

You feel strangely detached from the conversation in the kitchen, as if you're watching it take place on a screen at the Regal. The director cues you to go to your room, which you do, and to slam your door, which you don't because you do things your own way, choosing instead to shut it softly. Take that, Grandma, you say. You think about Jesús, wonder how he's doing. You heard he had several broken ribs, but who knows the truth. You wonder why Staci hasn't called—she usually texts every day. You don't have homework because Mr. Anders said that this week it's all zeros for you, young lady. You stand at your dresser and look at the engraving of Geleijn you ripped from the book and taped to your mirror. You see your reflection next to his, and you notice how your dark hair matches the circles under your eyes, how pale your skin glows. Is that what you look like? You lie on your bed. You hear Grandma Ediger complaining, your mom's soothing voice. You want to save Jesús, you think, to keep him from the boys at school, and you will, you completely will.

Family Things

For as long as I could remember, my grandparents lived in an enormous house surrounded by Grandma's asparagus patch and Grandpa's chemically-verdant lawn, on a quiet God-and-Country-fearing street in Wooster, Ohio. As a child, I spent many happy hours tinkering in their basement full of old tricycles, pig-gybanks, jigsaw puzzles, knickknacks and dusty boxes of junk politely referred to as "family things."

One Thanksgiving, a few years after I finished college, after my mother and aunts convinced Grandma and Grandpa to downsize to a smaller, more manageable place a mile or two away in another Rockwellian corner of Wooster, one with sufficient kitchen and basement space to accommodate Grandma and Grandpa's respective projects, the extended family lent its collective brawn to the moving effort. After an hour or so of loading couches and file cabinets onto the moving truck, I crept back to the parlor to ransack the boxes of old clothes headed for the Salvation Army. (The appearance of being busy was an effective and, I must say, clever defense mechanism against the unappealing prospect of being forced to scrub, dust, or mop something.) My efforts were rewarded with a few nice ties and an atrocious pair of white penny loafers.

By mid-afternoon, most of the family had returned to the new place to put Thanksgiving dinner on the table, and the old house sat nearly empty. Making one final pass through the living room, I noticed an ancient, enormous book lying on the floor, held shut with rubber straps. I asked Grandpa about it as we wrestled the last few bits of patio furniture out the screen door. He said it was an old German Bible; he figured he would give it to an Amish guy who had recently patched his roof. I almost walked off and forgot the matter, but I've always been fascinated by old books and foreign languages, and at the last minute I went back to the living room. A similar impulse once led me to purchase a French-Arabic copy of Khalil Gibran's *Paroles* in a Paris used bookstore—a decision I neither understand nor regret.

I knelt on the carpeted floor and carefully removed the rubber straps. My eyes widened as soon as I turned the first page. It wasn't a Bible; it was a copy of *Der blutige Schau-Platz, oder Märtyrer-Spiegel der Tauffs-Gesinnten* (now commonly known in abbreviated translation as *The Martyrs Mirror*), printed in Lancaster, Pennsylvania, in 1814.

Grandpa, did you already tell the Amish guy you would give him that old book? I asked.

Why, do you want it?

Yeah.

Grandpa shrugged, surprised, I think, that I showed any interest in the old book, but he said I could take it.

Family things. It's nice to pass them along, he said.

In the mid-seventeenth century, Dutch society was the wealthiest in Europe, thanks to its powerful navy and exotic colonies. It was enough to keep Tieleman Jansz van Braght awake at night. A young, conservative Mennonite preacher, van Braght was distressed to see his church gradually seduced by worldly concerns, infected with complacency, drifting, forgetting its past.

And so, in 1660, he published a gruesome book, titled in the original Dutch, *Het Bloedig Tooneel Der Doops-gesinde*. It was a reactionary work, documenting hundreds of horrific accounts of men, women, and children executed for their association with a Christian movement known as Anabaptism,[1] which had begun a little more than a century earlier.[2]

There was Simon de Kramer, burned at the stake in 1553 for his refusal to kneel before a parade of clergymen carrying consecrated communion wafers. There was Anneken Hendriks, first exiled from Amsterdam, then tied to a ladder and thrown onto a bed of coals with her mouth stuffed full of gunpowder. In 1569, Dirk Willems fled from prison across an ice-covered pond but stopped to rescue a pursuer who had broken through, only to be re-arrested and promptly burned to

---

1   A note on terminology: the name "Mennonite" was just coming into vogue when van Braght wrote the *Martyrs Mirror*. By then, the Anabaptist genus had begun to fracture into a number of distinct species like the Mennonites. Other prominent spiritual heirs of the early Anabaptists are the Amish, the Brethren, and the Hutterites. Today, after several more centuries of remarkable achievement in the field of church schism, there are dozens and dozens of distinct sub-denominations rooted in the Anabaptist movement.

2   Ed: Historian Joe Springer notes that the *Martyrs Mirror* is a continuation of a very widespread tradition of martyrological writing that was by no means limited to the Anabaptists.

death. The van der Leyen family from Ghent: brother David, burned, 1554; sister Tanneken, drowned, 1555; brother Lauwers, beheaded, 1559. All told, van Braght named 803 men, women, and children put to death for the crime of Anabaptism. Their stories, van Braght hoped, would scare his people straight.

∽

To place van Braght's mission in proper context, we have to jump back more than a century to Zurich, Switzerland. There, in January 1525, two young men named Conrad Grebel and Georg Blaurock baptized one another, convinced that in doing so they more closely observed the example of Christ than either the Roman Catholic or Protestant Churches. It was an unpopular move; authorities in Zurich viewed adult baptism as an act of insubordination and set about trying to squash the new heresy by any means necessary.

The first to die was Felix Manz, another early leader of the Anabaptists (whose name derived from the Greek for "re-baptize"). Manz was tied and cast into Zurich's Limmat River in 1527. Blaurock was burned at the stake in 1529; Grebel was only spared martyrdom by sudden illness—probably the plague.

The Anabaptist movement carried on, though, despite the fact that three of its most prominent early leaders were dead within five years of anabaptizing one another, and despite the state's enthusiastic pros-, pers- and ex-ecution of other subscribers to Anabaptist thought. By early 1527, they'd agreed upon a seven-article document codifying Anabaptist belief in adult baptism, separation from the world, the shunning of church members who fell into sin, and the rejection of violence.[3]

In 1536, a Dutch Catholic priest named Menno Simons converted to Anabaptism and became one of the church's most prominent leaders. Although his conversion forced him into hiding, he spent the rest of his life guiding the church from the underground, moving constantly, baptizing converts and writing widely. In spite of a large price on his head, Menno died a natural death in

---

3   A note on church history: this document, called the Schleitheim Confession, was written by 29-year-old Michael Sattler. Three months later, he was convicted of heresy in Rottenburg, Germany. Before burning Sattler to death, the executioner cut out his tongue and seared him with hot tongs. Two days later, his wife, Margaretha, was put to death by drowning. Even though they're juicy and salacious and sort of grotesquely fun, I think I'll stop with the execution accounts here—I'm sure you get the point.

1561. Over the next century, his followers began to call themselves Mennists, or Mennonists, and finally, Mennonites, which stuck and remains the broad label for the church, culture, and community in which I sprouted and grew.

~

But back again to 1660, Meneer van Braght and *Het Bloedig Tooneel*, published to protest the recent backsliding of the Low Country Mennonites. Though times were fat in Amsterdam,[4] life was hard for the southern Mennonites, concentrated in Switzerland, southwestern Germany, and eastern France.[5] Though their fortunes had risen and fallen over the previous century, these Mennonites never really found lasting prosperity and tolerance; by the early eighteenth century, they began a mass emigration to North America.

The Pennsylvania Colony was their primary destination; between 1707 and 1756, nearly 4,000 Mennonites from Switzerland and Germany settled in and around Germantown, Pennsylvania. William Penn, the colony's Quaker founder, was well-acquainted with religious persecution himself, and he welcomed the nonconformist Mennonites, who rejected violence and refused to swear fealty to earthly leaders.

By 1745, as England and France prepared yet again to make war, a group of these early American Mennonites themselves began to worry that their community was at risk of being swept astray. They wrote a letter to Dutch Mennonite leaders requesting assistance with translating *Het Bloedig Tooneel* into German; before the decade was out, *Der blutige Schau-Platz* was printed in Ephrata, Pennsylvania.[6]

A second German-language American edition came out in nearby Lancaster in 1814, and somehow a copy fell into the hands of a Lancaster County Amish family,[7] the Hartzlers, who eventually moved west to Wayne County, Ohio. My

---

4   A note on recreational toxicology: times are still fat in Amsterdam, take my Mennonite word for it.

5   A note on toponymy: Just for the record, this application of modern nation-state boundaries to this southern locus of Mennonitedom isn't historically accurate, but clarity is primary to my mission here, and political divisions were nothing if not obtuse in the aftermath of the Peace of Westphalia.

6   A note on geopolitico-linguistic irony: Yes, the first German edition of the *Martyrs Mirror* was printed in America by refugees who'd fled Germany (well, sort of—see the last footnote), became entangled in some nastiness between the English and the French, and turned to the Dutch for help.

7   A note on the Amish: Since the Amish-Mennonite distinction is poorly understood by the world at large, and since family lore has it that I'm a direct descendant of the first

great-great-grandfather Hartzler left the Amish church but kept the book and passed it on to his daughter, Hazel Mae, whose third son, Donald Moomaw (1923-), is my grandfather, who ended up with the book and stashed it in his bric-a-brac mother lode in the Kinney Street basement.

By the time Donald was born, however, the Moomaws were no longer good Mennonites. Somewhere along the way, the book brought from Pennsylvania had become confused with a German Bible, and Grandpa stared blankly back at me as I delivered an impromptu speech on the *Martyrs Mirror*'s subject, scope, and significance.

As best I can tell, the family's tenure as Mennonites came to an abrupt end over an out-of-wedlock pregnancy, though I've been advised several times not to dig around too much investigating the matter. Mom tells me there are lingering sensitivities, even though it happened (I think) about a century ago.

Anyhow, the scandalous Moomaws fell into apostasy and joined the Methodist Church, and by the time Grandpa was in his early twenties, he was piloting a heavy bomber over Germany in the last year of World War II. He went to Korea, made colonel, and now, well into his eighties, marches with an officers' honor guard during military funerals; his is certainly not a résumé consistent with the Schleitheim Confession.

When Mom went off to college, though, she re-scandalized the scandalous Moomaws[8] by reverting *back* to the Mennonites, because she was a peacenik and the Mennonite Church was the only one she found that officially opposed the Vietnam War. She joined the church (a move greatly upsetting to Col. Donald Moomaw, patriot, Republican, hawk, Freemason, curmudgeon, etc.), married my dad (who also converted as a young adult),[9] and then I came along—raised in

Amish bishop in the New World, I feel obligated to give them a little ink. In 1693, in Alsace, Jakob Ammann and his followers split from the Mennonite Church after a long and bitter fight over the doctrine of shunning nonbelievers. They came to North America at the same time and for the same reasons as the Swiss-German Mennonites, have since prospered as eye-catching oddities in modern U.S. society, and thereby cemented horses and buggies into the popular understanding of the essence of Mennonite-ness.

8   A note on the scandalous Moomaws: Wouldn't *The Scandalous Moomaws* be a great memoir title? This is not the time or the place, but I'm dying to disclose other entertaining and hard-to-believe scandal involving Uncle Jerry the hippie, Uncle Rich the End-times armchair theologian, and Grandma the octogenarian with newfound and amusing interest in wine and margaritas.

9   A note on pedigree: Dad, also né Methodist, has no Mennonite heritage whatsoever, which means I am, at best, an Anabaptist mongrel, and which adds further scandal to my tainted ancestry and makes me an unlikely guardian indeed of the old book I

the Mennonite Church, educated at a Mennonite high school, further-educated at a Mennonite college, Mennonite this, Mennonite that, my whole life long, ringing in my Mennonite ears.

And thus, 192 years after the old book's publication, when it came time for Grandma and Grandpa to downsize and discard those family things that the rest of the family didn't really want, I recognized and rescued the *Martyrs Mirror* lying there on the floor.

Family things. I'm glad you knew what it was, Grandpa said.

⁓

The modern connotations of religious martyrdom—that forty virgins and explosive belt and clash-of-civilizations stuff—aren't good, which makes it a strange thing off the bat to own a twenty-pound book that celebrates martyrs. What makes it particularly weird on a personal level is that I don't derive much inspiration from Lauwers van der Leyens and all those others who kept the faith as they lost their lives.

It was admirable of Dirk Willems, no doubt, to pull the guard from the icy water, but I don't need Dirk's story to sell me on the ideal of help for the stranger in distress. And Dirk's fiery death comes up short as a parable of personal sacrifice. It has aged to irrelevance. Dirk's faith through adversity is as applicable to my life as Dirk's Top 10 Tips for avoiding the plague. In the USA, in 2010, the government is not going to sear my tongue or gouge my eyes or burn me up or really hassle me much at all for being a Mennonite.

And that's another thing: I'm no more than a fence-sitting Mennonite. If faced with bodily harm, I'd definitely recant. I kicked my church habit a few years back once it became clear that church wasn't meeting any needs. It wasn't an angry sort of event or anything. Call it a change of pace. Call it the latest example of scandalous Moomaws flirting with a break from the past. Faith is sitting on the shelf for now, right beside my old copy of the *Martyrs Mirror*.

I pull it out sometimes, for show-and-tell with guests, who invariably thumb a few pages and say how "cool" it is. They are right—it practically reeks of antiquity and value. After a half-hour surfing through some of the Internet's dustier crannies, I figured it's probably worth about $800, and immediately felt a little whorish.

---

rescued from Grandpa. Tieleman Jansz is probably rolling in his grave, and I haven't even gotten to the section about my personal deficiencies of faith.

Sentimental value should never be denominated in USD, even—or perhaps especially—when the underlying sentiment defies explanation.

Sometimes at night I pull it down myself to feel the raised type, smell the lost decades, and contemplate its mysteries. I'd love to know more about how the book eventually fell into my grasp. I'd love even more to know why I hold it so tight. I turn it in my hands, a scuffed embodiment of uncertainty about who I am, a monument to contradiction, a talisman from the murky reaches of my own history, gnarled rootstock that might sprout again, an object of strange desire that caused me, on that November day in 2006, to kneel on the bare living room floor, lift it slowly and say, can I have this?

Family things. It's good to keep them around.

FIRE

Views from a Pond:
Dirk the Missionary
Ian Huebert

Legend II

These are the things you won't see
ever again: that dark starred tent, the way
the wind twirls the town hall's weathercock.
Trees.
The elegant church steeple. Look how it lifts
its pinnacle against the outraged sky.

The last crude pillars you will cling to
touched by tongues of fire
at your feet. Believers swear

those black twin stakes turned green
overnight, charred wood restored, bark brilliant,
branches alive with light-flecked whispering
leaves
the two of you will never see.

Ursula and Maria van Beckum
Deventer, 1544

TODD DAVIS

A Mennonite in the Garden

For Julia Spicher Kasdorf

We staked and tied our tomatoes
like the woman in your poem
who you said had her tongue

screwed to the roof of her mouth,[1]
and like that woman the tomatoes
came to harm, sacrificed to our hunger.

Even our children know Jan Luyken's
etchings, the heft of persecution, the reward
of history's painstaking script: Maeyken Wens

on a spit, flames rising from wood
likely cut and split by our own industriousness,
or Anneken Hendriks lashed to a ladder,

men trudging forward like mules, walking
the wooden staves until they stood upright.
With so much rain the fruit grows

too fast and too heavy, some of it
breaking the stalk without ripening.
Our neighbor's tomatoes have blight,

---

1   Maeyken Boosers.

leaves wilted, so we collect the green
from our broken stalks, make relish
and bring it to their door.

Why couldn't those women have remained
untouched, somehow God leaving
even the tomatoes unscathed?

The boy, who in my confusion, wanders
between these stories, plays a part
he never asked for: pear bestowed

through the dancing blaze, as if
forgiveness could conquer the anger
of such flames. We should know fire

isn't fastidious: fuel is fuel as it hisses,
then becomes ashes; soil in the garden
blacker for these efforts.

lilies and onions

they dance and jump in the fire, view the glistening sword with fearless hearts, speak and preach to the people with smiles on their faces; they sing psalms and other songs until their souls have departed, they die with joy, as if they were in happy company.
—johann faber of heilbronn

they sear her tongue
so she won't preach from
a burning pulpit. they
shatter her clay body with
hammer and tongs. they watch
satan whisper in her ear. it's
not a matter of courage: the city
of this world is a dungheap, naked
lords on thrones of shit.

on a bright morning she's trundled
to the town square. the lilies
are in bloom. women hawk onions
in the market, children
play tag, burghers eat pastry,
gawk and gossip. fire
makes love to her, the city flares.
i have chosen you.
the flames go cold.
her tormentors return to hearth
and family, waste away
with the disease
of freedom.

On Fire

Unicorns

On fire. That was Mom's expression. "Juliana, I hope you'll grow up to be on fire for God." Mom's hazel eyes shone with a strange light, radiated heat. Juliana had a child's tendency to take things literally. She considered: How would she look on fire? She pictured herself tied fast to a pole in a wilderness at night surrounded by savages with drums and war paint, jeering as they prepared to burn her at the stake. Flames licked at her ankles. Her face was placid and brave.

In real life it happened like this: Juliana wanted to collect unicorns, but her mother believed they were a vehicle through which evil spirits of the New Age could gain access to the souls of children. In the bathroom, Juliana found her mother's book that listed the numerous forces through which the New Age movement infiltrated popular culture and suckered in unwitting children: cartoons like Smurfs and Rainbow Brite, toy owls, fantasy books, unicorns, crystals.

Juliana's favorite toys were two unicorn-shaped erasers, one pale pink, one lavender. She played with them outside under the maple tree, in an imaginary kingdom. She didn't want to burn them. But she wanted to be a good and devout Christian. On fire for God.

"Are you sure you want to burn these?" her mother asked. She knew this was asking a lot.

"I don't want to. I *need* to," she said bravely.

"It seems like the right thing to do," her mother agreed.

After further discussion Juliana and her mother decided to build a bonfire on the gravel driveway and burn anything they owned that might be a refuge for evil spirits. Whose idea had it been?

Her mother, too, was making a sacrifice to the Lord that day. She'd put in glossy magazines of impossibly clean and expensive homes with colorful walls and matching furniture and no clutter—"house porn," her mother called it. Juliana wasn't really sure what pornography was, so gained the impression that porn had something to do with leaving fragile objects out in the open on coffee tables where they could easily be broken. Juliana's home was a white-walled parsonage furnished with church members' cast-off furniture supplemented by a few thrift store finds.

73

The ranch-style house had brown shag carpets that hid stains and nothing had been remodeled or changed since the house was built thirty years earlier.

At dusk, the bonfire's tongues licked up from the driveway. Juliana's eyes teared from the smoke. Heat covered her face, bare arms, and bare legs below her cut-off jeans. Her mother prayed to the God of Abraham, Isaac, and Jacob. Juliana pictured Abraham and Isaac in her mind just like they appeared in the big blue Bible storybook: Isaac, bound, on the altar with his father's knife raised toward his throat just before the angel of the Lord appeared to stay Abraham's hand and point out an alternative sacrifice, a ram caught by its horns. Now Juliana held the unicorn erasers above her head, hoping for divine intervention. No angel materialized to stop her. She tossed the unicorns into the flames. Part of her seemed to burn with them.

Desire

When Juliana was sixteen, she hoped to be burned at the stake. She'd got the idea from an old book she found when she and her mother packed their things to move from the country into town. Her mother didn't remember where the *Martyrs Mirror* had come from, perhaps from Uncle Howard. He'd been a Mennonite; weren't they a kind of Anabaptist? Juliana and her mother were non-denominational—but she told herself she would have been an Anabaptist in 1551, the year that Catharine was burned. To the Catholic monks who tried to persuade her to recant her Reformation beliefs, Catharine said: "I stand so firmly to my faith that for it, to the honor of God, I will suffer my self to be burned at the stake. What would you do for your faith? not much, I think. Hence repent, before you be brought to shame."

Juliana took Catharine's question to heart. What would she do for her faith? Would she have the courage to sacrifice everything, even her life?

On a cold November afternoon, Juliana walked home from school with Joseph Pascucci, the boy she had been dating, sort of, for three months. He had pale skin and dark hair and eyes like sunlight on an autumn morning. His body was lean and artistic, and his voice was rich like someone on the radio. Juliana's mother did not approve of him because he was a Catholic.

Juliana scraped her feet along Kurtz Street to hear the loudest possible swish swish of orange and red leaves scratching against the curb. "Do you smell that?" she exclaimed. "Detritus!" Her biology teacher had talked about detritus that day, how new life comes from old life when it breaks down. From blue sky floated more leaves, each burning bright red like flames. "Maple leaves make me think of martyrs, the way they burn their brightest right before they die."

"You're a piece of work," said Joe. But he took her hand as they walked, and warmth flowed from her palm through her arm and into her whole body. He seemed more real than Jesus did. Joe was living flesh and blood. Being near him made her feel more like flesh and blood too. Alive in her body. Was her interest in him based too much in the physical? She studied his profile as he hunched under his heavy backpack: a serious forehead, the nose with a bump half-way down for character, fine chin.

They hugged at the corner where they had to part ways; his house was a half-block one way, hers a block in the other direction. She hated to pull away from his embrace and walk alone, facing the wind. "I'll miss you." Was it wrong to be so attached to a person? Before Joseph, she'd relished walking alone, sometimes feeling a sense that God was walking with her. Now God seemed invisible, even imaginary, compared to Joseph's physicality. It occurred to her that perhaps God wanted her to break up with Joseph. It was a test, she thought, like the time when she had burned her unicorn toys. Like when the Lord asked Abraham to sacrifice Isaac. Like Catharine who was burned at the stake.

That evening after youth group, Juliana and Joseph stood outside the Potter's House in the cold. The lesson had been about sacrifice: what would you be willing to give up for God? One boy shared how he had melted several non-Christian CDs in the toaster. He'd meant to toast all of them, but ruined the toaster before he finished. He said it stank something awful. Outside, Juliana tried to explain to Joseph her need to sacrifice their relationship.

She spoke slowly, carefully, as she considered her words. "It's like when I was a kid, I had to burn my unicorns. They might have led me away from God so I burned them."

His shoulders hunched and his face turned away so she couldn't see him clearly. Then he looked straight at her. "You burned unicorns? That is the craziest thing I ever heard. Effing crazy."

His reaction startled her. She tried to think of a biblical story where a sacrifice rebelled. Isaac, Jepthah's daughter, Jesus. They had all cooperated. Isaac was spared, Jephthah's daughter wasn't, Jesus was complicated. What was she supposed to do now?

Her hands fluttered over her face. She hated that Joe would see her crying. She hated to lose control. The people in the *Martyrs Mirror* had never lost their composure. "I can't believe you said the F-word to me," she said through her choked throat. And now he was walking away.

She grabbed his arm and clung to it. Buried her face in his shoulder. He smelled so good, like some kind of spicy aftershave, and under that, his regular body scent.

He said something she couldn't hear. Cold winter air bit the back of her neck as she hugged him with both arms and wiped her wet face on his wool pea coat.

"Stay," she said. She looked up and saw that his cheeks were wet. She had never seen a guy cry before. She stood lightly on her toes to kiss him. They walked together all the way to her house where her mother and stepdad would not be home till much later. Though the night was cold, she felt warm all the way through. Burning hot.

The next morning, Juliana and Joseph met at the corner as usual, and walked to school. As they passed the red maple, Juliana noticed three orange plastic bags set in the angle of the street and driveway. One was partly open and leaves spilled out. The ground underneath the maple was raked bare.

Martyrdom

A few years later, Juliana held her young daughter, burning with fever, in her arms. The two of them waited in the hospital's urgent care waiting room. Rachel clutched a toy unicorn. The child had suffered a febrile seizure. The pediatrician told Juliana over the phone not to worry, that it was not rare for children under five to react to a high fever with a seizure, but to get the child a CT scan just in case. Since it wasn't an emergency, Joseph planned to wait till he got off work, then meet them at the hospital. Juliana wondered sometimes if she and Joe would still be together if they hadn't had Rachel. But what was the use of considering the hypothetical?

Rachel stroked the unicorn's sparkling mane. "Mama, I don't feel so well." Juliana longed to take her daughter's fever into herself. Let Rachel be okay.

She envied Great-Uncle Howard for his uncanny ability to take children's stomachaches. He didn't like to do it because it really worked, but sometimes when a child was sick, he would put one hand on the child's stomach and one on his own and mutter a special prayer under his breath. Minutes later the child would be skipping around the house asking for a peanut butter sandwich, while Uncle Howie lay on his side on the couch, eyes closed, hands clasped over his belly.

Now Juliana told Rachel about Uncle Howard as they sat on the black vinyl chairs and tried to tune out CNN news blaring from a television mounted over their heads. Juliana said she wished she could do Uncle Howie's trick and take her fever for her.

"No, Mommy. Don't say that!" Juliana loved Rachel's small chin when it quivered.

"Why not, sweetheart? It's what every mother wants to do for her child."

"Don't you ever try it." Too weak to hold her own head up, the little girl rested it against Juliana's palm. Rachel had inherited Joseph's black hair and serious forehead. Her eyes, hazel like her grandmother's, shone with a strange light.

"Shh, it's okay. I can't do it. But why don't you want me to?"

Rachel still leaned her head against her mother's hand, but her tiny voice was surprisingly strong. "That's what happened to Jesus. Every time he healed somebody, Jesus would get a little bit of what they had. When he healed the cripple, he got a little bit cripple. When he woke up the dead girl, he got a little bit dead. Then after he healed too many people, he got too much sickness and then he died."

"Is that what happened?"

"Mommy, promise me you won't take other people's sick on you because then you would die and I would rather die than live all alone without you. I need you." Her hot tears puddled into her mother's palm.

"Shh, shh. I won't do it, I promise. Shhh, it's okay. I'm right here to take care of you."

Her body was hot like a furnace. Juliana's cheek burned as she pressed it to her daughter's forehead. The things she had sacrificed for this child—graduate school, a career, that adolescent desire to be burned at the stake. She would do it again. Motherhood is its own kind of quiet martyrdom.

Through the large picture window, she watched outside for Joseph to come from the parking lot. A single maple tree glowed red-orange like it was on fire.

Leonhard Keyser, who would not burn

The priests spoke Latin to Leonhard Keyser
as he was wheeled in the cart to the fire
but he answered them in German
so the people could understand.

Then Leonhard Keyser leaned down from the cart,
plucked a flower with his tied hands, and said to the judge:

        Lord judge, here I pluck a flower;
        if you cannot burn both this flower and me
        then you must consider what you have done
        and repent.

And therefore when the wood was entirely consumed
his body was taken from the fire uninjured,
rolling out on the opposite side with
the unwithered flower in his hand,
his skin still smooth and white.

Then the three executioners cut him alive into pieces
which they cast into the fire, but they
succeeded only in burning the wood.

Jeremy Nafziger

Singing in the Mirror

I learned much of what I know about the Bible from singing. For example, "I know that my Redeemer lives" comes, in order, from the *Messiah*, from a folk hymn, and from Corinthians. Possibly Romans. And along those lines, I knew *Martyrs Mirror* as an opera before I read any of it.

The first I knew of *Martyrs' Mirror*, the opera,[1] we lived in Minnesota and traveled to Iowa, where my dad[2] sang in a performance that my sister and I didn't get to attend. I was very young and assumed a literal mirror. I pictured a martyr looking into it while being killed. In the performance, according to a few pictures I saw, my dad and three other martyrs were tied to a stake while wearing pilgrim's clothing, apparently in a high school gymnasium. There was only a vague, eventual connection to the only heavy, orange book on our shelf at home.

After that, my friend Kevin and I were at a playground, hiding in a gigantic tractor tire.

"What are you in church?" I said.

"What do you mean?"

"Like, Catholic or Lutheran or those . . . "

"Catholic," he said. He might not have been; I didn't realize that some people were none of these, and though it was a small town, it was a small town in well-western Minnesota, where the options were probably First, Second, or Faith Lutheran. We normally attended the latter, although sometimes we got up really early and drove far to a Mennonite church where I didn't know anyone in the Sunday school.

"We could play Catholics and Mennonites," I said. He looked confused. "Your people used to hunt us and execute us a long time ago."

He was more than happy for us both to be Mennonites then, running and hiding from his erstwhile co-religionists. It was quite a while later and even a few Mennonite history courses later that a friend of mine, a Catholic priest,

---

1   Alice Parker, *The Martyrs' Mirror* (Boston: E. C. Schirmer Music Co., 1973). Libretto by John Ruth, first performed in 1971.

2   Ken J. Nafziger.

pointed out that we should have been hiding from the Lutherans as well. As if one can really do that in Minnesota.

We moved to Virginia and my dad taught music and directed the choir at Eastern Mennonite College (EMC), and we only had to drive a few miles in any direction or a few miles more in any other direction to take our pick of Mennonite churches. *Martyrs Mirror*, the book, moved with us, unopened.

Then the college planned a performance of *Martyrs' Mirror*, the opera. Our family friend, Alice Parker, who wrote the music, was coming to conduct and she would stay in our basement. She had stayed with us before during a period in which I was working on tongue twisters. After she left, she sent back a page of some of the ones I'd told her, set to music. If it wasn't for the tune, I'd have long forgotten "Ethel, I have three thistles, three thistles in my mouth." You can also do it as a round.

Alice had visited us when the college did her opera *Family Reunion*. *Family Reunion* has lots of kids in the cast. I had been in that one before, back in Minnesota. I had one line to speak, none to sing alone. There weren't any solos for kids.

Martyrs' Mirror, the opera, on the other hand, has one big part for a boy soprano—the son of the doomed George and Catharina Blaurock. I didn't know this when my sister and I went to tryouts, as our dad apparently had a rule against mentioning too much to us that didn't get mentioned to the other kids. I think he was just keeping things fair, but the other kids probably knew more than we did because their parents read them the notes that got sent home.

The tryouts didn't involve cutting anyone out of the production but were more of a demonstration of people's willingness to show up. All the kids who came would be in the opera in some fashion, mostly as members of the crowd that attends the festival and executions. A bunch of faculty kids and others, all Mennonites as far as I remember, sang together while my dad and Barb, who was the director, walked around and listened.[3]

But for the part of the Blaurocks' son, the auditions were in fact tryouts. You have to be aware of competition for it to affect you, but even had I known, it would only have made a difference to me after I did or didn't win it—and that's not being competitive, that's being jealous, at which I was quite adept. But I had a relaxed to non-existent view of competition then. My general goal was to do well and do well

---

3   My dad hears singing so well that he can and does use this method of audition, sometimes even for his college chamber choir. It's pretty amazing. He doesn't even walk around—he can do it sitting at the front.

enough. I enjoyed Little League, for example, but I didn't have a sense of strategy; I just tried to get hits and catch the ball, and figured things would work out or not. I didn't have a winner's edge, that last bit that borders on violence that demands you not only do your best but that you do *better than*, that interior teammate's voice that says, while the competition is going on, "We're going to win this thing." Being *the* best, rather than *your* best, was to give in to the competition, which is of course what it means to compete, but that was something I didn't get.

While I lacked competitive, I did not lack comparative. See jealousy, aforementioned, which generally occurs after the fact. For examples: In fifth grade, I had been second in the school spelling bee, second to the cute sixth grader who played the same instrument, French horn, that I played in the younger band class. We both went to the county bee, where I was fourth and she won. You only had to be in the top five to get to the regional bee, which seemed eminently easy as I sat on the stage before it started. I think I missed *negotiate*, having earlier gotten a chuckle from the crowd when I asked for a definition of *inebriate*. The next year, I was second again in the school bee, behind Juliet who could have been Juliet on any stage. We both went to the county bee, and I was in the top five again.

Both times I was happy with my accomplishment—until later when I wondered why I didn't just stay in a while longer and win the thing. I mean, *negotiate*? But winning was beyond the scope of what I came to do. I maybe could have won, I maybe could have drawn other words, could definitely have studied more. But I didn't.

Both those years, I went to the regional bee in Waynesboro, and there you had to win outright to go to nationals in Washington, D.C. It just never seemed like that was going to happen. Nothing in my head even vaguely suggested that we were going to win this thing, and I bowed out fairly early both times. One year the word was *outmoded*.

The year of *Martyrs' Mirror*, the opera, I was in the eighth grade. Most of my good friends, Mennonite kids, had left John W. Wayland Middle School that year for Eastern Mennonite High School. I had wanted to go, too. It was a miserable year. I even wrote a letter to Dear Abby. I went to a school dance and at the end of it, with my nerve finally having arrived, asked a girl who I really liked to dance. She first checked with someone else, but fortunately (I guess), he was otherwise occupied. That was sort of how the year went, but somewhere in it, I was third at the school spelling bee, just good enough for the county bee, and I was third there (a career high), setting me up for another trip to Waynesboro in my last year (according to the broadcaster in my head) of eligibility. *Can the cagey veteran finally put together the performance that has eluded him all these years?* the voice continued.

Around the same time was that *Martyrs' Mirror* audition, and a few days after that, my mom asked my dad whether my sister and I were going to be in it, and he said yes. I wasn't going to be "the son," he said, but just in the crowd. This was the first I knew of the son, and I didn't know whose son, but I was disappointed. A kid named Randy was going to be the son. I barely knew him, but I was jealous.

But then things started to happen as if out of a noncompetitive, jealous person's dreams: I was going to win without having competed. It turned out Randy had something else going on the week of the performances. Maybe it was a family vacation. I remember being told by my dad that I was their next choice.[4] He seemed a little nervous, maybe because I wasn't the best choice, or because he didn't like telling his son that he wasn't the first choice.

However, the regional spelling bee and one of the performances were on the same day. I was asked to decide—no pressure either way.

Let's get this straight right away that this was no martyrdom situation. I'm not drawing a parallel of any kind. There were two equally good choices here, one of which I was going to have to give up sadly. There was not a good and righteous choice next to an evil, herd-following alternative. The fact was, I wasn't going to win the regional spelling bee and go to the national bee in Washington and stay in a hotel and all that. I talked to Barb once outside my dad's office and told her

---

4   That's exactly what he said. Many years later, I sang tenor in a 24-voice choir as-
     sembled by my dad to perform Bach's B-Minor Mass at the Eastern Mennonite
     University Bach Festival. At the first rehearsal, we each introduced ourselves and said
     which voice part we were singing. I said, "I'm Jeremy Nafziger, and I'm singing in
     the nepotism section." Everyone cracked up, but it's complicated. I sing pretty well
     and read music well, but there are lots of people who sing better and read better and
     don't get the chances I do. Then again, there are lots of reasons why people get jobs
     or promotions or other things when they aren't the best possible choice in all possible
     worlds. The "all possible worlds," it seems to me, is the key, since we don't live in all
     possible worlds. We live in the one where I was available and love to sing in my dad's
     choirs and often find it frustrating to sing for other conductors, and my dad a) knows
     I love it and b) is extremely fair. The evidence for b) is that I don't always get in to my
     dad's choirs. One year at the Bach Festival I didn't, and some people asked me why I
     didn't, and I said, "Who do you have to be related to to sing in this choir?" Another
     time, a couple tenors from the initial roster (who I would have picked over myself if
     I were making the list) couldn't make it, and I got to sing the St. Matthew. Which
     brings up another point—you really increase your odds of making a choir, even if
     you're not related to anyone, if you sing tenor.

that I was probably going to be in the opera, and she said she was glad I was "at least leaning" their way. In the end, I just dropped the spelling bee.

At the first staging rehearsal, in the Discipleship Center on the hill, I was relieved to find I didn't have to sing my part yet, just move to the right places. The bailiff, who was arresting George (a college student named Gary) and Catharina (a local woman named Susan), was a rather large college student who had just come from playing basketball. He was drenched with sweat. When Barb told him to grab George by the arm, George made him stand as far away from him as he could and still reach him.

I had a few rehearsals by myself with Marge, who taught voice at the college. I could sing the notes without too much trouble, surely more easily than I could have spelled words in Waynesboro. There was a problem, though: my voice. Sometimes it didn't work. As the notes got up to a very predictable pitch (the fourth-line D on a treble clef staff), it felt like the sound was striking a glass ceiling (which was *not* a term for something else when I was 13) built into the back of my throat. The tones that came out sounded like that glass had broken. I felt that ceiling wedged in my throat.

The most frustrating thing for a kid, I have noticed in my own children, is almost being able to do something. You never feel you're worse at something than right before you get better at it, when the old method won't accomplish what the improved one will, and you only know enough about the new one to know that it's going to completely replace the old. It's the price for maybe one day being better.

But your performance on a given day is only tangentially related to your prospects for future competence. I didn't have long—weeks, maybe—to get this voice thing figured out. There also wasn't much you could do about it. Marge called it "the break" and showed me ways to work through it or around it. The way you did it was to stop singing hard against the ceiling and to let the sound flip over it, into your head. We did short scales starting a few notes below the break and ending a few above it, and sometimes it went smoothly and sometimes it didn't, and I never knew which it was going to be until afterward, which was too late for live performing. I knew the feeling it had to have, and I could sing below it, and above it, but getting between the two was a crap-shoot. With Marge's help, the dice were slightly loaded, but that was all.

This was nerve-wracking and a little disheartening, but there wasn't much to do about it. It must have been the same for my dad, who was in charge of the music, to have his son exhibiting the potential for a disastrous performance; maybe it made it better that little of it was my fault, maybe that made it worse. He didn't give me much advice, except once. After a rehearsal, I was saying something about how it went and he interrupted me: "You have got to open your mouth."

I still do it today; I don't open my mouth much when I sing unless I make myself do it. Maybe that habit started when I was unsure of what would come out. Dad told me to practice the songs in the mirror. I did, or practiced opening my mouth at the mirror, not wanting to sing out loud in the house just then. Even looking at my own half-closed mouth, I couldn't open it wider. Worrying about the back of my throat wasn't helping the front of it. Seeing myself screwing this up was not helping me feel like I was not about to screw this up.

While Marge helped me understand how to sing, Barb explained my place in the action. It was considerably more simple, I thought—as simple as singing would have been if my voice weren't shooting craps. In the opera, the son is the voice of innocence. The kids in Alice's operas are guileless, and even their occasional misbehavior is of the good-hearted kind.

I could still credibly have been the voice of innocence. I was barely a teenager, and most afternoons I played football or Wiffle Ball in our backyard, and my parents never embarrassed me in front of anyone. I noticed girls but the closest I'd come to touching one was that school dance fiasco, and I didn't know what the options were should such a situation arise again. I didn't even know you had options. I got up early to do the paper route I'd had since fifth grade and would keep through high school. I studied when I didn't know the answers, I answered, I tried to listen in church, I was moved by holidays and both the end of school and the end of summer.

But not entirely. There were undercurrents. In something of a despair over the coming school year, with most of my friends at another school, I'd been baptized a few months earlier, which I didn't regret but felt either slightly foolish about or slightly stunned that it hadn't changed more than it did. Then there was politics—the state. I'd started reading *Bloom County*, which confirmed what some people had asked us on a street in Amsterdam on November 5, 1980: "How could you elect the cowboy?" The nuclear threat was absolutely real, and the cowboy joked about it, and even an eighth grader could see that nothing was actually going to trickle down. This concerned me. There was a difference between things going badly by accident (as they seemed to have done under Jimmy Carter) and going badly, even dangerously, on purpose.

And on the night of the dress rehearsal, I heard a little girl (guileless) in the choir ask Alice what was wrong with my voice.

Alice saw that I had overheard, even though the girl had asked quietly. So she answered in a tone that she knew I could hear. "Do you know what is happening to Jeremy? His voice is starting to change, and that's something that happens to boys. . . ." I didn't hear the rest; it was a perfect and unsettling answer at the same time.

Martyrs' Mirror, the opera, starts like this: A liturgical procession crosses the stage, while my "Friend" and I observe from the side.[5]

> Me: What beautiful robes.
> Friend: Yes, it's a special day: the Feast of the Adoration of the Host. . . .[6]
> Me: My Father says that is not part of Christ's teachings.
> Friend: Oh, but it is. Did He not say, "This is my body?"
> Me: But He didn't mean it to be carried around, and bowed down to.

The chorus kneels as the host passes by—all except George, my father. The monk tells him he is a dangerous man who will be prosecuted. When the procession exits, George preaches: "Brothers and sisters . . . a new day is upon us. We can read the Book, we can learn Christ's lesson. We can follow Him in life. . . . Christ gives us love that casts out fear."

In the next scene, the representatives of the state church/church state—the fat bailiff and the dapper monk (an English major with a beard)—read an edict from an emperor and a king to a bunch of sub-monarchs calling for the persecution and execution of the Anabaptists. I remember with how much relish the bailiff spat, "their *damned* opinions," which would *not* have passed the EMC administrative censors in another show.

My parents and I discuss the edict, singing our lines now. This whole scene is set below my break and I have no worries about this one, except for the one interval I consistently cannot hear or sing. "There is no other way," my father says.

"Will you be put in jail?" I ask. The "put in jail" is the tricky one, and it's harder with the orchestra. Alice helped me through this one, too. When I messed up the notes in the first performance, she took me aside minutes before the second one and said she was changing her cue to have the accompaniment sound before I sang, rather than our starting together. When I followed her

---

5 Capitalization in the original.
6 Ed: According to historian Joe Springer, "This would be the holiday known as 'Corpus Christi'—celebrated on the Thursday after Trinity Sunday (first Sunday after Pentecost), usually occurring in June."

exactly, she praised me afterward for getting it right with no rehearsal, and I felt moderately professional.

There's a Bible school scene with me and my mother and the children from the choir, who all sing their short lines well and without worrying about any vocal break-up. I quote a verse and it turns into an imitative stretch, me leading and the kids repeating for almost four pages in the score, all of it below my glass ceiling.

Next, the believers come to our house for a secret meeting. The other two martyrs are there, with Mayeken holding her baby. Her husband, Jan, is the song leader, the charismatic part of the ministry, sort of like that really cool youth pastor you had once; he leads a Tallis tune.[7] The bailiff comes and says he wants to get baptized, and is. Then he asks if he can go get his wife and kids.

"If you betray us, God will be your judge," says my father.

The hymn ends with "slaughtered by the score."

The bailiff returns. He wasn't getting his wife and kids after all: "NOW, you nest of singing baptizers,[8] you are under arrest!"

Father gets arrested first. Mother says, "God spare us our dear pastor," a rather impersonal reaction, and she is next. Jan speaks out about "treachery to innocent, God-fearing people" and is grabbed. Mayeken beseeches the bailiff to "Please, leave him," and she is the fourth.

The four prisoners can hear each other in prison, and since (as happens in an astonishing number of operas) they have the voices for a quartet, they sing

---

7 "How shallow former shadows" in the blue hymnal [*Hymnal: A Worship Book*], and the main instrumental theme in *Master and Commander*, the movie. There are almost a dozen hymns in the opera that I didn't remember were there until I looked at the score. One part of Alice's genius in music shows in how often you already know the tune, can learn the arrangement easily, and then never really care whether you hear the original version again. She could obliterate most of the hymnal this way and as long as we could still sing it in church, I wouldn't mind. She works these hymns into the piece deftly, without pandering—which would have been an easy thing to do, since a Mennonite audience knows them all. The range of stuff she and the indispensible John Ruth cover in the libretto is also impressive. After you hear *Martyrs' Mirror*, the opera, you only have to read *Martyrs Mirror*, the book, for specifics rather than for themes or theology.

8 "Singing baptizers" is awesome. I suggest changing all Anabaptist history books to claim that "Anabaptist" really means "singing baptizers." In what language does "ana-" mean "re-," anyway? I mean, besides Greek.

a hymn. This is the first appearance of "Mit Lust so will ich singen," or "I sing with exultation," which really is a martyr's text, written in prison and preserved in the *Ausbund*.[9] A small crowd gathers outside and sings with them.

Later, the four are interrogated. Another "damned" is dropped. They are tortured to the extent that they have to stop singing "A mighty fortress." A small group of sympathizers visits them in prison, bringing food and letters. Catharina never learned to write, she says, but she wants to send a token to her son: one of the pears that the group had brought. "Say his mother sent it to him from jail to show her parting love to her Son." She prays his life "will bring much fruit for Christ."[10]

The monk and bailiff return and condemn the four to death by fire. Mayeken loses it: Jan didn't tell her, she says, where it would lead. "I'm not strong enough to be a martyr."

This is human enough, to be sure. But it seems to me now that real martyrs do not have a choice. There are probably pathological cases who would die when they could live, just because dying would bring greater attention or glory to their cause. But the real ones aren't nearly so calculating. I question whether they even have causes, as we usually consider causes—stopping abortion, equality, cutting taxes, shrinking government, no nukes, abolishing the Federal Reserve. What they have are convictions. Pair those with a justice system that doesn't concern itself over niceties like evidence and intent and proportional punishment, and their only way out is to play nice with the state and the church, tell them what they want to hear. But there are those convictions—without them, they'd be Kevin and I hiding in a tire until dinner time. While certainly some who were martyred had less faith and conviction than others, it's just as certain that all those who were killed had more than the normal measure: enough not to have a choice when it came right down to it.

---

9   Ed: Hymnbook that includes songs written by and about the sixteenth-century Anabaptist martyrs; still in use today in Amish communities.

10 The martyrs in *Mirror*, the opera, are composites, except for George (d. 1529 in Tyrol)—and his real trial and execution were different than what happens in the opera (though the betrayal by an informant who wanted to go get his wife and kids did happen). There was a Jan Wouters (d. 1572, Dortrecht). There was a Maeyken Wouters (d. 1595), but she was executed with an older woman, not with her husband. And there isn't a Catharina Blaurock in the *Martyrs Mirror*, the book, but there is a Maeyken Boosers (d. 1564 in Belgium), executed at age 24. And *that* Maeyken sent a pear from prison to her very young son, who did not eat it, but kept it. It is in a museum in Amsterdam. The scene is sad but borderline manipulative in the opera—unless you know it's real. If you know the story, it's even sadder, along with amazing—but not surprising: How starving would a son have to be to eat the pear his mother sent him from prison while awaiting execution?

We come right down to it after intermission. The bells are ringing and it's market day, as innocently exposited by children skipping down the aisles singing, "Hooray, it's market day." Men are exhibiting wares, singing about the imminent demonstration of the state's power; the women join in the market day song as the jailers and the four condemned process from the back.

A man in the crowd asks Mayeken (who, by the way, is beautiful) for a goodbye kiss, followed by stage directions for "raucous laughter." My mother, in different words, tells them to shut up. To the monk's suggestion that they have "defied the emperor" she sings that "the emperor should rule—it is his duty. Yet there is one above the emperor. . . . Let us render unto Caesar, what is Caesar's, and unto God all that is rightfully His."

"At the end, the Son stands," say the staging notes. This is it.

"Be true to Christ, mother!" I call out from the crowd, in D. She answers, and the bailiff tells her to "keep moving." But the executioner, centurion at the crucifixion, says, "Let her have her say. She sounds like an honest woman." She sings me one of the verses from the Bible school scene.

> My friend comes to me: Will they truly Kill your Mother?
> Me: (F and marcato) She dies in Christ.
> Friend: She doesn't need to die. They would free her in a moment. They don't want to kill her.
> Executioner: True. That is true.
> Friend: Tell her, you tell her to live.

We're in E now and that means the D#s and the Es are on one side of my break and the rest of the song I'm about to sing is on the other. It is "Mit Lust" again, me and the woodwinds, the choir standing and watching and the stage is more or less mine, but I don't take it so much as stand on it.

> *But she would have to say*
> *that all that she believes is not true.*
> *She knows that Christ our Lord*
> *Himself was put to death on the Cross.*
> *How could she deny Him,*
> *and all that she believes?*
> *How could she deny Him?*
> *It is the only way.*
> Friend: I don't understand.
> Executioner: I envy her her faith and her Son.

That's the last son part in the opera. Between those last two lines, the son breaks through the guards and wraps his arms around his mother. I think I did it awkwardly, but the audience took the drama's emotion, which was considerable, rather than relying on what my acting ability—and 13-year-old awkwardness at hugging a woman—conveyed.

In the end, this all went pretty well. I heard a tape of it a few years later and thought it actually sounded good. My dad agreed and told me so. But here's what happened on the stage. The performances were on two weekends, Friday and Saturday. The first weekend, I got through without noticing anything around me other than that my voice did not perpetrate any major infractions. Then we had almost a week off, with maybe one walk-through rehearsal so we'd remember what we were doing.

During the break, I stopped worrying about what would happen in performance and started worrying about what would happen when it was over. I didn't think about my younger voice, which was probably going to hold out a few days more. I'd be in the choir at high school next year and I could learn to sing again in another clef.

But though my martyr parents died every night, they came back the next day and we did it again. At the last performance, they would really be dead, for all time. So would my old, young voice, and so would my character, something I've never thought of as separate from myself and did not until the last line of my song that last night. I've heard that acting isn't deciding what you would do in a situation, but deciding what your character would do, and method acting is, more or less, when those two are the same thing. My method was to completely choke up as soon as the song ended, sprint wildly and blindly to Susan, and hug her a long time, and hard like I meant it and I did. I had won something, even conquered. That my opera parents would soon be victorious over a stage reproduction of the state was the most moving thing I'd ever thought of, and that I would be bereft was the most real, real as a sob.

Martyrs' Mirror, the opera, went on. The men in the choir start an "evil heretics" mantra over which George and the women in the choir sing another hymn tune, "Christ's servants follow him in life," and Mayeken and George discuss whether I too will (one day, not that one) "have to die for [my] faith."

A small choir asks, "Could not these harmless citizens be spared? . . . Can they be murdered in the name of Christ?" The score calls it an "incipient riot" that builds to cries of "tear down the stakes" and "let them go." The crowd comes down around the stakes like a fog around hills, until Alice cuts them off mid-measure and they freeze silent.

Innocent Mayeken understands now, too. She walks toward the stake herself and sings from Isaiah, "Thou wilt keep him in perfect peace, whose mind is stayed on Thee." As she passes, the crowd unclenches fists, becomes bystanders. The children bring back the Bible school melody that I, the oldest kid and preacher's son, had taught them, this time to "God has put a song on her lips."

After all four martyrs turn down one more chance to recant—what choice did they have?—the final preparations begin. George asks whether someone will take a message to the brethren "in Moravia," that these four died rejoicing in the Lord. "They will be told," a man in the crowd calls, and the monk whirls to see who said it. Jan says his shoes are new, someone can use them. The executioner asks their forgiveness. "Step forward and do your work," George says. "We will meet the Bridegroom with our lamps burning." He sees, he sings, Revelation: the city of God coming to earth.

A torch is lit—"acetylene flame, 12 inches high, scary," according to the staging directions. The crowd chants "Fire!" and sings "The Lord will come with fire." Above it, we hear the American folk tune "Protection," one I never have to think about where I learned it first, with these lines I never forget:

> *The flames shall not hurt thee, I only design*
> *thy dross to consume, and thy gold to refine.*

"The rest is as a still frame at the end of a movie," according to the staging directions. The crowd helps the martyrs down from their stakes; they are dead, this is fantasy. A psalm: "O God for your sake they are killed all the day long." And from the balcony, hidden, the small chorus convinced, intertwined: "In all these things, we are more than conquerors through Him who loved us." The singers on stage and those upstairs exchange the confident negations—neither death, nor angels, nor principalities, nor things present, nor things to come, nor powers, nor depth, nor space, nor time, nor anything else. Nor confusion nor baptism, nor a change of key, change of voice. Nor reflection. We're going to win this thing.

Over a quiet hymn, a long list of martyrs is named. And then a prayer from the New Leader, and Mennonites that we are, we on stage and we in the balcony and we in the audience, stand and sing *mit lust*, sing with exultation.

Ars Moriendi

Babels Raets Mandamenten Worden
aldus Volbracht Door haer Dienaers . . .
—song for six Anabaptist martyrs

We six, in 1559,[1]
hummed the tune of "Zion Wilt
Thou Gather," suffering no small guilt
for savoring a verdict so divine.
To die as Christ—what luck! And what an art
to get the tongue to run with praise enough,
like a chicken with its head cut freshly off!
And what a wholesome sacerdotal sport
to wave away the burgher's casket of
exploding Chinese powder, which he meant
to girdle round our knees, whereby he'd prove
his disapproval of the punishment.
We said that we preferred the flames ascending,
like him who granted us this happy ending.

---

1   Ed: Composite characters.

Singing at the Fire

The song's impossible to sing
without hands becoming fists,
without the stone weight of pain
stabbing your gut like a sharp star,
without grace.

Seven martyrs made it up
in solitary cells. Each one composed a prayer
in a meter they must have agreed on. One
cries out in fear, one
begs God for help, another intercedes
fervently for the persecutors, pleads
for the faithful who will live.
One was a woman. Another a young boy. Picture them

singing while the flesh burns, the breath
lifting a melody, the stubborn tongue
in the seared mouth shaping the smoke-
blackened words.

No record's kept of the seven.
No one knows what the heart-wrenched angel writes
in blood in the lamb's book. No one knows the names
engraved on white stone. The sacred stone
those slain seven hold, to whom is given
the small unflinching light
of the morning star.

Seven martyrs
Schwäbisch Gmünd, 1529

JESSE NATHAN

Will We Burn? Will the River Run?

Break my hand and pray the river will save us. Don't let it go—
Ach! The sky is the color of pebbles the color of mice. They hate us.

But see how the river moves round the bend, into plain speech, horses into poems?
No, love. The sun is sunk. The river runs. Night falls like ash. No poems.

But I am your daughter!
I say time is a letter a stone wrote. I say time is a swimmer counting rafts in a river.

So? What if they light a fire to us and we don't burn?
A pebble is powerless. Who knew our pyres so soon would come?

Father, we could tread miles yet in this sunset. Why do you speak in a lonely tongue?
Because a pebble burdens, lovely and terrible. See the horizon, clouds in the shapes
    of fierce cats?

I am a girl awakened in the morning light of her life to a knock.
I am a man awakened in the middle of his life to the smell of fire.

WATER

Dirk Willems
Jan Luyken

BARBARA NICKEL

Maria of Monjou, 1552

I feel their rope around her naked thighs,
the mud slick on the bank. She won't forsake
that water down her neck, the blessing—*Baptized
in Christ*—as clerics fix a weighing rock.
I see her pressed under the river's braiding
currents, the shawls of leech and silt across
her back. A perch nibbles pieces. Shale blades
and shells erode the knots. By spring she's loose
in the sandy lobes of shallows where foxes come
to drink, nudge up small bones that run with seeds
of willow downstream and snag on rapids foaming
at the river's throat. Here all converges, seethes.
Close to the falls I feel a seam of mist
breathe down my arms to find my beating wrists.

Brides

Aeltgen Baten before they covered her
eyes and bound her cried out: Lord
what a beautiful city. She fell
shoved by her escort over the edge
of the Meuse bridge. Her body,
a plumbline's perfect weight, plunged
straight and sank. For faithful Aeltgen
drowning was a consummation.

Maeyken when she fell floated
so the story goes. Her young cheeks
bloomed like tulips, a soft south wind
made a sail of her skirts and like Ophelia
or the Lady of Shalott she drifted past
the bridge: the perfect bride, blind-
folded and like old Aeltgen chaste
when she reached the city.

Aeltgen Baten
Maeyken Wouters
thrown from the Meuse bridge
near Sonhoven, 1595

The Complete Water Deal

Baby Showers

I like to say My People, with capital letters and a fanfare if possible, since it gives me the aura of coming from a rare tribe lost in the wilderness, when in fact they were just a simple gang of farmers and merchants, who thought they might make a better living if God was on their side.

God was readily available back in the medieval day, not like today. You try getting a hold of God now and you have to punch an infinite number of buttons before you get to talk to a real human being. But back then, some parts of God had splintered off the standard model. The standard model had proved faulty, as evidenced by the appearance of two Popes at the same time, the invention of money, and the fact that He was late for supper. And so people began taking on the task of building utopias themselves, which a bit later led to the French Revolution, Socialism, Marxist communism, Zionism, Nazism, California, and the Mennonites.

My People—the latter, a gang clinging to the Nordsee by their skinny fingers—decided that the most important thing in this whole debate was water. So they began their own start-up since the God stocks were going through the roof, and sold it as the Complete Water Deal.

At least, that's how their competition saw it. Other start-ups—including the guy who got in on the ground floor, Mr. Luther—thought the whole thing was going too far.

Originally, as far back as Luther could remember, people had to have a shower when they were babies in order to get into the church club. In those days, water was as well liked as witches, and most serfs and princes and priests and harlots avoided the stuff like the plague. The church club at the time thought that one shower a lifetime should be enough for everyone, just as Bill Gates once thought that 64K would be about all anybody would ever need.

My People wanted everyone to take a bath.

They said that Jesus took a bath and John the Baptist took a bath before they were allowed in the club, so why shouldn't we? Of course, My People had a stronger than medievally normal odor about them because they were farmers in a marsh, and bathing may have had its practical applications as well. Plus, being dike makers, they were used to getting soaked.

Unfortunately, there was a name mix-up that started at this point when My People didn't know they'd last this long, thinking it was perhaps a fad, and so didn't register a name. Because of this, they got mixed up with every other protesting club in the 1500s, which was quite easy since everyone was confused anyway, having just come out of the Dark Ages.[1] But at the beginning, they simply called themselves The Brothers. Unfortunately, it was kind of a secret name and nobody else knew what to call them, so they were alternately labeled the Doopsgesindes (Those With Water on the Brain), Anabaptists (The Re-sprinklers), or simply the Double-Dipping Brudders.

Soon a trend began that named groups of believers after the people they followed, like Luther, Buddha, Christ, Judah, and Atheos. Thus, a few years later the Mennonites arose around Menno Simons, and following the tradition really should have been called Simonites, but that was too close to Samsonite and Simoniz, which would eventually be copyrighted by luggage and car polish companies respectively, and anyway both involved the sins of traveling and cars. When Mennonites kept splintering to outdo each other in not having pride, the same naming technique was used. This led to Jacob Hutter spawning the Hutterites in the same century. The Hutterites are still around today and are relatively easy to spot, since they live in communes but are allowed to drive vehicles, although they limit themselves to GMC Suburbans and John Deere combines. They also believe that the golden age of man was marked by beards, long skirts, aprons, and polka-dotted headscarves in the tradition of communists. In the next century, Jacob Ammann split off from the Swiss Mennonites to invent the Amish, probably the most famous Mennonites thanks to their love of horses, fear of electricity, and Kelly McGillis, all very understandable obsessions as far as I'm concerned. Then in the nineteenth century John Holdeman took another group backwards in time to create the Holdemans, who rejected neckties and whitewall tires and favored black bonnets, but found communal living too intimate. In

---

1   Ed: Historian Joe Springer notes: "Rempel's style is such that we probably should not worry too much about historical accuracy . . . . 'Dark Ages' is a nebulous term, but when referring to Western Europe [the era was] probably over at least 150 years before the Reformation." Likewise, *Doopsgesindes* for *Doopsgesinden*, *Brudders* for *Brüder*, whitewall tires in the nineteenth century, full conflation of Peasant's War and Anabaptist movement, etc., should be taken with a poetic grain of salt.

the twentieth century, Evangelical Mennonites began, who I believe were named after my mother, Evangeline, due to her outgoing nature and tendency to tell everyone what to do.

But no matter what name was used, in the 1500s the Holy Roman Church Club could only equate this radical concept of bathing with the equally reprehensible idea of sharing; and then My People really got carried away and decided that bathing and sharing *at the same time* would be a neat idea, kind of like the 1970s fad of showering with a friend.

The ramifications of this were too much for the Emperor Charles V, the Pope, and Mr. Luther and his friends, and they immediately began killing the stinky farmers whenever possible. As this was the end of the Dark Ages, killing and torturing were done with modern inventions. A popular method was to invite everyone to a public barbeque, where My People were the main course; nifty barbeque tools were used too, with the application of hot coals or glowing pincers to pull out tongues. Fire was quite popular for execution at the time as it purified the soul, much as barbequing steak insures there are no bacteria. However, Anabaptists who recanted were shown mercy and had their heads cut off instead; women were often tied up in a hemp bag, and *then* given a bath. Also, the homes of Anabaptists or their sympathizers were burned to the ground or razed. Today it may be difficult to understand why these methods of helping people with their religious choices were used, except for the razing of homes, which is currently enjoying a renaissance in Palestine.

To fully comprehend those times, you have to put yourself in the shoes of a medieval peasant, much as you may find them ill fitting and smelly. Your whole life is centered on one goal: not dying. To reach this goal, however, there are numerous things you have to do. You have to be a slave and pay the Prince taxes, which are currently about 99 percent of your income. You have to find enough food to eat, although you don't have any money left and the Prince regularly takes your harvest, never mind your daughters. On top of that, in 1523–24 you experience two crop failures. With the money that's left over from your dry stalks of grass, you now have to pay the church club a hefty tithe to support a priest living high on your hog. Even God is apparently also trading in cash, and willing to take down payments on purgatory to erect magnificent cathedrals where you can go and not understand anything. If you try to hunt an animal you are hunted in turn, since the Prince needs the animals for his amusement, and the animals stink less than you. The firewood that keeps you alive during the winter must be bought at double the going price, while forests grow untouched behind you—the Prince, again. And the land you held together—sharing it with the community—is bought up by Princes and, worst of all crimes, is subdivided and given names like Forestview Place.

This is essentially the list of grievances proclaimed during the Peasant's Revolt. In 1525, up to 75,000 peasants were murdered for the crime of wanting a better life. Do these people never learn?

The Swim Team

Despite all these hardships, including but not limited to the difficulty of getting indoor plumbing, My People stuck to the Complete Water Deal with admirable tenacity. So much so that today, almost five hundred years later, while many Anabaptist beliefs and customs have come and gone, swimming for salvation is still front and center in the church.

I brought my Quebecois girlfriend, Geneviève, to my hometown last year, and she came to the church where I was dipped. She'd been to church before of course, a real one, with incense and robes and Latin and virgins and everything. I'd gone with her to a Catholic sprinkling, and the priest had flirted with me. But this was her first time with the Simple People. I'd told her a few things here and there about what to expect, and she had no idea what I was talking about.

"So they have specialties," she said. It sounded like a Blue Plate at the diner.

"Yeah," I said. "For instance, the church has no decoration to speak of." My parents were decorators and would have loved to get the contract, but the church only put in new carpet and drapery once every thirty years. The last époque I'd seen was the Seventies.

"My mom used to believe incense was of the devil. Possibly still does. Granted, sandalwood is pretty dicey. Also, Birkenstocks used to be grounds for getting the schaft."

"The schaft?"

"The Bruderschaft. The meeting of the brudders. Cancelled your subscription. Revoked membership. Barred from the joint."

"For sandals?" She checked out my feet. I was wearing Danish farm shoes. Clogs. Very macho, in Denmark.

Then there was the bathtub at the front of the church.

"Wait a minute," my girlfriend said. "You mean you go in the water?"

"Right in. All the way down."

"Do they give you a bathing suit?"

"Nope. Sunday best. White shirt and tie. Better to pull you up with if you lose it."

The bathtub, about the size of Hugh Hefner's hot tub, was located about ten feet up flush behind the wall, with a glass front about three feet high. Four steps led into the water. There was a hidden microphone somewhere, and all the ambient noise that accompanies a bath was relayed through the church. The best part in watching other people go down was waiting for the water to splash over the glass and into the choir. It didn't always happen. It took one of three types: those afraid of water who would fight the experience; differently challenged kids who were always splashing anyway; and people whose girth simply displaced the bathtub water.

I got baptized there when I was about sixteen, which was seen as kind of the age of reason when you could decide things for yourself. My age of reason only occurred about twenty years later, but I was anxious to get in the water. Around that time I had met a girl from the Big City who belonged to a Swim Team, which I found enticingly exotic, largely because at the time there was no swimming pool in my hometown, but also because she looked great in a bathing suit. It became my mission to join a swim team myself, where I could stand around the Olympic sized pool wearing almost no clothes, exchanging witticisms and staring at her and her friends. Unfortunately I was unable to pursue the idea much further, not only for lack of a pool, but also I wasn't particularly interested in swimming, never mind training and competing.

There were meetings with the pastor before the baptism so we could understand the seriousness of our decision. We were to understand that not only were we making a public pronouncement about our religious beliefs, we were also becoming a member of the Church Club.

"Do we get bathing suits?" I asked.

There were eight people going in the tub before me, and being unversed in metaphor I was a little suspicious about the whole cleansing aspect of it. But I had little choice. It was the only Swim Team in town. I tried to generate some of the excitement of hanging out with my fellow athletes at pool side, and asked what kind of entry they were going to try, and how many laps they thought we might have to do, but was largely ignored since most were busy adjusting their nose plugs and wondering how cold the water would be. While there were no judges with scorecards, I knew my peers had taken the rare move of coming down from their usual perch in the last row of the church balcony and sitting in the front rows. This was not because of a spiritual resurgence on their part, but because a number of young girls were joining the Club as well, and the whole thing had the potential to turn into an Anabaptist wet T-shirt contest.

Except for being the center of attention for a few minutes, the Swim Team thing was disappointing. There were no badges, no snapping of towels in the changing room after, and I soon gave up my athletic ambitions for other pursuits. In my last year in high school and my last year in my hometown, a real pool was finally built. On graduation night, a Bad Influence and I jumped the fence and went skinny-dipping.

Just as we were exalting in our freedom, a flashlight shone on my bare butt.

"Get out of the water," said one of the two Mounties, who was a woman.

My ancestors' lives passed before my eyes. Were they still hunting us? We climbed out of the pool naked and shriveled.

"There's been some vandalism here," the Mounties explained. "We've been monitoring the pool for some time."

"Oh, we're not Vandals," I said. "They came more from the eastern part of Germany, and sacked Rome."

"We're making a public pronouncement," said my friend.

"That's right," I said. "It's a club thing. Can we get our bathing suits?"

That was my real baptism, and after that I moved out of my hometown for good.

Maurice Mierau

The difference between a martyr and a suicide

The sack bursting open off
a high bridge to expel this
man I admire, a martyr—

not an eloquent suicide

(not that he didn't cling to the sack
his fingers an unspeakable confession
playing an inaudible instrument),

the town executioner struck him blind
with a stick: oh how you murder me—[1]

this man like a frog falling heavily
into stagnant water, I pity you,
the sack bursting open—

a martyr who could not live
in the flesh
drowning in it.

---

1   Jan Jans Brant

Morus Rubra

The morning after the fire, Oney Friesen sees a tree she doesn't recognize a quarter mile away in a neighboring hayfield. It's bent over at the trunk, as if a long-forgotten storm attempted to pull this tree out by its roots, but only managed to twist the trunk into a painful angle. She thought of Oma's[1] hands; arthritis had curled her fingers into a similar position before she died.

She wonders how she could have missed such a tree in plains of pastures and hayfields devoid of trees other than *Maclura pomifera*—hedge apple trees. She wonders if this circle of the earth is filled with trees that remain to be seen.

Up close, the leaves on the tree are thinned from the summer heat and provide an irregular shade. Oney guesses it's an *Acer negundo*—ash-leaf maple—but she can't be sure without Oma's eye. Oma had known the name of every weed, tree and grass that she came upon. She called them by their Latin names: *Amaranthus spinosus, Parietaria pensylvanica, Ambrosia artemisiifolia, Morus rubra.*

Oney wonders who owns this field. She scans the horizon, as if that will reveal the owner's identity.

Jack would've known, she mutters to herself. Her younger brother had been the wanderer of the family, riding his bike around every farmstead within a ten-mile radius and introducing himself to everyone he saw. *Glad-handing like a billijch Laundeskaunsla—a cheap politician*, their oma had said once. *As if he's no longer a true Mennonite and going to run for city council.* She sounded pleased beneath her frown at the thought.

When Oney told Jack what their grandmother had said, he grinned and repeated the *Plautdietsch*—Low German—phrase under his breath: *billijch Laundeskaunsla, billijch Laundeskaunsla, billijch Laundeskaunsla, billijch Laundeskaunsla.*

There's a hollow near the base of the tree. Oney settles into that hollow and leans against the trunk. Then she sighs and wiggles down until her head fits in the hollow. The sifted heat focuses on one part of her body, then another. Puffs of wind slip in under the canopy of holes, lifting and dropping sweaty strands

---

1   Ed: Grandmother.

of her hair that has grown in finer, lighter than before. As if the terror of the accident has evaporated all pigment.

Oney raises her left hand and examines it carefully in the forgiving shade. The whole thumb is gone, and her index and middle fingers are merely stubs. The scars are thin; they were pink at first, but have now faded and sunk into her flesh. It seems as if there had never been anything in those spaces that Oney had so carelessly worn.

Oney closes her eyes and rests her right hand on her right breast. She has slept like this for years, as though her chest needed extra protection beyond a quilt and darkness. After the accident, she wore a cast for two weeks and slept with her left hand over her head as the orthopedic surgeon instructed.

The first night her hand was freed from the cast, Oney had a vivid dream: she was at a nameless beach with a blinding sun and the softest sand she'd ever encountered. She dug and dug into this sand, amazed at the way the grains slid through her fingers. She tried to shape a hill out of the sand, but it kept slipping through her fingers. She began to dig faster into the sand, but it remained as flat and still as before.

When Oney woke up, she realized her shirt had risen above her breasts, and her hands were digging into them; her right breast was sore from the scratches of her right hand, but her left breast remained untouched. Oney stroked her left breast slowly. The sand returned. Over and over she crossed the base, then the crest, then the other side. The nerves of her amputated fingers searched for contact. When they only found air, they pulled what they could from it. That was what air felt like to an injured nerve, she decided. It felt like sand.

Now she rests her left hand lightly on her heart. The amputated fingers rear with imagined contact; her pulse speeds up and pushes against her palm. She waits a moment and listens for the artless wind, but the wind has stopped. It has left her canopy of holes. Like Jack and Oma, it has gone where she cannot follow.

Oney lost her fingers earlier that summer, just as the wheat turned platinum and every combine stood poised to begin the harvest that wouldn't arrive because of the rain.

It had rained for days. Sometimes it would walk lightly across the roof. Others it let loose a volley that pounded the windows and flattened the *Digitaria sanguinalis*—crabgrass—that roamed everywhere on the farmyard except for the rectangle in front of Oma's double-wide behind their house. Oma hated *Digitaria sanguinalis*.

Oney was in the kitchen eating a sandwich when Jack bounded in. Let's take the canoe down the river, he said, rummaging through a cabinet, his muddied shoes squeaking on the kitchen tiles. He was only fourteen, three years younger than Oney, but his voice and big hands and ears suggested he was much older.

Oney laughed. Calling Mulberry Creek a river was one of the things that amused and sometimes annoyed her about Jack. Jack lived in a world where a hike in the Flint Hills was a trek through the Amazon rainforest and a lazy canoe cruise equaled white-water rafting in the Rockies.

I know it's wet out there, he continued, pulling out two ponchos and a pair of hip boots. But the river is the highest I've seen it, so maybe this time we can actually ride the whole way to Ulysses.

Usually a canoe trip down Mulberry Creek involved more walking than rowing, so Oney could see why this would be tempting. How are we supposed to get back here? If the current's too strong, it'll be hard to paddle back.

I could call Uncle Evan and see if he'll be around to drive us back.

Still cradling the ponchos and boots, Jack grabbed the phone and punched the number in with his giant thumbs. After a few seconds, he hung up. Well, the phone's busy, so that means he's around.

Before the accident, Oma decided to teach her grandchildren about plants and martyrs. Life and death, Oma said. They go together, you see?

She had a huge garden only a few feet from her double-wide. The garden was like a miniature Eden, filled with every vegetable that would take to the arid soil. When they were finished with their chores in the garden, Oma would walk Oney and Jack around the pasture, pointing out the many different kinds of grass that one small space of land could contain. They couldn't leave the pasture until both of them had named at least three things correctly: *Scirpus atrovirens, Aristida purpurascens, Andropogon gerardii.*

When Oney asked Oma why she insisted on using Latin names for plants, Oma looked at her in surprise as if she had just asked why one should wear shoes in the snow.

Your opa[2] once took a Latin course by correspondence while he was in seminary, and I would help him study, she said. Then I saw how so much Latin was everywhere—including the seed catalogues. Latin names are more clear than English.

---

2   Ed: Grandfather.

Some folks think Bermuda is Buffalo when you're talking grass since they look so alike. But if I say *Cynodon dactylon* or *Buchloe dactyloides*, anyone who knows Latin can really know what I'm talking about. You can't mistake them anymore.

Oma didn't need to quiz Jack for very long, because he was a fast learner, unlike Oney. But he would join them on his bike anyway, the wheels hissing in the grasses throughout Oney's interrogation.

What's this, Honey? Oma would ask, calling Oney by her given name. Oma insisted on proper names for plants and humans.

Parietaria pensylvanica?

No!

Amaranthus spinosus?

No, Oney, Jack whispered into her ear. It's *Ambrosia artemisiifolia*—can't you tell by the leaves?

No cheating! Oma shouted, trying to swat at him with her straw hat. Jack only laughed and pedaled away, listing the grasses and weeds that he wheeled over: *Salsola tragus! Parietaria pensylvanica! Elymus virginicus!*

In the evenings, they sat in Oma's cramped living room as she took out books filled with the names and photographs of people who'd lived in the Molotschna Colony in Russia. She had maps of the villages in the colony, and pointed out where their ancestors—the Friesens, Josts, Kaufmans, Wiebes, Sieberts—had lived.

Why did they leave? Oney asked. The houses in the pictures were squat and neat; they stood in rows in a neighborly fashion, with stretches of fields behind. She glanced out of the window and wondered why anyone would want to leave such a place for this patch of Kansas desert.

They had to. The government said we could no longer have German schools. Things were changing—our ancestors saw what was coming down the road. Oma looked at Oney and Jack with ferocity and whispered: *Cossacks. Communists.*

Jack laughed and said: But we don't speak German anymore, so it wasn't worth it anyway.

It wasn't the language that was important. It was the meaning *behind* the end of the German schools. They wanted to assimilate us—make us Russians.

Oney was sure Oma had never met a Russian in her life, but Oma's face when she spoke about Russians seemed to say they were the dirtiest, vilest of all people.

Do you know they say that we brought *Salsola tragus* with us when we came here? To this day I believe some Russians mixed it with our Turkey Red wheat before we left. Just to spite us.

Salsola tragus? Oney asked.

Russian thistle, Jack whispered.

Invariably, Oma read out of the *Martyrs Mirror*, a giant book filled with illustrations of people dying in various ways: flaying, drowning, hanging, burning. Oma read the stories of the martyrs strangely—with a mixture of pride and disdain for their fates in her voice. As though Oma, unlike the martyrs, could have convinced the torturers to join her in the struggle for the true Gospel.

The day before the accident, they came upon the story of Lame Sijntgen.[3] Oma handed Oney the book, pointed to the text and closed her eyes. Oney dutifully read: *Thus it happened, after manifold trials and temptations which they suffered for Christ's sake, that they were sentenced to death by the rulers of darkness, and beheaded with the sword in the court's castle. And as Sijntgen was lame, she was carried upon the scaffold in a chair, and as she held up her folded hands rather high, a brother (named Natanael de Tollenaer, a brother of Joost de Tollenaer) cried, "Lamb, look out for your bands"; and so they also cut off her two thumbs.*

Oney stopped reading. Oma, what does that mean? What was he saying?[4] What?

Lamb, look out for your bands.

Jack looked over Oney's shoulder. *Lamb, look out for your bands,* he confirmed to Oma, as if Oney's translation hadn't held enough clout. Oney slammed the book shut. Jack laughed at her scowl and ambled out of the room.

Do you know what he meant?

I'm not sure.

Why did they cut off her thumbs, since they were going to kill her anyway?

I don't know. Extra punishment—something to keep people scared. I wouldn't have let them carry me, that's all I know. Oma reached for the book and opened it. I would've crawled if necessary, she told the pages. If I had to die in such a way, I'd do it on my own terms.

The hood of Oney's poncho kept slipping off her head, so her hair was drenched by the time they dragged the canoe from the pickup bed to the creek. The creek was at least twenty yards across and six feet deep. The rocks lining the bottom had completely disappeared; the current ran without stopping to chat among its neighbors as was its habit. Instead, it rushed to its unseen destination. Sev-

---

3   Sijntgen Barninge.

4   Ed: Misprint in an online text version of the *Martyrs Mirror;* it should read "look out for your hands."

eral times the water flung itself up against the trunks of *Populus deltoids* and flashed its white underbelly.

Jack dropped two emaciated life vests into the bottom before Oney climbed in. She eyed them with suspicion. We really should buy real ones, she said.

They're fine for this. Anyone who drowns in this is just stupid, Jack replied. He had been swimming since the age of three. Their momma claimed he intently watched the older kids for about ten minutes before leaping into the deep end of the community swimming pool and imitating the breast stroke almost immediately. Oney hadn't witnessed this feat, but somehow she didn't doubt it. He had been the one to teach *her* to swim after two swimming instructors failed. She suspected the trick had been that he hadn't shown her his perfection. He just waded next to her and made quiet suggestions.

Jack pushed the canoe into the current and jumped in. For a moment the canoe twisted and rocked and seemed ready to flip over. Oney briefly gripped the sides, only to pull them back with a yelp. When Jack had repaired the rusted sides of the canoe, he failed to wrap some of the aluminum patches near the rim properly. Oney's left hand had caught on one. She looked at her palm; a bright red stripe crossed the base of it to the flesh between her fore and middle finger.

What happened?

Your patches caught my hand, that's what happened, she snarled. Oney held up her hand. You didn't bend the edges over the rim like I told you!

You never told me that!

Well, even if I didn't, it seems a pretty obvious safety hazard. Oney craned her head to see if they were still in view of the pickup. We need to go back.

Why?

Why? I cut my hand is why!

Jack glanced back. It's not that bad, he said.

I need to have it cleaned, Oney insisted.

There's water all around you.

Who knows what's in this creek!

There's a first-aid kit in the tackle box, he said. He shored the paddle and craned his neck behind him, searching for the box. We can really clean it when we get to Uncle Evan's, okay? He found the tackle box and produced it with a flourish that nearly caused him to fall backwards.

Oney barked a painful laugh. She remembered what Oma had said about Jack having the mouth of a *billijch Laundeskaunsla*, running for city council— he won her over with his easy voice, his willingness to look ridiculous when the moment called for it.

With one hand, Oney rummaged through the battered fishing tackle box. After a moment's search, she pulled out a baggie with first-aid items: five adhesive bandages, gauze, four aspirin and a nearly-finished roll of duct-tape. Oney taped up her hand with the gauze and the duct-tape, and swallowed the aspirin that were scattered in the bottom of the bag. She leaned back in the canoe and looked up in the sky. The rain had turned heavy again; it fell against her eyelashes and leaked into her eyes, making the trees above melt into a steady milk of green that deepened and lightened with every breath she let pass through her lips.

Oney held up her bandaged hand. The pain seemed distant, as though she had heard about it from a far-off eyewitness. She spread out her arms and imagined she was flying. The wind resurrected the sleeves of her poncho and directed her southward. The current grew wilder, but she wasn't in a hurry. For once, she wanted to drift over the smothered rocks without an end-point in sight. She had graduated from high school a year early and was going to a Quaker college in Vermont that fall—a school she hadn't seen, but which had granted her a full scholarship.

Oney felt that she had been waiting since birth for the drive to Vermont that would pull her away from this circle of earth with empty horizons that penned in its inhabitants beneath the eye of God. *It is he that sitteth upon the circle of the earth, and the inhabitants thereof are as grasshoppers; that stretcheth out the heavens as a curtain, and spreadeth them out as a tent to dwell in: That bringeth the princes to nothing; he maketh the judges of the earth as vanity. Yea, they shall not be planted; yea, they shall not be sown: yea, their stock shall not take root in the earth: and he shall also blow upon them, and they shall wither, and the whirlwind shall take them away as stubble,*[5] Oney muttered to herself.

When she was younger, Oma made her memorize entire chapters of the Bible to repeat on command. To give comfort in times of trouble, Oma said.

Oney suspected she had gotten that line from a Bible-pushing pamphlet—it didn't sound like Oma-language. Oma-language was filled with the dissonance of researched Latin and smatterings of *Plautdietsch* from her childhood.

Oney never remembered the verses that were supposed to bring you nearer to God—only the words of wrath and disdain for the human race were printed in her brain. All she knew from that passage was that God desired to leave the earth empty and unplanted—to create the wasted landscape that surrounded her daily.

More than once Oney wondered what it was about a God who considered men to be insects upon the earth that made a martyr out of Lame Sijntgen.

---

5   Isaiah 40:22-24 KJV.

What she had seen that Oney did not. Oney hoped that at college in that new tree-crowded place called Vermont she might see what she'd been blind to here, surrounded by grassy space.

But now she felt she could drift in the circle for a series of lifetimes. She finally understood why Jack was drawn to this creek with his leaky canoe: it was because you always decided when to drift, when to return. Going home was your choice—no one could reverse the course southward. Because of the rain, the *Morus rubra*—red mulberry trees—that lined Mulberry Creek were freely dropping their fruit in the canoe. The fruit sighed with each landing, glad for the journey's end.

Oney laughed. We really should buy a decent canoe. One with a tent on the top.

Jack looked back at her. Yeah, he admitted, I know. There's a reason this thing was abandoned. I just thought it'd be really neat if I fixed up an old one, you know.

Yeah, Oney said, grinning at his use of the word *neat*. He sounded like Oma when she learned that Oney was headed for a Quaker college: *Well, I don't know much about Quakers but they seem enough like Mennonites. I think it will be neat to live among all those trees!*

Later, Oney knew she should've been thinking ahead for Jack. A bend in the creek hid a small metal bridge that swung low over the water. Usually they had to either lay down in the canoe and let it slide over them or pick up the canoe and climb over the bridge if the water was too high. She always had to remind him of this as soon as they came within sight of the bend. But she didn't this time, since her eyesight was blurred and directed at the sky.

Oney!

Oney sat up. The bridge was nearly level with the water. The water was frothing and spitting into the air—for the first time in her life she heard docile Mulberry Creek growl.

Jack was frantically trying to paddle them upstream, his oversized hands clutching the oar so tight his usually reddened knuckles were white. Oney realized how young he was; his charming self-confidence fooled so many into thinking he was mature and ready to handle the world. But he wasn't. He was young and thought he could beat Mulberry Creek.

This is stupid! Jack! Forget it! Let's get out! Her legs flexed beneath her, ready to jump.

The canoe turned slightly to the right.

There, Oney! See, Oney—Jack looked back at her, grinning. As he turned, the canoe readjusted itself toward the bridge. He snapped his head around.

Jack! Oney yelled. Jack, jump! She rolled out of the canoe and clung to the side with her injured hand. The metal bit ferociously through the duct tape; if there was pain, Oney didn't notice.

Jack threw the oar into the water and swiveled around to face Oney. He struggled to his feet, crouched and hurled himself at her, but his right foot caught on the center yoke so he fell on his face. Then he straddled the side of the hull and tried to roll out like Oney, but his hip boot had caught on something and wouldn't come loose.

Help me! he shouted before the scream of metal against metal took over. The water wedged him between the bridge and the canoe. The current flashed its underbelly against his face and drove itself into his mouth.

Oney let go of the canoe and stretched out her arms to lock Jack into herself. Her bandaged left hand touched his right shoulder and squeezed, but the duct tape slid him out of her grasp. The current caught her poncho and dragged her beneath the bridge.

She thought she was dead. Death was colder than expected; angrier, as it pricked each nerve so that she felt she was on fire rather than submerged by a usually languid stream. The water filled her surprised mouth with a vengeance, ripping her lips from her teeth and pouring past her tongue into the center of what had once been a girl called Oney.

For several hours Oney floated down the rapids of Mulberry Creek. Some teenagers found her caught by the low-slung branches of a *Morus Rubra*. They thought she was dead until she raised her head and asked where Jack was.

The cut was much deeper than she'd thought. Her hand had doubled in size. Her head was bloody from the rocks the current had failed to avoid. When she returned home a week later, her arm was in a sling and her shaved head was wrapped in gauze.

Her parents, aunts, and cousins coursed around her the moment she came home, pouring words into the empty spaces that Jack had filled. Oma stood to one side, muttering the same two words: *billijch Laundeskaunsla billijch Laundeskaunsla billijch Laundeskaunsla.*

Oma did not talk about Jack after the accident, for which Oney was grateful. Her parents wanted to talk about him daily, but Oma and Oney remained silent.

Do you ever miss Jack? she asked Oma only once as they weeded the garden.

Yes, of course.

You don't talk about him.

Oma gave her a sideways glance. Neither do you.

Why don't you talk about him?

Because I haven't been able to let him go just yet.

Why do you have to let him go?

It's not right to hang on to people when they die. It keeps you from getting on with your own life.

So how will you know when you've let him go?

When I've decided how I'm going to remember his life.

Do you have an idea of how you'll do it?

Not yet. But I'll know when I think of it.

They surrounded themselves with words of other languages while they waited. During the day they sat in the garden and muttered together about *Daucus carota, Brassica oleracea, Brassica rapa, Raphanus sativus* and *Spinacea oleracea*. Oney clumsily weeded the *Brassica rapa* with her right hand; Oma clawed through the *Lactuca sativa* with her arthritic hands and put the inedible leaves in a basket for compost. In the evening came the unpronounceable names of people who died for the glory of God: *Francoys van Leuven, Hansken van Oudenaerden, Grietgen van Sluys, Jan van Ackeren, Michiel van Bruyssel.*

Oney wondered if the martyrs had been afraid; every story she read stated how often they went to their deaths singing praises to God. She remembered Jack's flash of a face as she passed him by: lips round and blue, eyes circled in red, cheeks half-submerged in their final destination. Was that the look of death martyrs wore before the fire or the axe? Or was there a special look given by God to his True Servants? Would the martyrs think Jack's death as ridiculously stupid as Oney did?

Lamb, look out for your bands, she often said to herself in a sing-song voice at night as she drew her hand across her sandy breasts. *Lamb, look out for your bands.*

Oney wondered how Lame Sijntgen had stood that final torture—if she sang a hymn the moment the executioner severed her thumbs, or if she screamed into the empty sky for relief.

When Oney woke up in the recovery room after the accident she had not known her fingers were amputated. What she did know was that the pain in her hand began at the tip of her forefinger and slowly dripped down her arm into her shoulder, headed for her cramped heart.

It hurts! It hurts! It hurts! she screamed. It's going to my heart! Stop it! Stop it! Stop it!

Later, Oney wondered if the martyrs would have been ashamed of her.

The county sheriff dumped the battered remains of the canoe on the Friesens' yard two weeks after the accident, though her parents had requested its destruction. Oney had been taking a nap and did not wake up until the tow truck rattled away.

She approached the canoe, staring at the twisted hull, the warped patches that Jack had poorly soldered. It had seemed so large when Oney and Jack first brought it home, as if you could easily sail such a craft across any sea, any ocean, any bit of a creek that straggled out from beneath canopies of *Morus rubra*.

Oney reached out with her good hand—a shiver went through her fingers into the weak metal. The hull responded with a sigh as it rocked twice. She touched it again with more force. This one moved the hull an inch to the right. She put her full hand on it next and gave it a true shove. The skeleton skittered across the gravel. Oney found herself pushing the canoe across the yard; she plowed it over a corner of her oma's garden; she crashed it through a forgotten section of a barbed-wire fence and across an acre of *Scirpus atrovirens,* *Aristida purpurascens,* and *Andropogon gerardii* until she came to a hedgerow at the southern end of the pasture.

Her throat hurt, but she hadn't screamed once. She felt like she hadn't breathed in a long time. She wondered if this was how the martyrs had screamed—at such a pitch that no one could hear them. Not even God would hear such a searing cut of pain.

While Oney and her parents were driving to Vermont, Oma died of a heart attack. Momma and Poppa had left her dorm room only an hour before the residence director knocked on her door and handed her the phone.

A neighbor, Carl Kliewer, had gotten some of Oma's mail by mistake, and found her.

She must've been there for a while, because she was covered in ants. His voice echoed strangely, as if he were speaking into a can rather than a phone. I think she probably fell in the driveway—that's where her glasses were—but she crawled to the garden, next to the lettuce. I don't know why she didn't head for her house—it was closer.

Oney laughed. Her laughter echoed back to her; it sounded much happier than she expected. She could picture Oma gripping the gravel as she blindly pulled herself toward her personal heaven rather than to the telephone just inside the door of her double-wide. Oma did not need to be carried into an ambulance to a sterile death. She had chosen to join the course southward.

Oney? Are you okay? Carl asked.

I'm fine, really, she said into the echoing space between Vermont and Kansas.

Will you be coming back?

She didn't have to come back—no one would know in this place what she hadn't done.

Yeah. I will.

As she flew back to Kansas that night, she smiled at the blackened landscape below, amazed at how she had made her choice with such ease.

Oma had cornered Oney a few minutes before she and her parents left for Vermont. Here, she whispered, shoving an envelope into Oney's hands.

What's this? Oney asked.

What do you think? Seeds. *Morus rubra* seeds. Plant one somewhere in each state before you get to Vermont for me.

Why?

It's how I'm choosing to remember Jack. He always wanted to wander around, be a *billijch Laundeskaunsla*. Now I can think of him doing it with you, floating with a current of *Morus rubra*. It'll be neat.

Oney got home more than a day before her parents did. She was glad, because she knew how she was going to remember Jack and Oma. She imagined they would both be pleased. Oney went into her brother's room and gathered all of Jack's camping gear into a box: boots, books, sleeping bag, shirts, pants, hat, cooking equipment, maps of trails he'd never followed, travel guides, travel journals, notebooks with awkwardly drawn maps.

Oma's double-wide already smelled unused when Oney opened the door. She found the book of the martyrs and grabbed one of the produce baskets. Oney stumbled through the garden and harvested the last bits of Oma's garden. *Daucus carota, Brassica oleracea, Brassica rapa, Raphanus sativus, Spinacea oleracea, Lamb, look out for your bands!* she whispered to herself.

She pulled Jack's bike and the little trailer he had made in a welding workshop out of the tool shed and filled it with as much as it could hold. It was harder than she expected to pedal through the thick grasses she could not name in the swiftly fading sunlight.

The canoe was tipped to one side against the hedgerow, as if it had attempted to escape more than once. Oney pulled it away from the hedge and cleared every stray bit of grass from its circumference before piling Jack and Oma's lives into it.

The fire wouldn't start at first, so she scrambled around the pasture and picked up anything dry enough to burn. When it did catch, the fire mostly smoldered with the smell of melting plastic, frying *Allium cepa*—onions—and nylon.

Oney went to the bike trailer and found Oma's book; she fed the foundering blaze with its pages slowly. The paper crackled in the fire like applause from above. Oney figured the martyrs would've approved. They knew what Oma had tried to tell Oney with the seeds of *Morus rubra*: it did not do to remember how someone died, but how someone lived. Oney wondered if that was why Lame Sijntgen allowed herself to be carried to death. She had made her own choice long before. How she died didn't matter.

For a few moments the flame soared into the reddish purple sky, lighting her hands with a surreal glow—as if she had leapt into the heart of it already. The nerves of her stumped hand pulled her closer. She wanted to plant her left hand into the fire's center, to see what would happen if she touched that flicker of blue. She hovered over the blue, stretched out her trembling hand and dipped her invisible fingers into the martyrs' flame. It felt as if someone was driving a length of barbed wire through her finger to the top of her head. Oney screamed into the air, hoping the molecules of her breath would merge into the deepest blue of the fire. That it would carry her voice upwards, to the place the martyrs called Heaven.

Under the *Acer negundo*, Oney flexes her hands above her breasts. Her remaining fingers seem a little stronger, as if they have finally taken the place they'd always been meant to have. She's wondered about the best way to tell a stranger how her fingers were lost: cutting herself on the hull of a canoe seems a stupid way to end a finger, to end a life. She still wishes she had lost them bravely— by saving Jack's life, rather than simply sliding by, propelled by the arms of a ridiculous poncho—perhaps for a sacrifice that made the absence worthwhile.

Still flexing each muscle, she settles her hands on her chest, but today when she draws her left hand across her left breast, the sandy sensation she expects is gone. She repeats the gesture over and over, and then across other parts of her body that are shaped like the dunes of unknown beaches. The sand has disappeared.

Oney holds her hand to the light and smiles. The emptiness that fills the spaces where her fingers once were seems a little freer since the dip into the blue flame.

Lamb, look out for your hands! Natanael de Tollenaer had shouted to the crippled martyr who held her hands high. Oney wonders if Lame Sijntgen had been holding her hands up in prayer or victory. Oney hopes for the latter. Her executioners had to do her one final service: carry her to her death like a fallen hero. Oney wonders what she saw as they held her high above the ground: faces turned upward as if to God; the circle of heaven and earth holding mountains and seas; perhaps this distant figure beneath the *Acer negundo* that had chosen to survive the storm.

JESSE NATHAN

In McPherson County

what do I do with you, rusted chains
and museum-lost tongue screws of Europe?
My question forms, smoke from a faraway fire.
My lover says nothing. We work under
underlit clouds, humongous sky
full of anonymous smoke. Sunscreen,
bandanas, in summer wheat we guzzle Crush
and pick rye. Our heads throb, grizzled by heat.
A week of sun has pushed our crop
from emerald green to blond.

•

Curtain of cloud.
Curtain of water.
Curtain of weather.

•

A storm gives dimension to the sky. Thickens it.
By eight our faces are blanketed with chaff, the sunflowers
stare up like satellites and we undress
fast but do not kiss in an upstairs bedroom.
We sleep under thunder and gloom. It'll be a soaker. Won't work
the fields tomorrow. She mumbles
sleep, dammit—and I risk rest 'til I rise
and stand naked at the curtainless panes
awakened at two and again at four-thirty to angry rain,

dismembered limbs of trees streaking by. Wires of lightning
light swathes of field, tractors stagger in the mud.

•

switchgrass sage aster eastern gamma
alfalfa sumac larkspur bluestem thistle
milkweed ironweed bindweed dandelion
beardtongue dogwood blue wild indigo . . .
Drenched. Flattened. A mess of nerves.

•

She clears the sleep
from her voice like cobwebs. By seven-thirty
the sky will break blue and soggy smells of straw
will hang, she says. Purple, unearthed worms
will squirm under foot. She says at eight
we'll wade the ditches. Slog the puddles.
See the strewn heads of sunflowers
flung upon the earth.

Flowers of Amsterdam

For the sake of the Gospel,
the book says. 1549. Pieter, Johann
and Barbara are tied to the stake.[1]
Their bodies flare out in a triple bloom,
still flare out in the mind, the recalcitrant
flesh still acrid. And Catherine drowns
in the canal, her skirts billowing out
over her tied legs like a lily.

Now vast markets of flowers, a harbor
where once a shipload of grain
was exchanged for a single tulip bulb.
City of night when the streets open
their black laps for the painted blooms,
when music rides the blue and swollen veins,
washed and languid houses that double
in the watery streets.

City of choices. Which fire, which perfume,
and at what price? Catherine cries out
over the water. Each one must choose,
she calls into our bright throats,
each one for himself. And how
do you choose when a whirlpool sucks you in,
into the purple corridors of the iris,
the cool swarm of apple orchards?

---

1   Six brethren and two sisters, d. 1549, Amsterdam; Catherine comes from imagina-
    tion or a forgotten source.

"Careful of the feast's tomorrow," Van Gogh
writes near the end, after the yellow skies.
"For my own work I am risking my life,
and my mind is half-gone. . . . But what do you want?"

What do you want? The one way to live,
the one unequivocal rose in this life
of mirrors, in this city of water where
the day is now nearly gone and the floodgates
already open. The dark elms dip their hair
into the rising tide and the laden boats
drift with the current. But here and there
one moves against it, one figure in a boat,
the twin oars quietly opening the water's
glistening petals, opening a secret passage
in the deep and watery place.

WOUNDS

Views from a Pond:
Dirk the Patriot
Ian Huebert

children like us

the exiled the disinherited
the ones with broken knees
children like us whose skin
is not their own whose flesh
remembers the generations
& their tears who are filled
with the world's longing &
call it love who bruise too
easily like fresh fruit the
gifted the innocent the broken
hearted who hear voices in
the trees who've seen the sky
become transparent at sunset
& know eternity in their bones
the beautiful the lost whose
cries keep the earth alive whose
flesh is like grass like flaming
the orphaned the poor in spirit
suffering earth's children

ANN HOSTETLER

Living Sacrifice

"We are more than the sum total of our wounds."
The priest's voice echoes through the nearly empty
cathedral nave. From where I kneel

I look up to Tiffany windows,
angels with lilac wings and golden hair
gesturing toward a city of light.

I remember the *Martyrs Mirror,*
ancestors who entered flames singing,
who refused to sit in a temple of images.

Blasphemy to imagine them pictured here with bonfire,
rack, tongue screw emblazoned in sun-licked colors.
Images pressed into my brain

as they were pressed on the freckled
pages of the seventeenth century Dutch edition
my father brought home to show us.

This is how others suffered
to keep the faith. Last night
my daughter called from 12,000 miles away

to tell me that she slit her arm
from elbow to wrist, but she's okay.
The priest's words flood back.

Who taught her that pain validates anything?
I want to tell her that writing on the body is not writing.
That people are not martyred, they are murdered.

Damn it. The body
is just a body
and each of us has only one.

Bastard Son of a Priest

Felix[1] grew up behind the church,
with his teenage mother walked
across the alleyway to the back door
of the cathedral whenever Father beckoned.

The man in robes reached
for what he shouldn't have touched.
His mother prayed each night, her son
breathing beside her, for deliverance.

Where her prayers took the shape of encouragement,
young Felix learned his path to love
in his father's Latin and Greek.
He studied well and learned to turn his words against the church.

When deliverance came, into that final baptism
in the River Limmat, Felix' mother sang
encouragement in her first moment of ecstasy and relief
since that dark embrace in the confessional.

Fortunately for his soul
Felix thought she sang for his salvation.

---

1 Felix Manz.

Rhoda Janzen

The Martyr Box

They used to strap gun
powder to the knees
of Anabaptists, a small
but civil courtesy before
the flame, whereupon
the martyrs would

explode in merry
laughter. At ten I took
a test, the Butler
Mennonite Brethren
Spiritual Gifts
Questionnaire. Up

came the martyr box
like a pink and personal
valentine, the fuchsia
heart for pain, the burn
to stand one's ground
in clover. Here's my

advice. Let them kill
you every day for
fifteen years. Slip
through the world
unseen, the ant that
wanders off the line.

To others, the grand
booboiseries of
Shakespeare—ambition,
lust, the marriage plot.
But the martyr minds
her winter in the fine

tormented space beneath
the stage, where it's
dark as a cawl and one
must squint. True: death
is a mouth that needs
a mint. Call it a rotten

sacrament. These
cuts, lord knows,
refine one's attitude.
And you'll find
that death improves
the mood. In fact

one does much better
if one lives to die in
a dense hair sweater.
Do take me down
to the grave, where
dark crumbs roll.

Death is a night
through which I sing,
curled in my box like
a dahlia bulb with a
blackened eye and
a dream of spring.

STEPHANIE KREHBIEL

Staying Alive:
How Martyrdom Made Me a Warrior

We are supposed to be cheerfully yearning for death and in the meantime, until that blessed day, our lives are meant to be facsimiles of death or at least the dying process.

A Mennonite telephone survey might consist of questions like, would you prefer to live or die a cruel death, and if you answer 'live' the Menno doing the survey hangs up on you.

—Miriam Toews, A Complicated Kindness[1]

We never had the *Martyrs Mirror* in our house. I've never asked why, but I think it's because my parents just don't think that tales of gruesome torture and death make for fun or particularly edifying reading. Perhaps they felt that, generally speaking, there was enough depressing stuff in everyday life to keep us busy without dragging the Anabaptist martyrs into it. Maybe they both got their fill of Mennonite history from going to church and participating in the life of a Mennonite college—maybe they just didn't groove on sixteenth-century etchings. Whatever their reasons, I'm grateful. If they'd used it for bedtime stories, I'd be *really* messed up.

Due to this lack of zeal for Anabaptist martyr history from my immediate family, I didn't realize how passionate, negative, and unexamined my relationship to the martyr stories was until my twenty-fifth year. It was 2001, the year I started writing about Mennonites as part of my graduate work. So in September of that year, I had Mennonite history and culture on the brain already—after the 9/11 attacks, I found myself in the throes of a cultural and historical obsession I was dying to escape.

Prior to 2001, the last time I really got into it with the Anabaptist martyrs was during the buildup to the first Gulf War. It was my freshman year of high school. A few weeks after Iraq invaded Kuwait, my Sunday school began a semester devoted exclusively to the study of the *Martyrs Mirror*. While our public school classmates ran around in "These Colors Don't Run" T-shirts, threatening to beat up wusses,

---

1 Miriam Toews, *A Complicated Kindness* (New York: Counterpoint, 2004), 5.

we contemplated the finer points of victimization. As far as our teacher was concerned, the martyr stories were the lynchpin of Mennonite identity. He presented
us with overheads demonstrating the various functions of Inquisition-era torture
instruments, graphic tales of stake-burnings and heads exploding from mouths full
of gunpowder. I felt certain, as I left class those Sundays, that we were the only teenagers in America whose religious education involved diagrams of the tongue clamp.

I am trying to remember what I felt that semester. Given my current relationship to these stories, and my feelings about the way Mennonites use them, I
imagine I must have felt trauma. I'm more easily traumatized now, though, having
seen more of the world and its ugliness, than I was at fourteen. I remember that I
was encouraged to identify with the martyrs and, when the inevitable anti-pacifist
taunting came at school, that I did so. But martyrdom didn't actually mean anything to me, any more than war meant anything to me. I could play with them
both as concepts and sites of allegiance without true emotional engagement. It's a
gift of being young and sheltered, the chance to play like this. Since my country has
gone back to war, it has not been so easy.

I hesitate to give my own post-9/11 story too much weight. So many people suffered, and continue to suffer, as a result of what happened on that day, and my
own suffering has been mercifully unremarkable. But like many Americans of my
post-Vietnam generation, I still view my life in two categories: that which came
before, and that which came after. My experience that fall impacted how I think
about almost everything, and transformed how I think about martyrdom; there
is no place else to begin.

Simply put, after 9/11, I broke down. From a clinical perspective—a perspective I was obliged to seek, for only through mood-altering medication was
I able to regain enough functionality to stay in graduate school—I suffered
from generalized anxiety disorder and bouts of situational depression. It took
a psychiatrist five minutes to come up with this diagnosis. *Fine*, I thought,
whatever. I come from a generation of psychiatric patients; everyone I knew was
on something for something. I found nothing exotic or shameful in the labels
themselves. The clinical labels placed on my moods were the medical world's
way of imposing sense on the chaotic place I was in, and I was content to accept this version of sense as a means to an end, that end being the medication
for which I was frankly desperate.

Medication pulled me out a non-functional abyss, but even as I started moving through the world like a normal human being again, I found that almost everything I did in the course of a day took an enormous effort. The weight of dread made it hard to move, though I couldn't sleep either. Campus was a minefield of obstacles; I found myself practically unable, for instance, to walk past the bulletin board at the back of the library that bore photocopied front pages of the *Detroit Free Press* and the *New York Times*, for every headline broadcasted how dark things were getting. It became a nightly ritual of will to walk past that bulletin board on my way to the parking lot, steeling myself, making myself breathe like I did in yoga class, then reading, while my guts dropped into my shoes, how a war was starting, how another terror warning was being issued, how the attorney general was encouraging us all to police each other.

It was like nothing I'd ever experienced before, and yet it felt menacingly familiar, this atmosphere of fear and endless suspicion, in which neighbor spies on neighbor, in which difference and dissent are viewed as deadly pathogens. If there was such a thing as a real world, this was probably closer to it than the version I'd been living for the past twenty-five years. Suddenly the cost of Anabaptist inheritance seemed clear. When a nation went nuts and the authorities whipped the populace into frenzy over threats both real and imagined, we were always among the hunted, weren't we? And the hunt had unquestionably begun; I had only to look to my Arab and Muslim neighbors to see that. The city's mosque was plagued with bomb threats; houses in the Arab neighborhood were shot at; a Muslim friend of a friend was visited by thugs in the night and escaped assault only through skillful words and quick thinking. That, of course, was just in our city.

On the one hand, I knew my white skin and mainstream appearance gave me protection all too easy to take for granted, and in fact I'd been plenty critical in the past of middle-class, white Mennonites who played at being persecuted minorities. On the other hand, I had the martyrs, who I'd been encouraged, through methods both overt and subtle, to regard as my spiritual forebears. The martyrs, who said things like, "This is the true way to eternal life, which is found by so few, and walked by a still smaller number; for it is too narrow for them, and would cause their flesh too much pain."[2]

My ecumenical nature shuddered at the smugness of that, but there was logic in it, too. It was clearer than ever that "the world," as an Anabaptist might put it, was still ready with its stakes and racks and tongue clamps. I wouldn't have

---

2   Thieleman J. van Braght, *The Bloody Theater or Martyrs Mirror of the Defenseless Christians* (Scottdale, PA: Herald Press, 2001), 617. Words of Jan Jans Brant.

to qualify for the martyr Jan Jans Brant's version of the narrow path to be seen as a threat by a paranoid "patriot."

I had no problem seeing the faces of the old inquisitors in the Bush Administration or its lackeys; indeed I was unable to shake the association. The inquisitor was a potent archetype in my mind, fed not only by the *Martyrs Mirror*, but my teenaged fascination with the Salem witch trials, when I devoured *The Crucible* and every other piece of fiction I could find on the subject, disturbed but unable to shake my identification with the pilloried, tortured, and burned. Now I had my own inquisitor, his imagined visage a sort of breeding accident between John Ashcroft and Savanarola. As my own personal creation, albeit one based in fact, my inquisitor had access to everything in my apartment. He read the titles on my bookshelf: my yoga books, my Marxist anthropology, my Mennonite hymnal. He read my email inbox: messages from distressed, insurrectionist liberals, friends from Middle Eastern countries, the Palestine branch of Christian Peacemaker Teams.

I'd lost the sense of my home as a safe place, but campus remained just as terrifying, particularly when I was teaching. As it happened, I was leading discussion sections for a course on Rastafari, an intensely biblical, separatist faith born out of crushing oppression. My job was to open my undergraduate students' minds to the concerns of the oppressed. As I heard them discussing the pros and cons of dropping nuclear weapons on Afghanistan, I realized what I was up against. They were so ignorant that it took my breath away; around them I felt I was in entirely hostile company, as though they might call the FBI if they didn't like my lecture.

If this seems excessive, remember how crazy things were in the fall of 2001. People didn't even trust the air they were breathing, let alone their teachers.

I wanted to stay silent, to protect myself, and this shamed me. The martyrs were glorified because they spoke with breathtaking confidence; every account I'd ever read in the *Martyrs Mirror* emphasizes the courage, even ecstasy, with which they faced their gruesome fates. "The Lord takes away all fear; I did not know what to do for joy, when I was sentenced," said Maeyken Wens, burned in Antwerp in 1573.[3]

Joy? Now looking back, I think this is the cruelest use of the *Martyrs Mirror* to which I fell prey: the idea that not only do our beliefs invite painful death, but that we should give it a rapturous welcome. Jesus Christ himself didn't live up to these standards. "My Father, if it be possible, let this cup pass from me," he said in Gethsemane (Matt 26:39). And on the cross: "My God, my God, why hast thou forsaken me?" (Matt 27:46 KJV).

---

3   van Braght, 983.

The martyrs occasionally expressed fear in their letters, but the *Martyrs Mirror* historians rarely permitted their heroes such lapses in faith. There's something spooky about Maeyken Wens, about George Raeck, who if the book is to be believed, "cheerfully stepped forward to the executioner, and exclaimed with a joyful heart, 'Here I forsake wife and children, house and home, body and life, for faith and the divine truth.' "[4]

I had just gotten married. As my husband and I walked side by side in peace marches, signed petitions and wrote letters to our senators pleading them to check Bush's authority, I pictured one of us captured, whisked to a secret prison somewhere, separating us as ordinary couples have been separated by cruel governments throughout history. I thought of Michael and Margaretha Sattler, of the thousands who vanished in the Dirty Wars supported by American politicians who were again in power, of the innocent Muslim men now being torn from their families by decree of our own so-called Justice Department. I had a good imagination, and obsessively pictured us in their shoes. It got bad; I feared for him whenever we were apart, even though we were rarely further from each other than the opposite ends of campus. Apparently, George Raeck's wasn't a brand of joy I had mastered.

I associated my Mennonite-ness with victimization. I'm not sure how that happened. No one who taught me what it means to be Mennonite, not even my old Sunday school teacher, meant to portray Anabaptism as an affliction that marks one for death. A strange thing, that a faith founded on the principle of adult baptism now felt imposed, a burden rather than a choice. I resented how the martyrs were taught to me, as heroes whose gory demises should somehow fortify me against evil. I longed to forget about them, but it was too late for that. Their deaths played in my mind as I lay awake at night. For all the fresh death in the news, it was still their deaths that made me imagine my own, and I wasn't a better person for it. I was becoming as suspicious as the red-blooded, flag-waving Americans I was so sure were out to get me.

Here again was the question of silence, which was such a temptation in those fearful moments. What kind of a person would I be, were I to give up my activism, duck under the radar? More importantly, what end would my silence serve? I remembered the slogan of the '90s AIDS awareness campaign: "Silence = Death." This had been a guiding principle through my years as an American liberal: we have to keep talking about what's happening, lest the truth be left behind in favor

---

4   van Braght, 646.

of someone's ideology. Yet from the martyr stories, I absorbed the opposite lesson, that to speak out is to invite death, even to welcome it. The moral confusion engendered by this message is surely evident in Mennonite history. For all our adulation of our rabble-rousing founders, silence enabled our survival across continents and centuries. I was stuck in that paradox now, unable to imagine a source of hope or faith that might set me free.

~

Stories get under my skin more than they should. Were I not cursed with such an overactive imagination, the martyr stories might have faded from memory, replaced by something newer, perhaps, and less troublesome. But I am who I am—a woman who hears a story of stake-burning and feels the heat of the flames, a woman for whom the press and cut of a tongue clamp seems not so far away nor improbable.

"Past lives," said a friend to me once. "Maybe you *were* one of those martyrs." Anything is possible, I suppose, but Jeff Gundy, in describing his own relationship to the martyr stories, offers less speculative reasoning I find more apt: "If you grew up with such tales shaping your view of the world and of human society, as I did, you might also find it hard to be easy in the world even when your own persecutions were limited to an occasional trivial remark. . . . You might find yourself wondering who was really on your side, even as you were going about most of your days with very little to distinguish you from every other American. You might always carry a faint sense of reserve, a suspicion of 'the world,' a thread of conviction that you were somehow not *supposed* to belong."[5]

Gundy's reflection points to what I consider one of the most morally questionable aspects of martyr pedagogy, if you will, as it's often practiced by Mennonites. It's the myth of exclusivity, the idea that these old histories are badges that distinguish us permanently from the general populace. This conceit may have been forgivable in separatists with little knowledge of the outside world. Today, however, we have no excuse for speaking or acting as though we're the only ones with a history—or present—of religious or political persecution. I don't mean to denigrate their courage, or make light of the horrors they faced, when I say that the martyrs were extraordinary in the most ordinary of ways; they died because they professed

---

5   Jeff Gundy, "Cathedrals, Churches, Caves: Notes on Architecture, History, and Worship." In *Scattering Point: The World in a Mennonite Eye* (Albany: SUNY Press, 2003), 16-17.

the wrong allegiance and refused to keep quiet about it, as have any number of people from any number of cultures throughout history. If anything, the martyr stories should remind us of our commonality with non-Mennonite others. I've rarely heard them used for that purpose.

But I'm not the first Mennonite to criticize the way these stories have been used. Melvin Goering's "Dying to Be Pure: The Martyr Story" points out how ill-served modern Mennonites are by the two-kingdom ethic celebrated in the martyr stories.[6]

Jim Juhnke's "Rightly Remembering a Martyr Heritage" takes on the Mennonites' tendency to demonize the descendants of our ancestors' oppressors,[7] and Julia Kasdorf's brilliant essay "Writing Like a Mennonite," while hardly a position paper, convinced me that I wasn't crazy for seeing the martyr stories as a means of stifling Mennonites' creative and political expression.[8]

In the non-literary realm, members of the Mennonite congregation I attended at the time of the 9/11 attacks cautioned against using the martyr stories as a paradigm for interpreting our relationship to the rest of the American public. If we did so, they warned, we would lose opportunities to collaborate with peaceable non-Mennonites. Of course they were right.

Yet how easily I fell into the paradigm myself. It troubles me, as I look back on the fall of 2001, that when the time came to be a real witness for peace and compassion, I was derailed by morbid, isolating fears. It's tempting to blame myself, or old Sunday school teachers, or various venerable Mennonite institutions, or even George W. Bush (who deserves so much blame anyway, a little bit extra can't hurt). In the end, what matters is that the martyr paradigm hurt me. It wasn't a useful story to tell myself.

My susceptibility to stories is my weakness or my strength, depending on how widely I read. If the martyr stories were the only great tales of moral struggle that I ever really internalized, I would have likely stayed in a state of paralysis. But

---

6   Melvin Goering, "Dying to Be Pure: The Martyr Story," *Mennonite Life* 47 (December 1992): 9-15.

7   James C. Juhnke, "Rightly Remembering a Martyr Heritage," *Mennonite Life* 58 (September 2003).

8   Julia Kasdorf, "Writing Like a Mennonite," in *The Body and the Book: Writing from a Mennonite Life* (Baltimore: Johns Hopkins Press, 2001).

the world is full of tales of moral struggle, and as I moved back into the world I found more of them, sometimes in unexpected places.

I once believed, as do many Mennonites, that the folklore and stories we repeat in our families and communities should be devoid of metaphors that cast the spiritual aspirant as a warrior and the spiritual struggle as a battle. (Violence, on the other hand, could be instructive—so long as our identification with the victim was made explicit.) Spurred on by my own spiritual crisis, however, I've come to see this view as a kind of fundamentalism. There's a reason why battle metaphors have so much appeal and narrative versatility: lots of things happen in battles. Infinite possibilities for decision making occur, usually without the benefits of great moral clarity. Victims and perpetrators are sometimes the same people. Real life looks a lot like this.

The martyr stories are based in fact, but the dominant role they play in Mennonite faith and culture has elevated them to the level of folklore and myth. The martyr has become a central archetype in collective Mennonite identity; we're at the point where the way we repeat these stories says far more about who we are than do the histories themselves. It's for this reason that I cannot confront the martyr stories solely as history. (Indeed, I'm ill-qualified to confront them as such, for I'm not a historian.) And from my standpoint, the first thing to look for in a cherished metaphor or archetype is utility. Is it making it easier or more difficult to react to my circumstances with compassion and wisdom? Does it give me flexibility to handle the unexpected? Is it helping me to create positive change in the world?

As is probably evident by now, I don't find the Anabaptist martyr a very useful archetype. For one thing, her sights are set so fervently on the next world that she gives me few clues about how to deal with this one; a morbid certainty hangs over her entire existence. Of course, there's no point in denying death, or the reality of violence. But the martyr keeps me fixated on violent death—not only its meaning, but its mechanics. I once brought my (non-Mennonite) graduate advisor a copy of Kasdorf's, "Writing like a Mennonite." After reading it, he remarked to me, with a degree of alarm, that the *Martyrs Mirror* sounded pornographic. My advisor, who did research in Haiti amidst social unrest and flying bullets, is not one to shy away from the realities of oppression and violence. I think, though, that he was correct in spotting the perversity of repeating the gruesome details of these individuals' deaths whilst maintaining a strong and persistent identification with their victimhood. Maybe it's easier for men to find inspiration in the martyr archetype without taking it so personally. As a young woman in this misogynist, pornography-drenched culture, though, I'm at no loss for narratives that depict splayed, exploited bodies that look like mine. The *Martyrs Mirror* offers me no refuge.

I suppose it's evidence that whatever force guides us on our spiritual paths has a sense of humor: after years of indulging in reprehensible forms of high culture snobbery (my own version of the two-kingdom ethic) I found the most powerful antidote to my martyr-induced malaise in television's *Buffy the Vampire Slayer*.[9]

Buffy is a supernaturally gifted young woman, charged with the mission of protecting the world from demons that embody real-world ills, from misogyny to militarism to petty bureaucracy. Though she's unique in her gifts, she's unable to save the world alone. Her friends are as vital to the narrative as she is, and it's their combined efforts that keep the insidious forces at bay. Buffy never gets a free ride, morally speaking; she can and does misstep, occasionally abuses her power, and struggles to balance action and compassion. The only given is her potential to change the world for good. Her success is always dependent on her ability to work with others, to engage the world rather than setting herself above and beyond it.

Buffy had a seven-season run, so there was plenty of time to address the complications that arise when confronting a complicated world with our high ideals. In one of the final season's episodes, for instance, Buffy has a rare moment of candor with a disconcertingly insightful vampire that she can't stop conversing with long enough to slay properly. She confesses her difficulty in connecting to the world she's sworn to protect. She feels unworthy of her power, as though it's something she should be punished for, and thus she feels unworthy of her friends. Yet she can't really value their opinions, she admits, because as the chosen Slayer, she feels her own knowledge, her own path, to be superior. Faced with this tormented logic, the vampire sizes her up. "You have a superiority complex, and you have an inferiority complex about it," he concludes.[10]

The only way to make that dialogue pithier, from a Mennonite perspective, would be to tell Buffy she had an inferiority complex, and a superiority complex about it. Either way, I recognize that tangle of humility and hubris, alienation and

---

9 This show, which ran from 1997 to 2003, has garnered a great deal of academic attention in recent years. Rhona Wilcox's *Why Buffy Matters: The Art of Buffy the Vampire Slayer* (London: I. B. Tauris, 2005) and *Fighting the Forces: What's at Stake in Buffy the Vampire Slayer,* edited by Wilcox and David Lavery (Lanham, MD: Rowman and Littlefield, 2002) both explore the show's themes in more depth.

10 *Buffy the Vampire Slayer.* Season 7, episode 7, "Conversations with Dead People." First broadcast 12 November 2002 by UPN. Directed by Nick Marck and written by Jane Espenson and Drew Goddard.

obligation, in the world but not of the world—what a relief to see it onscreen, shown for the mess it is rather than distilled into black and white categories that never hold up in real life.

Watching Buffy, I see the versatility of the warrior archetype, how it can accommodate, even illuminate, the realities of human error, doubt, and personal accountability. The warrior archetype also resonates with me because it's a model of action and resistance. The word *resistance* doesn't air well in some Mennonite circles; people associate it exclusively with violence, but I think this is a mistake. I know of no other word that adequately captures the action of standing up against oppression, even if that stand is peaceably taken. Perhaps *activism*, but this word is mostly reserved for outward political action. *Resistance* also encompasses the movements of the soul. I don't embrace violence, but resistance is at the core of my being. If I don't name it, I fear I will lose it.

Of course, I'm not going to convince any Mennonites to start showing *Buffy the Vampire Slayer* in Sunday school, and that's hardly my intent. But I will say this: I need stories that give me hope. I also need stories that offer me agency, the power to act and to create change. The best stories, the honest ones, won't hide the sometimes deadly cost of defying oppression. But here's the point I believe is essential to morally instructive stories: the purpose of the action is to make the world a better place. Death may be a consequence, but death is not the point. The thing I dislike about the way the martyr stories are told in Mennonite circles is how we've come to focus on the dying, as though dying is a thing that makes us great. If that's really it, then we might as well skip the rest—we might as well just lie down and die.

In "Dying to Be Pure," Goering asserts that Mennonites need to get over the aspiration to purity so celebrated in the martyr stories. "Promoting a more peaceful world, not just avoiding personal participation in war, requires deep involvement in social and political movements that soil the purity of intention and idea with the reality of action. Avoidance of such involvement, implicit in the assumptions of the martyr tradition, places purity of self above the cry of the poor and oppressed."[11]

I'd only add how high the stakes have gotten. If you're shrinking at my assertion that a Hollywood vampire slayer has given me more solid guidance than the martyred founders of my faith, all I can say is that despite its fantasti-

---

11   Goering, 14.

cal elements I find Buffy's world a lot more recognizable than sixteenth-century Europe. Buffy's world is on the verge of collapse, and only through the dedicated work of a motley, diverse, and decidedly impure community of ordinary people can it be saved. Like Buffy, the world I see around me is begging for action, not retreat or neutrality. I'm grateful for a story that not only asserts the agency of every person, even the seemingly powerless, but also demonstrates over and over the futility of thinking we're alone in our battles.

For all this, I can certainly understand the reticence with which peace-minded Mennonites approach battle and warrior metaphors (though I need hardly add they'd find plenty of them in the *Martyrs Mirror*). These days the Christian right seems more steeped in warrior language than ever: "prayer warriors," "culture warriors," "God's mighty warriors." The predecessor of these warriors, as far as I can see, is the medieval crusader, traveling to Middle Eastern lands to force people to Christianity with the end of a sword. A friend recently showed me a solicitation sent to her by that most unfortunately named of organizations, the national Campus Crusade for Christ. It described the pressing need for mission work in Iraq, explaining that young people there were in desperate need of Jesus. I'd argue that they are in desperate need of clean air and water, decent food, and personal safety, thanks in large part to the insane war inflicted upon them by politicians no doubt supported by the same well-intentioned people who wrote this earnest plea for cash. In the end, it seems the martyr and warrior archetypes both harbor the same dangerous potential: to make us locate evil solely in the Other and imagine ourselves pure, be we sword-bearers or victims.

But throwing out metaphor hardly seems a solution. We need metaphors like we need water—it's our literalism that gets us in trouble. So I'll carry the sword, though only in metaphor. Why? Because it represents power. I won't disassociate myself from power, though I know it can be abused. I have power. Intellect is power. Communication is power. Forgiveness is power. Teach me to wield power well, not to deny it.

The environmental and social justice activist Starhawk, a veteran of nonviolent direct action, deconstructs power in a way I find useful. "Power-over," as Starhawk defines it, is the power of greed and domination. This kind of power is threatening the survival of our planet, and obviously it needs to be confronted. Can we confront this power without a power of our own? We don't have to, according to Starhawk. In *Webs of Power: Notes from the Global Uprising*, she writes,

> another type of power exists as well: power-from-within, empowerment, our ability to create, to imagine, to feel, to make choices. When we act

together in an empowered way, we develop collective power. Through personal and collective empowerment, we can fight against, dismantle, and transform the systems of domination that perpetuate oppression.[12]

I doubt I would have agreed with the early Anabaptists on everything, but I suspect that many of them understood power-from-within and used it consciously. How else would they have had the courage to defy authority with such flagrance? For that matter, who understood power-from-within better than their ideal, Jesus Christ? I've always been proud of Mennonites for trying sincerely to emulate Jesus' empowering work rather than fixating on his death and victimhood like the Mel Gibsons of the world. Why do we still do it with our martyrs? Surely martyrdom is not the most important thing they have to teach us.

I think it's time to claim our power, to stop thinking of ourselves as "defenseless Christians" when in fact our decisions impact this fragile planet as much as those of our neighbors. We are of the world, and the world can't wait forever.

---

12   Starhawk, *Webs of Power: Notes from the Global Uprising* (Gabriola, BC: New Society Publishers, 2002), 231.

Debra Gingerich

Migraines and Other Mennonite Pains

Forgive your parents for marrying cousins whose parents married cousins. Don't run track or vote or swear oaths or take jury duty (if you can help it). Don't act proud or pretty. Memorize every tortured drawing in the *Martyrs Mirror*. Put on hand-sewn trousers or cape dresses. Don't marry a Catholic. Pray to Jesus like he is your best friend. Know what it means to be a disciple. Dirk Willems knew (burned to death after saving his captor). Love your enemies. Convert disciples (but not those with new ideas). Keep your hands in fruitful soil, and wake by dawn for milking. Don't step beyond the invisible line drawn in the bishop's dirt. Sit through long sermons on wooden benches. Lijsken Dircks endured more than that (drowned the day after birthing a son). Pick up your cross and shoulder it. Get tied to the stake, dumped head first into cesspools, laughed at for wearing a dress with sneakers. Read the Bible in English and some kind of German. Know what it says and follow every letter. The pain is nothing you can't stand.

scapegoat

someone had to die because that's
what the story was someone had
to die sometimes it was enough
if you went crazy for a while or
cut off your hand accidentally with
a chainsaw or something terrible
happened like someone's children
getting killed in a housefire or a
fatal car accident *an act of God*
people would say wisely
nodding their heads it wasn't enough that
one time on the hill one man's death
taking the place of all it had to be
repeated in every generation every
family someone had to die pull all
his hair out run off become a thief
go bad usually the sensitive angry
one the stray out of the ninety nine
nothing like a black sheep to make
a yellowish flock feel white ah but
the best deaths were the innocents
the babies the daughters with the
golden hair & most of all mothers
sweet white ghost mothers cheerfully
sacrificing themselves to the world
denying themselves into goodness
so the rest of the black sinful clan
could be saved by their dying

ANN HOSTETLER

For Those Who Would Save the World

Give up perfection for just one day.
Feel yourself a creature of flesh and bone,
walk around in the cold, wind chafing
your face, joints jarring as your worn
soles pound concrete.
Keep walking till you face
your deepest failure—not
with clenched fists, not blinded
by shame, but with a detached
curiosity that opens to
compassion. Finger
the glazed wound tenderly
as you would caress the gash
in Christ's side. Wear it lightly
as God's fingerprints. You see
one doesn't have to travel far
to know suffering, though you
may carry it to the ends of the desert
before you discover it's yours.
Before you discover the light
failure lets into the darkness.
Polished by forgiveness our failures
are the only possible windows
through which to truly see
another human soul. All else is mirrors
and an endless craving
for reflection of worthiness.
Remember—Christ was wounded
so he could be like you.

TONGUE

Views from a Pond:
Dirk the Escapist
Ian Huebert

Annie E. Wenger-Nabigon

Dungeon

Barbara[1] wasn't lost, sold or tortured,
just confined to the dungeon
without water for her tongue.
She never had a funeral;
the authorities knew where her bones rested.
Her husband, Jacob,
Lost his tongue, sold as a galley slave,
eventually fed the fish
in the deep blue dungeon.

---

1   Ed: These are composite characters. For an account of Anabaptists who became gal-
    ley slaves, see the *Martyrs Mirror,* 1126. Wenger-Nabigon writes: "When I reread the
    Martyrs Mirror, I was struck by the accounts of Anabaptist prisoners who were left to
    languish in prison, completely dependent on family and friends to bring them food,
    sometimes having to sneak it in, or pay to have the food given to the prisoner."

Tongue Screw[1]

From *Sweeter Than All the World*

Antwerp, Flanders 1573
Danzig 1638

I was born in Antwerp, Flanders, in our small stone house on the Oudenaerde Ganck in 1570. They named me Jan Adam Wens. It was the horrid time when the Spanish Fury burned in the Low Countries, driven by the merciless inquisition of Antoine, Cardinal Granvelle of Utrecht, and the Spanish armies led by Fernando Alvaraz, Duke of Alva. King Philip II of Spain and Portugal considered himself the champion of the Counter-Reformation; his armies slaughtered infidel and heretic alike, and he paid his mercenaries with shiploads of gold and silver brought from the Americas. Death by labor in the mines of the New World, death by religious rage in the Old; my brother Adriaen Wens was fifteen years old and I was three when, early in the morning, our mother was led out to be killed.

In the Grand Square of Antwerp, where the unfinished spire of Our Lady Cathedral towered over the tall seven-stepped houses facing the new city hall, Adriaen climbed up on a bench, holding me as our mother had written him in her last letter: "Take Hansken on your arm now and then for me." He was trying to lift me high so that together we could see her burn. But when the executioner chained our mother to the stake piled around with firewood, Adriaen fainted and fell to the cobblestones, and of course no one in the crowd noticed. So neither of us actually saw it happen.

October 6, 1573. I remember nothing, not even how my head cracked. I was only three.

On the other hand, my wife, Janneken, says she remembers everything. Both how on September 6 of that year her father Hans van Munstdorp was burned alone in such a huge fire that it drove the watchers into the side streets and they

---

1   Ed: Rudy Wiebe cites Horst Penner and Peter Klassen for most of the Danzig history included in this piece. A good English source is Klassen's *A Homeland for Strangers* (Fresno, CA: Center for Mennonite Brethren Studies, 1989).

feared for the surrounding buildings, and also the four well-controlled fires—the executioner had a month of burning experience—which much more slowly, and with great torture, destroyed her mother Janneken Munstdorp and my mother Maeyken Wens, together with her sisters, my aunts Mariken and Lijsken Lievens.

"It's impossible," I say to Janneken. "You weren't born when they killed your father, and only a month old for your mother."

"I know, I know," she answers in her low, soft voice, her small face looking at me as fierce as any bishop. "But I saw."

"How?"

"I saw him because my mother saw, I was in her womb. That's why they didn't burn her and my father together. For her, they waited till I was born and they found a wet-nurse."

"I know that—but how can you say you saw even then? You were barely a month."

"The nurse took me to the square."

"But I was three years, and I remember nothing!"

"If you don't remember, how do you know what happened?"

"Adriaen told me."

"But he told you, many times, he fainted and fell. You have the scars to prove it."

"He saw enough, before and after."

And usually, I don't have to say any more. I can't. We sit opposite each other in our hearth, warm, silent together. She knits, I stir the fire and raise or lower the kettle on the kettlehook, so it sings. Adriaen told me all he ever will; he's no longer alive. And when Janneken and I speak of that time, sometimes years apart, we talk the way a wife and husband do who have lived through forty-seven years together and who know they will continue to circle back, again and again, to those horrible memories, sometimes by accident, sometimes when it seems they can, momentarily, bear them: this is how we were born, it is our one life. If we cannot by the mercy of God forget, then we have only this past by His grace to remember.

Sometimes, when I'm at work splitting or polishing stone, trying to shape it exactly into what it needs to be, I see my scarred hands and tools chipping away forever at what already exists: our immovable past. Which surrounds Janneken and me like an immense plain of irreducible stone. Hand, hammer, chisel, stone and the years of our life, we keep on trying to split and shape them right; so they will fit.

Fit into what? How? If you could remember perfectly, could you shape a horror the way you work a stone? Shape it for what? To build what?

"They would have killed your father too," Janneken says suddenly, directly to my thoughts. "If he hadn't fled to Friesland."

"Then why—my mother knew that—why did she write to him, asking him to visit her in prison? He never came."

"He sent Adriaen and you, he knew they wouldn't hurt children, especially unbaptized ones."

Why do I have no memory? Not so much as a slant of darkness in her cell, a smell of stone. When I was fourteen and our father died, Adriaen decided we must leave even Friesland forever, and he took me back to Antwerp so I would have some memory of the place where our mother died. The roadstead of the Scheldt River was full of more ships than I could count, their ordered sails tied up or opened white as the clouds of heaven. But we had no time to watch them glide by, we were staring at the stone walls of Het Steen Castle rising out of the harbor water. Stones well cut, expertly laid, its great arched halls could have been filled with choirs singing praise to God over the water to encourage travelers leaving for the measureless oceans of the globe. A king's castle for seven hundred years, and now a dungeon. Defenseless Christians chained there to groan, their bodies beaten open and rotting.

Like our mother. Arrested in April, tortured for six months and burned in October. Adriaen told me I was with her inside that stone twice, for several weeks.

Janneken says, "It was all they could do. Your father escaped Antwerp alive, he worked to send money so the four women had better food and a cleaner cell." She smiles at me, certainly the living memory of her mother's face, with no chisel needed. "So I didn't have to be born among the rats in the holes below the river."

"Six months. She smuggled out two letters, and he never came to her once."

"How do you know he never?"

I don't. That's the trouble. No matter how often you turn over what memories you have, you still never know any more; you never know enough to recognize what more you will want, what more you will desperately need to know, later. And when the later arrives and stretches into endless future, what can you do?

Remember what you cannot forget. Every bit you have. When the evening light fell low across Antwerp harbor, the water blazed like polished steel against the castle, and finally Adriaen and I walked away. Through the narrow, high streets to the Grand Market. It was safe enough then, just a young man and a boy walking. The winged, slate slope of the city hall roof, its carved arches and windows, and the tight, beautifully peaked buildings all around us, as if in the level light we were standing inside the darkness of an immense, blazing crown. The Cathedral spire was still not complete; the Calvinists momentarily controlled the city and they had been throwing the Papist furniture out of the church while Antoine Cardinal Granvelle and Philip II were busy ashing Catholic heretics in other parts of the Low Countries. In southern Europe the Calvinists burned Anabaptist believers—rebaptizers, as they called them—as quick as did the Catholics, but not in Antwerp. They used other means, like allowing them no work and hoping they would either starve or leave.

Adriaen showed me where the bench had stood that he climbed on. Where we both, he told me, strained to look over heads to the four tall stakes. They made the four women climb up; they had brought them in carts along the same street from the castle that we had just walked. The fountain was not built yet, nor the statue over it representing the Roman soldier holding the chopped-off giant's hand high over the Scheldt and, in his defiance of tyranny, about to act out the city's name, *hand werpan,* that is, "throw the hand away."

Adriaen and I stood there. Perhaps he prayed. I told my mind, "Here is the place, here," but it would think nothing. After a time he walked away, into another street. Ten slow steps and we were on an open triangle of cobblestones. I looked up and up, bending back, looking: it was the magnificent Cathedral of Our Lady.

Named otherwise by the Calvinists, at that moment. But as soon as the last Anabaptist-Mennonites were gone and Alexander Farnese and his army in their turn destroyed the Calvinists and most of the beautiful city for the continuing glory of the Roman Catholic faith, Our Lady would arise once more inside her enormous stone diadem. Wearing her blue and gold robes, her crown three times taller than her head, her tiny crowned Child held high on her left arm. If, as they affirm, the Virgin and the Child neither sleep nor faint, how many thousands of people have they been forced to watch burn? They say eighteen thousand by the Duke of Alva alone.

I have learned the tender prayer that can be prayed to Our Lady: "Heavenly Mother Mary, in his last hour on the Cross, your divine Son Jesus committed us to your motherly care. We pray to you, reveal your holiness in this your city, Antwerp." But the prayer helps me little. I have no motherly care to forget.

Janneken says, "But Jan Adam, you do. Adriaen and I have told you the stories."

Sometimes my mind sinks, it refuses even those. The four chained and violated women whom Janneken says she "knew" for the five months they endured in their dungeon before she was born, and the short month after.

"Your mother wrote to you," Janneken insists. "'My dear children, kiss one another once for me, for remembrance. Be kind, I pray you, to your afflicted father all the days of your life, and do not grieve him.' "

"Adriaen's son has that letter, both the second and first."

She answers, "But you saw the words she wrote, you memorized them. She wrote, 'What I say to the oldest, I say to the youngest. By me, your mother who gave you birth in much pain.' "

And I answer her back, "And your mother wrote your sister, at one o'clock in the morning on the day of her death, 'Here are knitting needles for my daughter. Keep them, and do the best with her, my little lamb which I bore under my heart.' "

"Yes," Janneken says, the needles clicking steadily. "I lay in her lap when she wrote that."

I know the letters by heart, but in a way they will never be more than a memory of paper, of shriveling ink. Not touch or feeling. But I do know the feel of the ship that brought Adriaen's family and me to Danzig in 1584, its sway and riding of long swells, the sails cracking full, and the ship's lean down before the wind to drive the chisel of its prow *smash!* through the froth into the blue, away. The journey-Danzig was the wealthy Hansa city-state on the Vistula River, a mile inland from the Baltic Sea, protected by low walls and the salty river delta called the Werder. The Danzigers wanted more productive land for their grain trade, and so they welcomed the Mennonites to dike, drain and farm the Werder more intensively, but inside the confined city they also needed more of the tall houses the Dutch knew how to build side by side on narrow land. So, when I turned fifteen, Adriaen hired me to a builder's stoneyard, on the channel where the Motlawa River flows through the southern wall of the city to form the harbor inside.

I was a laborer. Climbing down onto the barges heaped high with shifting stone, I grappled chains around each rock so it could be hoisted onto the docks of the stoneyard. I had never seen a mountain, nor will I, but as I clambered and balanced among those immense rocks I began to comprehend the jagged spread of the massifs from which they had been cut. My wooden shoes hooked on their sharp edges, my arms were dusted raw from reaching around them. It came to me then that, as far as it was possible for me to think, here the textures of infinity rubbed my fingers.

The Dutch Mennonites who fled to Danzig to escape persecution could work in the city, but were not allowed to live or own property inside it because they were not citizens. So they built their villages outside the walls, as close to them as they could, the Frisians in Neugarten west of the Hagel's Hill, and we Flemish in Schottland just outside the southern Petershagen Gate in the shadow of the Bishop's Hill. It was here, in church one summer Sunday, that I met Janneken.

Met her *again*, she told me. The first time, she said, was in the death cell of our mothers. I cannot even remember her saying that, though she has reminded me often. I remember only her standing there, the wide folds of her long brown dress skirted with a white apron, her reddish hair gathered up under a white cap covering her ears, her small, pointed mouth moving. I did nothing but lift rocks all day, and suddenly before me was a manifestation: I felt as if God Himself had taken my head between His two hands, twisted it right and spoken into my face:

"Jan Adam Wens, look at this delicate woman. She is your wife."

Janneken helped me understand and accept what my father had undeniably bequeathed my body: his mason's hands. I became an apprentice in the Danzig guild of stonecutters. Hand and chisel and rule and line and hammer, I learned not only to see mountains in the stone I handled, but I became content, sometimes almost happy, to shape them. Feel them, in turn, determine the very muscle of my hands and arms and back.

That was the best thing I learned, and perhaps also the most limiting. Because seeing mountains in a stone could not teach me to recognize the smaller, delicately beautiful shapes that the greatest of Mennonite stone masters discovered there. The first master was Willem van den Blocke; he had fled Antwerp to escape the Duke of Alva, and Danzig gave him many building commissions, including the magnificent High Gate through which the annual procession of the King of Poland entered the city. I never worked for old Master Willem, but I cut stone for his son, Abraham van den Blocke. He was, if not as gifted a sculptor as his father, certainly a greater architect; better even than Adam Wiebe of Harlingen would be.

Once, toward the end of Abraham's life, when under Adam Wiebe's rebuilding of the city core we were fashioning the Neptune Fountain on the Royal Processional Route, Abraham said to me, "I thank God for you, Jan Adam. Every day. I can draw the design for a fountain, and Wiebe can bring up the water, but only you can cut the stone perfectly."

He created the figure of Neptune, his trident and small basin, and had it cast in bronze in Augsburg. I built the wide stone base for the fountain where it still stands after 370 years of war and rebuilding, on the Long Street where it broadens into the central Long Market. I also cut the intricate facade of the Arthuis building opposite the fountain, which has been called the most exquisite Renaissance building that still exists north of Italy. Perhaps it is. When the sunlight reflects across its stones, I always thought any soul must feel its flawless serenity.

Janneken is so tiny, I am so large; across from me at our hearth, she is singing. She threads that old Flemish skipping song into the click of her knitting:

> Oh, the lice, the lice,
> They were worse than mice,
> For they visited once,
> And they were not nice,
> The high and mighty Bishop of Ronse.

And I sing the proverb of the Bishop Pieter Titelman after her:

> Pieter, Pieter Longnose,
> Your nose, so high it rears,
> The wind blows through your empty head
> And out through both your ears.

"One evening," continues Janneken, "the high and mighty Bishop of Ronse drove his carriage into an inn." Her voice is lilting as if she were telling this to our six children again, the stories they and their children after them will carry in their blood into coming generations. "And there the Bishop met the Bailiff of Kortrijck, who was already sitting inside, eating an enormous supper of lamb and boiled and rare roasted beef, and chicken and seven kinds of cheeses, both sharp and salty, with mussels as a side dish and white, white bread so soft to sop up all the lip-smacking juices."

I join in her telling, the way we often played the roles together. "'My most merciful Bishop,' said the Bailiff, bowing low to hide his smile, 'you are travelling again.' "

Janneken answers: "'Of course,' said the Bishop as the fawning innkeeper lifted his fur cloak, so fine and churchly heavy, from his broad shoulders. And then he sat down at the table, for the Bailiff was after all close enough to his rank that he could quite properly sit and even eat with him. 'Know you not,' the Bishop told the Bailiff, misusing the words of Jesus, 'that I must be about my Father's business?'"

I speak as the Bailiff: "Of course, my Lord Bishop! So you are again travelling throughout the land in your sacred concern for souls. And perhaps hunting out and capturing heretics again, is that right?"

She says: "The Bishop answered, 'You know me well, my son,' and sighed wearily, folding his large, soft hands as if in prayer over his great, round belly. 'The Church must be ever vigilant, it can never rest at ease when sin would abound.'"

I say: "The Bailiff hid his mouth behind his hand and said in a puzzled tone, 'My Lord, I, like you, travel much in my line of duty. I arrest evil men, thieves, murderers, corrupt merchants, violent lawbreakers. Now, I must have at least nine, sometimes twelve men with me in order to effect an arrest, but you never travel with more than two servants and your skilful smith to forge and fit the necessary manacles. If I travelled with so few men, I would not live for a day. How is it possible for you?' "

She says: "The Bishop fondled his great diamond rings one by one, and smiled at such ignorance. 'I need have no fear,' he said. 'Wherever I go, I bear the authority of God Himself, and I arrest only good people who have never yet offered me danger.' "

I say: "'But my Lord,' answered the Bailiff, ever more puzzled, 'if I arrest all the bad people, and you all the good, who then in our land shall escape captivity?' "

Janneken's needles are at rest; I follow her gaze into the low blue flames of our evening fire. She continues:

"And not long thereafter, God Himself visited the high and mighty Bishop of Ronse in his princely palace at Kortrijck, visited him with a miracle. He became infested with lice. They grew on his body like grass, in such terrifying numbers that not even his numberless servants could bring him enough linen to keep him clean, nor wash his body free of them. The more lice they scraped from him, the more the lice multiplied. Days, weeks, months . . . and at last he died, in his splendid bishop's bed, a most horrible death."

My wife glances at me; is there a slight smile at the tips of her lips? The fire burns too darkly, I cannot tell. I take my turn to complete the story:

"Four women came, albeit in great fear, to lay out the Bishop for burial. And it was to them that the second miracle was revealed. When they drew back the blankets, they discovered his poor shrunken body, but not a single louse."[2]

Janneken and I tell each other this amazing little story quite often; the way we told it to our children, now grown and living around us. For we consider ourselves the third miracle: we found each other in Danzig, far from Antwerp and twenty years after our mothers gave their final encouragement to each other as they were chained, each to her stake. Encouragement with their looks only, and

---

2   See the *Martyrs Mirror*, 1095, for van Braght's version of this tale.

groans; they could not sing or call out their faith to each other through the rising fire because their mouths were transfixed by iron tongue screws.

After I was old enough to know the story, Adriaen told me how he recovered from his faint, got on his feet and found there was no one in the Grand Market. Just the charred stubs of the execution posts and ashes, smoking. I must have stayed beside him all that time, he said, because I came with my bleeding head and watched him search in the ash heap.

I asked him, "What were you looking for?"

He raised me, and even after I grew to be taller than he, and later much broader, he remained my Big Brother, full of exact facts and wise decisions. He said, "There was no . . . reason, I was blind with tears, I couldn't see, not at that moment. I saw nothing happen, and now there was nothing . . . the square was empty, no one there, smoke going up from the stump and ashes where I saw her being chained, and suddenly I knew that the dear Lord Jesus had come, He had lifted our mother up in His arms straight to heaven, that was what had happened, she had vanished and so everyone had just left, gone home, and I kicked those stupid ashes, they were nothing! and my foot hit something sharp and hot and I cried out, I was kicking embers away from the black stump over the cobblestones, but then you came closer and bent over. You picked it up."

I know I did. I have deep scars. I see them every day because I work closely with my hands. I must have picked up the tongue screw with my right hand because my right thumb and two fingers are scarred, and then I dropped it into the palm of my left hand because it is burned even deeper. Adriaen told me he could smell my left hand burning, but I did not make a sound.

My Master Abraham van den Blocke died on January 28, 1628, only a week after his father Master Willem. Though neither had been permitted to live in Danzig, because they were not citizens and were neither Catholic nor Lutheran, they were given the high honour of full city funerals, and burial inside the massive Cathedral of St. Mary.

My mother, Maeyken Wens, has no gravestone; nor do her sisters, Mariken and Lijsken Lievens; nor does my wife's mother, Janneken van Munstdorp. They were translated by fire from earth to heaven, they parted from us and a pillar of cloud received them out of our sight. But the place of their translation remains: the "hand werpan" fountain in the Grand Market in Antwerp, Belgium, stands on the spot.

Janneken and I have the knitting needles, and also the iron tongue screw.

Sometimes I hold it in my hand. My gnarled fore and middle fingers fit into it as precisely as my mother's tongue for which it was especially forged. Janneken tells me this: there is no need for memory.

Cardinal Granvelle had ordered that there was to be no more testifying to the crowds by condemned heretics during their procession to the place of execution; there was in particular to be no more singing, especially of martyr songs. They were too disturbing for the church faithful. Therefore, on the ordered day of execution the skilful smith of the Bishop of Ronse came to the cell in Het Steen Castle with his portable charcoal smithy. The executioner commanded my mother to put out her tongue. She said:

"Love God above all. He Who is, and shall ever be."

And then she did that.

The smith pushed the curled iron onto her tongue until the flanges spread her lips as wide and hard as possible.[3] He pulled it off, hammered it a little tighter, then forced it on again. He was silent, efficient, well accustomed to intimate work on a shuddering woman's face. He screwed the vise down to the point of steady blood, and finally, to make certain it would never slip off, with tongs he took from out of his fire a white-hot iron. He laid that iron on the tip of my mother's tongue.

---

3   See the *Martyrs Mirror,* 1038.

Communion

The Zurich Anabaptist dissidents officially broke with Ulrich Zwingli by rebaptizing themselves. An earlier act of rebellion, however, was eating sausage during Lent in 1522.

Eve bit the apple—
but you fed each other sausage.

Were you gleeful that night,
like naughty children?
Or solemn,
as weight of stained glass centuries
shattered with every mouthful?

I can speculate—but this I'm sure of:
Sausage tastes *good.*

Your mouths were filled with
juice,
spices,
salt like sweat on skin.
You licked greasy-slick lips afterwards,
satiated.

When the flames licked at your feet years later,
when the water rushed in to fill choking lungs,
did you want another chance?
Did you think about your families?

Or, as darkness closed in,
did you suddenly remember that giddy, strange night,
taste the salt
on your tongue . . .

Becca J. R. Lachman

When Red Rushes Up

True humility is neither thinking too highly of one's self
nor thinking too little of one's self, but rather
not thinking of one's self at all. —Amish proverb

What does *a woman want?* —Sigmund Freud

Silence scares me most.
You see, I come from
a long line of martyrs
who gave up their lives to be
heard. Some women
were drowned at night in secret,
their testimonies grown
too powerful. Even with tongues
screwed tightly down, a mother's body
still begged for crowds to admire
            and fear such faith.

Burned, baked, stretched and smothered,
they made their public offerings, turned back
on splitting ice to save
their executioners
in order to sit at their heavenly
banquet. Or to follow a man
across the country, raise
his children, cook his potatoes
just the way he likes them.
           I come from

persecution set ghosting
in lungs and feet so heavy black-
purple, it's impossible to boil it
out of us. Look at the way
some tongues are still
                missing.

I carry these two apples with me
daily: cheeks that still expect me
to stand in ready flames with all
that is said or asking for it—or, even
worse—*un*said, since I might be taken
as prideful or clinging or my mother's
mother, Eve's ready
hand. All these things and more
rush to my face like fire. Shameful
ripening. Ripening,
mirrored: the silence
for which I'm piling up
                the stones.

JULIA SPICHER KASDORF

Writing Like a Mennonite

Others were tortured, refusing to accept release, in order to obtain a better resur-
rection. Others suffered mocking and flogging, and even chains and imprisonment.
They were stoned to death, they were sawn in two, they were killed by the sword;
they went about in skins of sheep and goats, destitute, persecuted, tormented—of
whom the world was not worthy. They wandered in deserts and mountains, and in
caves and holes in the ground.—Hebrews 11:35-38 NRSV

I

Long ago someone called Mennonites *die Stillen im Lande* (the quiet in the
land), a phrase that conveys the sense of a silent and defenseless community
set against a noisy, violent world—and, at least for some, the name stuck. The
phrase probably comes from Psalm 35:20, which is a complaint against an
articulate enemy who uses language to persecute voiceless pacifists: "For they
do not speak peace, but they conceive deceitful words against those who are
quiet in the land." Until the traditional Anabaptist principles of nonresistance
and community led some Mennonite people to become engaged with the anti-
war and civil rights movements of the 1960s, Mennonites considered silence
to be an appropriate attitude toward the wider world and a necessary means
of survival in it—whether they inhabited deeply rooted farm communities in
Pennsylvania or endured migrations across Europe or between the Americas.
This attitude was borne of actual experience: Anabaptist migrant groups in
Europe were often allowed to settle in new areas only if they promised not to
proselytize or testify to their beliefs. They could live on the land as long as they
remained quiet. In early America, a similar habit persisted.

Silence and seclusion became a strategy of living peaceably with the wider
world as well as a means of keeping peace within the community. In the Pennsylvania Amish-Mennonite ethos I know, seductive and eloquent discourse was
distrusted and considered a possible form of coercion. The choices a person made
in daily life wrote the text that mattered most. Conflicts in family or community
seemed to be smothered in silence, and because disturbing or minority views
were rarely expressed in public, they could exist in their own quiet space on the

margins, a kind of "don't ask, don't tell" policy for differences of many kinds. If deviant members refused to keep quiet, conflict could be fractious and bitter. In *Disquiet in the Land: Cultural Conflict in American Mennonite Communities,* Fred Kniss catalogues 208 examples of quarrels over issues ranging from the implementation of Sunday schools and participation in military service, to dress and language used in Mennonite Church communities in four eastern states between 1870 and 1985.[1] He concludes that conflicts often spring from two competing impulses in Mennonite life and thought: traditionalism, with its emphasis on moral, biblical, and collective authority; and communalism, expressed by pacifism, concern for justice, congregationalism, and mutual aid. A vivid example of this tension can be seen in current debates about how to respond to churches that openly accept gay and lesbian members: traditionalists opt for expulsion and excommunication, while some communalists argue for dialogue or even inclusion. Whereas schism can tear a community limb from limb and leave lasting scars for decades, at least it provides a means for both groups of people to disagree and still retain their sense of belonging to a fragment of the original community. For an individual, the cost of articulating a dissenting view is much greater. Rather than stir up trouble, draw unnecessary attention to themselves, or risk ostracism, individuals—especially if they were women—have often chosen to keep their most troubling thoughts to themselves.

I have another, more visceral sense of silence. I am still a child—at seven, at ten, and at fifteen—walking home from the school bus. The kindly grandfather figure of the neighborhood waves to me as he does every day, that gesture not so much a greeting as a way to lure me to his porch. Most days I resist, wave sweetly, and keep walking up the hill toward home as if I do not understand his desire. I am torn between not wanting to visit him and wanting to be good and obedient to a grown-up whom my family respects. So other days I comply, as I do this day. He leads me through the screen door to steps that descend to the cellar, where he will show me an elaborate miniature railroad set up for Christmas or a lathe where he turns wooden candleholders or the workbench where he grows seedlings each spring. Then he will pin me against a wall and stab his tongue against my teeth, which will be clenched tight, as I try to breathe. His tongue will taste sweet from chewing tobacco; his breath will heave as he presses his body against mine. I will never open my mouth to speak or scream, because I think that if I open my mouth his tongue will shoot down my throat like a snake.

---

1   Fred Kniss, *Disquiet in the Land: Cultural Conflict in American Mennonite Communities* (New Brunswick, NJ: Rutgers University Press, 1997).

Experience comes to a child simply, literally; only much later does it burst on me as a metaphor that has structured my thought and influenced my perceptions all these years. Now I wonder whether my quiet ancestors kept their mouths clamped shut for fear that another's tongue would plunge down their throats. Is this why the shift from oral German dialects to English or Russian or Spanish or Portuguese has always been so painful in Mennonite communities and families? I wonder if a memory of trauma and fear of violation has kept Mennonites from producing imaginative literature until recently, even though they have been living in literate and safely landed communities in America since colonial times. John Ruth has recounted many other reasons for our failure to write in times past: a legacy of iconoclasm from the Radical Reformation, a distrust of the assimilating influence of education and high culture, a devaluation of the individual voice in the service of the collective religious community, a deep commitment to facts and plain speech, and the folk culture's underlying values of practicality, hard work, and thrift.[2] Nevertheless, as plain dress, a strange dialect, and the geographical separation of valleys or remote prairie villages have delineated safety zones for vulnerable Mennonite bodies in times past, so the absence of literary activity has hidden Mennonite hearts and minds from the curious gaze of others. In the absence of published fiction and poetry, outsiders have no access to the experience and imagination of the community. Perhaps the refusal of previous generations to publish imaginative work was another kind of cultural resistance, borne of distrust and of a fear that literature would somehow expose the interior life of the community—or of the individual—and thereby make them vulnerable to violation.

When the man was done, I would let his wood-framed cellar door slam shut and walk home through the backyards, thinking, "Well, that was not so bad. It was only my body." I think that the martyr stories taught me that wonderful splintering trick: it is only the body. In one of my favorite engravings, it is only the body of Anneken Hendriks tied to a ladder that forever tips headfirst into a fire of the Spanish Inquisition, her hands pressed together in prayer. In another

---

2   John Ruth in *Mennonite Identity and Literary Art* (Scottdale, PA: Herald Press, 1978) outlines the most obvious traditional resistances to literature among Mennonite peoples, including an amnesia of the oral literature resulting from the language shift from Pennsylvania German to English, and numerous religious and cultural scruples. Since the late 1970s, serious, imaginative literature by Mennonite writers has begun to blossom and has enjoyed both a popular reception and scholarly attention from Mennonite readers.

story, Maeyken Wens knows it is only a body that her children will miss after she burns at the stake, her tongue clamped so that she cannot speak. "Fear not them which kill the body," it says in Maeyken's section of the *Martyrs Mirror,* paraphrasing Matthew 10:28: "And fear not them which kill the body but are not able to kill the soul; but rather fear him which is able to destroy both soul and body in hell."[3] They can burn the body but not the soul. You may gaze at my body, even touch it if you must, but you will not know my soul: my essential self exists safely apart from my body and from you. Therapists call this splintering of consciousness *dissociation* and count it among the common psychological strategies employed by those who survive physical trauma.

Once, after a reading I gave from *Eve's Striptease,* a tall, distinguished-looking woman with silvery hair approached me and simply said, "I had an experience like yours, but I do not speak of it. I stand on my silence." And she seemed to have found solid ground to stand on. Rather than endure the feelings of violation that invariably accompany revelation of childhood sexual mistreatment, she chose to keep a dignified silence. Although sometimes mistaken for compliance, the refusal to speak in defense of oneself can be a fierce form of resistance, as when Jesus refused to speak before Pilate or when he hung on the cross and "opened not his mouth . . . as a sheep before her shearers is dumb" (Isaiah 53:7 KJV). Certainly this stance has helped to consolidate identity and has served as a means of resistance for Mennonites; silence is a worthy weapon for a pacifist body that carries memories of physical violation. Following the literal teachings of Jesus, Mennonites have refused for centuries to defend themselves with any sort of visible force—including the force of language in legal courts.

When two thieves approached the end of a wharf off Manhattan's west side where I was sitting with my writer friend Donald, my first thought was not to speak or fight but to flee, leaving him behind. Approaching a couple of men down the pier, I could find no words to explain what was happening to us or why I wanted to stand there with them, mute as I was. Meanwhile, because Donald had no money, the thieves came for me, and the two men nearby scattered, confused and sensing trouble. While the male thief held Donald, his female partner shoved my shoulders and chest, but I refused to give up the seven dollars in my purse. I was sure that only fingers poked in their coat pockets, not guns. Exasperated, Donald finally convinced me to give them whatever was in my wallet, and then they sprinted toward shore, where a police car happened to be cruising by.

---

3   Theileman J. van Braght, *The Bloody Theater or Martyrs Mirror . . . ,* trans. Joseph F. Sohm (Scottdale, PA: Herald Press, 1977), 982.

Donald ran after them and hopped into the back of one of the police cars, which took off in pursuit of the thieves. I remained behind on the pier, and a kind man named Gabriel, who had witnessed the chase, stayed with me until the police returned. In parting, he asked me to be sure to testify against the thieves if they were apprehended. Drug addicts often robbed gay men in that neighborhood, he explained, and the cops were rarely sympathetic.

Later, at the station house, the policemen assured me that my testimony would send the man, who was on parole, "up the river" to a penitentiary for several years because his pretend pistol elevated the theft to a felony. During the next few days I searched for alternatives, but it was nearly impossible to make the city's victim services workers understand that I was unsure about whether to testify against my predator. I had no memory of my parents ever talking to the police; it just seemed to be something we don't do. The more I dealt with the criminal justice system, whose workers were unguardedly bigoted, the more deeply I identified with the African-American man and his female accomplice who had escaped. The assistant district attorney explained that the decision to press charges was the state's, not mine, and threatened to subpoena my testimony.

My conscience remained unsettled until the morning I phoned a Mennonite acquaintance who worked as a chaplain at the city's prison on Riker's Island. In a voice still blurry with sleep, he suggested that my refusing to testify might be the worst form of pride: taking responsibility for another's choice. It may be an especially Mennonite temptation to assume that we can make peace in the world by absorbing its violence onto our own bodies. His advice resonated with my memories from a Mennonite college in the early 1980s, when a couple of my classmates who had refused to register for the draft faced criminal charges, and one Anabaptist leader suggested that North American boys could make peace by actually placing their bodies between military lines in El Salvador.

In the end, I testified before a grand jury, and the case was later settled without trial. Leaving the courthouse that clear autumn afternoon, I was swept with a surprising sense of relief. It seemed impossible that all I had to do was just to say what had happened. I hadn't expected the jurors to believe my story, so I wore the most innocent floral print church dress in my closet. Partly I had blamed myself for the mugging, as if two writers out on a pier watching the sun go down over New Jersey somehow deserved to be punished. Indeed, most New Yorkers gave me that sense, as they instantly asked, "What were you doing out there at dusk?" (That placing of blame on the victim is urban magical thinking that traces effect to cause and thereby allows the speaker to distance himself from the episode, believing that he is safe from random acts of violence.) I didn't tell my parents about the robbery until long afterward, not wanting to worry them or confirm a sense that my home was unsafe.

Nonetheless, walking away from the court room into Chinatown's chaotic streets, I felt oddly light and shaken. The secret I carried from childhood remained buried, but I now know that it must have been tangled up in my heady sense of relief. I had simply said what happened to me, and I had been believed, not blamed. I'd even heard one of the jurors let out a moan of sympathy and exasperation when I told the prosecutor how much money was in my purse. On the way back to my office, I stopped to watch a worker release garments from the window of a third-story sweatshop. Red silk blouses on hangers gracefully glided down a line to a man loading a truck below, scarlet tongues flapping in the wind.

Stranger than my sense of relief that day is the fact that the robbery took place several hours after I learned that my first book would be published. Donald's first novel also found a publisher later that year, and ever since then, we have referred to book publications as "muggings." It is impossible to prepare for the sudden terror and vulnerability that comes with the news that one's thoughts will become print. Even when a book is consciously written with that goal in mind, the event of publication can feel like a violation—especially to authors who are driven to write because their tongues are somehow tied. Until the publication of *Sleeping Preacher,* I had been content to confide my ideas about family, history, and Mennonite culture to a notebook page. But on the Tuesday after Labor Day in 1991, a morning phone call from the University of Pittsburgh Press and an evening robbery made it impossible for me to remain silent—in several senses.

A poem included in that first collection revealed to my family for the first time what had occurred in the home of that elderly neighbor man. My parents' concern about raising us away from the traditional community had been soothed by kind neighbors like him—a Mason, not a Mennonite, yet every bit as generous and kind to my brothers and me as a grandfather might have been. For two decades my silence had protected them and also had protected him. Growing up, I had simply absorbed his assault on my spirit and body and had hidden my knowledge away in some secret place. I wanted to disturb no one. Perhaps even then I sensed that, for my parents, the choice to raise children away from their community of origin was a risk. My silence supported their hope that life is more complex than the dualism that would divide experience between the safety of the sect and the danger of the world. Indeed, within that one man I knew both kindness and coercion, a contradiction that to this day I cannot explain and must simply accept. Several times in college I had tried to write about it—once as a poem, once as a narrative sketch—but both pieces remained undeveloped. It was not until the summer I was twenty-six, at the MacDowell artists' colony in New Hampshire for the first time, that I wrote "The Interesting Thing," a poem I included in my book.

To bring this kind of information to light, even in writing, is never simple. When an ancient violation is finally named, people are at a loss about what to do: what to remember and what to forget, whether there is any way to make amends, or whether retribution will only continue a cycle of violation. It is difficult to know what brings healing and justice. At the personal level, these questions are complex. At the local and national level, I see them everywhere as my mind's eye moves down the cities of the Eastern Seaboard to the American South, from Haiti to South America, across the ocean to Western Europe and the former Soviet Union and the Balkans, down the coast and around the cape of South Africa, up to the Middle East and across the subcontinent of India and Pakistan, across Burma to Cambodia, Vietnam, and the People's Republic of China. If it is impossible to correct the horrible things that people have done to one another, then why even try? Consider the recent Japanese apology to Korean women pressed into prostitution during World War II or the rehabilitation of the victims of the 1692 Salem witch trials in New England. Do these gestures offer any critique of history's cruel cycles of violence? Do they prevent future abuses? Yet the cost of not remembering and telling those stories—at least for me—is the unconscious repetition of violence, on the self and onto others.

One evening, after a day of solitary work at MacDowell, I was sitting at a small bar table with three other writers from the artists' colony, listening as one told how he had gotten expelled from Brooklyn College in the 1960s for publishing an underground newspaper. Although I don't like to smoke, I had a cigarette in my hand when one of the men asked the storyteller, "Why did they kick you out—for printing the word *c---*?" The force of that word caused me to swiftly reach across the table and press my smoldering cigarette into the speaker's chest. "Jesus, Mary, and Joseph!" the Irish poet cursed. The rest of us froze, silent, until someone finally said, "Any man can go to a colony and have an affair, but how many men get burned with a cigarette?"

That he would link violence with sex through some vague association of excess in that moment is incisive. In a situation where I was surrounded by older and more accomplished male authors, I took up a cigarette—shape of a pen, shape of a penis—and burned a man's body because he had uttered the word that names and degrades female difference. The myth of female castration—that women are only castrated men, males without potency—is as powerfully embedded in Western culture as Oedipus, Angela Carter reminds us. This myth, which supports erotic violence and male domination, is "an imaginary fact that pervades the whole of men's attitude toward women and our attitude to ourselves, that transforms women from human beings into wounded creatures who are born to bleed."[4]

The next morning the Irish poet appeared at breakfast with a salved wound the size of a dime shining angry red where his shirt hung open. He needed to speak with me, he said. He needed to know why I had done it. I hardly knew him, so how could I have known that he wouldn't hurt me in response to such a reckless deed? I told him that I was sorry, terribly sorry, but in fact I felt only surprise at my capacity to enact that cliché of contemporary torturers. Although we have remained on good terms through the years, the poor man had to explain the episode to himself in the end, writing a villanelle called, "What Does it Mean to be Touched by Fire?" The end rhymes that I recall—fire, desire, conspire—all suggest pain, sex, and collusion.

It would take many years for me to begin to see the ways that violence is linked not only to sex but also to writing. Writing is a process by which suppressed feelings come to consciousness, sometimes painfully. I believe that it is no coincidence that I committed an act both cruel and erotic—at least in some metaphoric sense—when I was just beginning to write out of my own memories of trauma. It is as though I had swallowed a hook long ago and the force with which I was tugging at the line to pull memory loose from my flesh caused me to lash out with a monstrous, unconscious gesture. As the mugging painfully forced me to speak on my own behalf, so childhood violation was gradually pushing me toward articulation, the way a splinter will work its way to the skin's surface, festering, trying to heal. The wound becomes a mouth that finally speaks its testimony, thereby transforming a mute, confused victim into a subject with a clear vision of her experience and a literate voice.

II

That trauma can both confine one to silence and compel one to find articulation is clear in the brief history of Mennonite literature. Apart from some devotional books, the first, and by far most important work by Mennonite authors is *The Bloody*

---

4   Angela Carter, *The Sadeian Woman and the Ideology of Pornography* (New York: Harper and Row, 1978), 23.

Theater or Martyrs Mirror of the Defenseless Christians Who Baptized Only Upon Confession of Faith, and Who Suffered and Died for the Testimony of Jesus, Their Savior, from the Time of Christ to the Year A.D. 1660. First published in 1660 in an edition of 1,000 copies, this enormous book contains texts composed by or about individuals enduring torture, on trial, or awaiting execution. Commonly called only *Martyrs Mirror,* the book's full title is useful for the way it defines the words *Anabaptist*—a Christian pacifist who practices adult baptism—and *martyr*—one who dies testifying for beliefs. Elsewhere much has been made of the way this title underlines the spectacle of martyrdom, which unfolded in public, according to a civil and religious script.[5] Yet the word which interests me most is *testimony.*

In cases where court records are preserved, the "testimony" of the martyrs in this book is quite literal. Yet all of the 4,011 "died for the testimony of Jesus." In some cases, their testimony is preserved in letters and verse written to relatives and fellow believers. For illiterate people, martyrdom itself became a kind of writing with the body, because the martyrs' words and actions were converted into textual form as a consequence of the physical ordeals they chose to endure. For Anabaptist sisters, martyrdom represented a choice to enact the ultimate sacrifice that placed them on equal ground with their brethren. A third or more of the sixteenth-century martyrs were women, and in some regions during the worst periods of persecution, as many as four in ten of the martyrs were female.[6] For instance, Anneken Hendriks is described in *Martyrs Mirror* as Anneken de Vlaster, a housewife from Frisia who could neither read nor write. Yet her dramatic death in Amsterdam in October of 1571 ensured that her words were inscribed forever. The fifty-three-year-old woman, who probably worked as a linen weaver, was so loud and verbal about her faith that the authorities stuffed her mouth with gunpowder to keep her from giving "good witness" to spectators at her execution. The account does not say whether her skull mercifully exploded when her ladder-bound body fell into the flames, but we know that she did not silently store her convictions there. Her words and courage inspired Dutch Mennonites to write a hymn that narrates her execution. In addition, fifty-three hymn texts were written by imprisoned Anabaptists awaiting execution and preserved in the *Ausbund,* a 1564 worship book still used by the Amish.

---

5   John S. Oyer and Robert S. Kreider, *The Mirror of the Martyrs* (Intercourse, PA: Good Books, 1990), 13.

6   C. Arnold Snyder and Linda A. Huebert Hecht, eds., Introduction to *Profiles of Anabaptist Women* (Kitchener, ON: Canadian Corporation for Studies in Religion/ Wilfrid Laurier University Press), 12.

Even after the Anabaptist era, trauma continued to be a means of articulation and inscription at those times when it did not silence the community altogether. Whereas the Mennonites and Amish who migrated to America during the colonial period published next to no literature for a broader audience until well after World War II, those who had migrated to colonies in Russia during the eighteenth century did publish, but mostly after their communities were destroyed. "The tragic upheaval of war and revolution and the destruction of the Mennonite commonwealth in Russia shocked the Mennonite literary imagination into life as nothing had since the age of martyrdom," observed Al Reimer in a 1993 survey of North American Mennonite writing.[7] During the 1920s and 1930s, a few émigré authors, mostly located in the Canadian West, tried to make sense of that traumatic loss by writing and publishing literature, often in *Plautdietsch,* the German-based mother tongue of their Russian childhoods. Like other literatures of loss—Isaac Bashevis Singer's Yiddish novels come to mind—this work preserved the memory of an ethnic homeland, often portrayed as Edenic.

In these literary efforts, and through countless oral repetitions of violence and dislocation narratives that are still repeated in Mennonite communities, I see spontaneous attempts by individuals to heal the consequences of trauma. From the time of Freud's first work with hysterics, and from early research into shell-shock, the inability to speak has been associated with trauma. Almost from the start, doctors believed that the physioneurosis caused by terror could be reversed with words. It seems that while normal memory exists in narrative structures, the memories of trauma lack context or language and persist only as vivid sensations or images. If these memories and feelings can be articulated and shaped into narrative form, they can thereby be integrated into the rest of a life's experience. A 1992 study by Harvard physician Judith Herman links research into private traumas such as domestic violence and public traumas such as terrorism. Herman relates current work with torture survivors in Chile, where therapists have helped victims to write detailed narrative accounts of their mistreatment and then to relive the experiences by speaking them within a supportive community. "The action of telling a story in the safety of a protected relationship can actually produce a change in the abnormal processing of the traumatic memory," she writes.[8] I wonder whether *Martyrs Mirror* has sometimes served this purpose at a collective level, for it seems that the book was most often printed in conjunction

7   Al Reimer, *Mennonite Literary Voices: Past and Present* (North Newton, KS: Bethel College Press, 1993), 15.
8   Judith Herman, MD, *Trauma and Recovery* (New York: Basic Books, 1992), 83.

with an impending war, the need for stories felt most keenly in relation to the community's fresh fears of persecution.

It would also follow that in those times when the community has refused to hear traumatic stories, it has hindered healing. I think of the Mennonites who remained in Soviet Russia after the 1920s migrations and who therefore faced the brutalities of Stalin's regime: collectivization, cultural and religious repression, and the systematic deportation or execution of most able-bodied men. By 1941, the invasion of the German army enabled these Mennonite villages, dominated by women then, to open their churches and conduct school in their own language. For a time, the occupying troops took Mennonite women to be their translators, assistants, and mistresses. When the German army began to retreat in 1943, German-speaking people followed the army in a trek toward Germany, certain they would be killed if they did not stay ahead of advancing Russian troops. A number of these women—some with children, some widowed, some separated from husbands who had been deported to labor camps—emigrated to Mennonite communities in Canada. Although many of these women were eventually integrated into the Canadian communities, they were not warmly received on their arrival after the war. Because of their dubious marital status, many were denied membership in Mennonite churches, and no one wanted to listen to their stories of violence, combat, sexual assault, or impropriety. A desire for peace and purity prevented the community from helping these women to heal, their trauma compounded by abandonment and isolation in an era when common wisdom advised survivors to forget the past and count their blessings. Even now, as full members of the community, most of these women have chosen not to speak about their experiences of war or their initial encounters with Canadian Mennonites.

In 1994 Pamela Klassen published a powerful ethnographic study based on the stories of two of these women.[9] Oddly enough, I first read this book while waiting to be called for jury duty, sitting on a mahogany pew in the massive main hall of Brooklyn's criminal court. I was so moved by the tragedy of the women's experience and Klassen's skillful analysis that I wept, my body curled over the paperback, in the din of that chaotic public space. When my name was called to sit for a lawsuit, I told the attorneys that I come from a Mennonite background, and they dismissed me from the case immediately, knowing of the sect's reputation for being nonlitigious, noncooperative, and apart from civil society.

---

9   Pamela Klassen, *Going by the Moon and the Stars* (Waterloo, ON: Wilfrid Laurier University Press, 1994). See Marlene Epp, *Women Without Men: Mennonite Refugees of the Second World War* (Toronto: University of Toronto Press, 2000).

A serious work of literature by a Mennonite critiquing Mennonite experience was not published for broad distribution in a language that could be understood by the dominant culture until Rudy Wiebe's *Peace Shall Destroy Many* appeared in 1962—this was 302 years after the *Martyrs Mirror* was published in the Netherlands for readers of Dutch.[10] When this book appeared, Wiebe received a letter from B. B. Janz, the venerable church leader who had negotiated with authorities for two years to arrange the 1923 migration of Mennonites from Russia to Canada. In his fine Gothic German hand, Janz asked Wiebe why he would publish a book in the English language that cast the Mennonite settlers in such an unflattering light. His chief concern was grave: if images such as these were broadly available, and if the Canadians decided that they could no longer offer a home to Mennonites, where in the world would they ever find another place to live?

Subsequently, and especially in recent years, Mennonite writers have proliferated and flourished like prairie grasses in the Canadian West, where they are often celebrated as pioneering rebel-heroes. If they are vulnerable at all, the terror comes from an internalized threat. Poet Di Brandt has said that she believed Mennonites from her farm village would kill her if she published her first book of poems, *questions i asked my mother.* Can she actually mean that Low German-speaking farmers from Rhineland, Manitoba, would find her house in Winnipeg or Windsor and knock on her door in the night, stamping their dung-clotted boots on her porch? Do they carry shotguns or pitchforks in her imagination, I wonder? The frequency with which she has mentioned this fear in public—once in a reading that I heard in 1990, three times in her 1995 collection of essays, *Dancing Naked*—suggests that it must be true in some sense, however unlikely in another. Her fear contains the truth of myth. Because she seized the authority of literature and persecuted her community by telling its secrets and exposing its shame, it must punish her in turn—as happened after Rudy Wiebe's first novel, as happened to the martyrs of old.

Before the publication of *Sleeping Preacher*, I also dreaded my book's reception in the Mennonite community, although it turned out to be warmer than I ever imagined. Given my context, perhaps I needed to imagine punishment in order to

---

10   Other works of fiction were published by North American Mennonite writers before
      Peace Shall Destroy Many, but this book marks a turning point because it was regarded
      as a literary rather than a popular work, it explores Mennonite experience directly, it
      was broadly distributed, and it engaged readers both within and beyond the Mennonite
      community.

cast myself in the position of author. This reminds me of a short but famous essay by Michel Foucault in which he traces the evolution of contemporary notions of authorship. Long before copyright designated the individual ownership of texts, he writes, the name of an actual author—not the name of the king or of a religious or mythic figure—was ascribed to a text only when it was considered transgressive and subject to censorship and punishment. Writing was regarded as an act fraught with risk, enacted on a field defined by the opposing poles of sacred or profane, lawful or unlawful.[11] I am not prepared to evaluate this idea in terms of historical fact, but its truth as a myth seems clear enough, and I would add to Foucault's list of oppositions, another: those ideas that are supportive of the community and those that are threatening to it. Moreover, I have noticed that, within the community, those writers who are regarded as transgressive seem to be taken most seriously by their Mennonite readers, as if the vague threat of punishment were a mark of authenticity or excellence. The terror of punishment for Mennonite writers—whether real or imagined—seems to invigorate creativity as persecution and trauma engendered Mennonite literature longer ago. "The more ye mow us down, the more we grow," wrote the second-century church father Tertullian. "The blood of the martyrs is the seed of the church."[12]

I have begun to question the disturbing consequences of this martyr identity, however, with the assistance of Lois Frey, a Mennonite-turned-Quaker therapist who has studied creativity and trauma for more than twenty years. She believes that trauma either destroys creativity by making a child too afraid to risk new experiences; or, if it is not so overwhelming, trauma may enable a child to grow, both in strength and in creativity, through the various ways she finds of mastering her injury. Frey wonders what causes a child to turn in either of these opposite directions, and a few years ago she turned her attention to Mennonites, whom she believes have inherited "encapsulated trauma." Symptoms of this inheritance that she recognizes in the Mennonite culture of her childhood include splitting of the self, impaired capacity for fantasy and symbolization, literal and concrete thinking, defensive occupation with the mundane, and memory behaviors that tend to repeat the trauma. The response to a memory of trauma is the curtail-

---

11 The essay originally appeared in the *Bulletin de la Société français de Philosophie* 63, no. 3 (1969), 73-104, and was first delivered as a lecture in 1969. "What is an Author?" can be found in Michel Foucault, *Language, Counter-Memory, Practice: Selected Essays and Interviews,* ed. and trans. Donald F. Bouchard (Ithaca: Cornell University Press, 1977).

12 Quoted in Oyer and Kreider, *Mirror of the Martyrs*, 9.

ing of creativity and a self-protective and fearful refusal to take risks. Cautious behaviors that once protected endangered beings thereby "retraumatize" them.

One aspect of the Mennonite inheritance Frey has named the "persecutor/ martyr introject." *Introjection* is a process whereby things from the world—actual persecutors and martyrs, for instance—become embedded in the unconscious as a pattern of behavior persisting for generations. Among Mennonites, Frey believes, a collective history of victimization, social ostracism, and persecution has written a persecutor/martyr script that gets replayed within the community or within a family every time an individual is censored or marginalized. To break beyond the victim/perpetrator introject, one must integrate both identities within the self. Confronting experience through the production of art is one means of escaping the scripted, narrow roles of victim and perpetrator. Moreover, an artwork's ability to express ambiguity and paradox enables an individual to recognize that she is capable of playing both roles. The production of artistic works thus enables a person to integrate the opposite identities into a whole and complex personality capable of confident, public expression.[13]

In many respects, I agree with Frey's assertions, but I am uneasy about the large claims they make for artistic work. It may appear in her public performance that the poet has become confident and capable; the voice in the poem or on stage seems to have mastered the injury at once immersed in it and in control of it. Louise Glück brilliantly recounts this apparent "revenge on circumstance": "For a brief period, the natural arrangement is reversed: the artist no longer acted upon but acting; the last word, for the moment, seized back from fate or chance. Control of the past: as though the dead martyrs were to stand up in the arena and say, 'Suppose, on the other hand . . .' No process I can name so completely defeats the authority of event."[14]

Of course, this triumphal moment exists only within the process of writing and within the written text. This is because writing enables the author to

---

13   For several years during the early 1990s, Lois conducted a small discussion group of Mennonites who had grown up in conservative homes and who are successful in highly creative vocations. We met a few times a year for a full day at a time to reflect on our memories of the community and on the nature of creativity. Her initial hypothesis in this study was that the experience of being culturally marginal enables a person to function more creatively because they are used to being different and coping with issues of loneliness. Her research was reported in a paper delivered at The Quiet in the Land Conference (Millersville University, 1995) and later published as "Creativity: From Victim to Reconstructor," *Mennonot* 7 (spring 1996), 18-20.

14   Louise Glück, "The Idea of Courage," in *Proofs and Theories* (New York: Ecco Press, 1994), 25.

transcend the limits of her body and to evade the demands that others may place upon her. A written text cannot be made to change in response to others; it does not fail to speak out of fear, nor can it alter in response to the loving attention of a reader. Moreover, it exists in a time and in a space quite apart from the body of its author.

Unbeknownst to me, you read this book, for instance; even after my death, it will exist. Although much is made of the "writer's voice," text is not speech. In fact, as the ultimate disconnection from the life world, the ultimate dissociation, writing may be the most brilliant splintering trick of all. It has taken me some time to grasp the fact that, in this way, my cure has also been my curse.

This split is another way that writing may be bound to violence. In order to write, an author gives up her conversations with the world, withdrawing for a time from the company of those she loves and from the pleasures and pains of living. French novelist, playwright, and mother Hêlêne Cixous admits, "Between the writer and his or her family the question is always one of departing while remaining present, of being absent while in full presence, of escaping, of abandon. It is both utterly banal and the thing we don't want to know or say. A writer has no children; I have no children when I write."[15]

I think of Maeyken Wens, most disturbing to me of the Anabaptist martyrs because her story glorifies a choice to abandon her children rather than recant. Could she not have practiced some form of the splintering trick: comply with the authorities yet still believe whatever she wanted in silence, for the sake of her sons? As much as I want to argue for the heroic voice, I also regret her choice, unable to imagine what it must have meant in her time. Maeyken Wens' letters to her family are preserved in the *Martyrs Mirror*, but most startling is the written narrative of fifteen-year-old Adriaen. Standing with three-year-old Hans on his arm to witness their mother's execution, Adriaen fainted and only revived when the fire had burned to a smoking heap. Searching the coals of his mother's execution fire, Adriaen found the contraption made of two blades that were screwed together to secure her tongue. Today this relic remains in the possession of Dutch Mennonites in Amsterdam, a phallic-shaped symbol of brutal force and silence, which, like the cross, is transformed by tradition into a beloved emblem of sacrifice and witness. The engraving in *Martyrs Mirror* shows, not the martyr Maeyken, but an almost comical view of Adriaen's broad behind as he reaches for the tongue screw in the smoldering coals, while Hans, still wearing a baby's dress, looks on.

---

15   Hêlêne Cixous, *Three Steps on the Ladder of Writing* (New York: Columbia University Press, 1993), 21.

In an essay about the staggering numbers of Christian martyrs who, during the twentieth century, suffered under regimes on all points of the political spectrum, poet Dana Gioia reveals an etymological fact that I find very interesting. Historically, the word *martyr* carries no trace of suffering or death. Its root means only "witness"—witness to a truth. "The martyr's task is not armed resistance; nor is it even passive suffering," Gioia writes. "Persecution and death are only the by-products of the martyr's true role—to witness the truth uncompromised."[16]

For many people, the deathbed is the only place where they finally can bear to reveal the truths they have silently carried all of their lives. Facing death, they are finally free to speak with the clarity of those Anabaptist martyrs who gave "good witness" when facing the flames of an executioner's fire. Hélène Cixous identifies death—or an awareness of mortality—as the first rung on the ladder of writing.[17] This is the ladder, tipping toward the fire, on which Anneken Hendriks was bound. The author must lean into the scorching truth of her own mortality in order to write. She must write the book that threatens to cost her her life.

The implications of the martyr's example are absolute: one must bear witness to the only truth one sees. It is a matter of consequence that the word *witness* means not only "to see," but also "to speak." To write like a martyr means, not to choose death, but to choose to bear life—giving witness, to communicate the truth of one's own vision or insight, to affirm its value with confidence, no matter how arrogant or disturbing it may be, "and the truth shall make you free" (John 8:32 KJV). When my poem about the old neighbor was finally published, it shattered my family's perceptions of a person whom they had known to be only benevolent and generous. That is a violent act. No wonder the one who disturbs a perceived truth is felt to be an aggressor.

I also know that, by speaking of that molestation, I risk becoming defined and marked by its shame. But how different is that experience from any unfortunate thing that happens to a child on her way to becoming an adult? It may be no different, except in the scope of its consequences, from what happened to me at the age of twelve, while hiking a mountain trail at church camp, when a copperhead bite transformed me from a child who could catch garter snakes with her brothers into a child with recurring nightmares of a floor so thick with serpents that it undulated; of copperheads so smart they could read my mind, which was plotting an escape; of snakes that turned and attacked when I opened my mouth to cry for

16   Dana Gioia, "To Witness the Truth Uncompromised: Reflections on the Modern Martyrs," *Image* 13 (Spring 96): 71-73.

17   Cixous, *Three Steps*, 36-37.

help and no sound came out. Even now, terror rushes through my body whenever a snake flashes on the television screen or I see a patch of snake skin slither under the leaves in my garden. Metaphoric associations aside, does the snake bite brand me in the eyes of my readers any less than the touch of an old man? Or does everything always and only collapse into the shapes of familiar narrative plots?

III

As a community carries memories of trauma, so does an individual's body, often accompanied by deep and contradictory desires to deny and declare the pain.[18] As a little girl, I found in the martyr stories a way to survive: It is only my body you can touch. The split between body and spirit that I learned in such a visceral way exactly parallels the split between experience and words that developed centuries ago with the technology of writing. The disembodied medium of letters has enabled me to loosen from my body's recesses those old wounds, to re-create them on a page, and, eventually, to speak. Yet whatever I learned from my own texts, whatever I am able to say there, is only partial if I cannot also speak with others. "Writing is the only cure," an old maxim says, and I used to believe this, until I realized that writing was only part of a long training for the day when I would be able to talk. I bore on my body a violence until I could write; I bore witness in writing until I could speak.

Among the few material objects I have from that old neighbor man is a huge 1927 unabridged dictionary with elaborate Art Deco ornaments on its spine. On the title page are these words, inscribed in his inky cursive:

> *This book is my pride and joy*
> *Presented to Julia Spicher*
> *Dec. 6, 1980*
> *Remember me.*

It was a gift for my seventeenth birthday. By then I had been scribbling in school tablets for years, writing to make sense of the fragmented and silent parts of my life, removing language from my own body and inscribing it on that safe, quiet space of the page, where I could assemble and view it again. When he gave me that gift with its heartfelt inscription to remember him, did he assume that I would also remain quiet about the liberties he had taken with

---

18 "The conflict between the will to deny horrible events and the will to proclaim them aloud is the central dialectic of psychological trauma" (Herman, *Trauma and Recovery,* 1).

my body for a decade? That secret may have been more damaging than the touch of a pedophile's hand for the ways it has gagged my mouth and bound my body, isolating me in silence. Did he think I would fail to remember myself?

The tight-lipped survival strategy of my childhood is no longer useful, and in the martyr stories, I now see, not submission and silence, but men and women who spoke with their words and with their bodies, who refused to hold their tongues or keep the peace. Although I have succumbed to both temptations, I now write not for revenge—following popular tales of victim and monster—nor for redemption—following a Christian paradigm that is often too swift to be true. Following my perpetrator's advice, I write simply to remember and to bear witness.

The meaning of the word *memory* for me is enriched when I see that its tangled Indo-European roots run through the Latin *memor* (mindful); the Greek *martus* (witness), which became *martyr;* as well as the Germanic and Old English *murnam* (to grieve). We write to bring things in mind, to witness, and eventually, to grieve. Thus, I learn to refuse the abusive one within myself who will always beckon me back into that house. Though I may be tempted to be nice and comply, how can I return to that hushed place, when I would rather stay out on the road, offering myself to conversation and relationship as a martyr offers her body to flames? I must find my own life's pleasures, unable to recant or let some other tongue go down my throat.

Camp Hill
2000

The Woman with the Screw in Her Mouth Speaks

When people are starving, they go inside. This is the only way
to survive. Conserve. Save. Go to the quiet place in yourself
and wait for the day food comes. Wait without hoping,
for hope takes energy and you have very little to spare.

We went inside, too, but we wrapped our silence around a kernel
of fear. This fear fed us, and for this we were grateful. It made us
shrewd and cautious, not dim-witted like those who starve,
nor desperate. For us were the orderly rows of corn, the tight cluster
of farm buildings. Our barns were clean and painted white, bright white.
No one was going to find a blemish, an opening, a crooked row,
a reason. For the most part, outsiders would not see us, and
when they did, they would see only perfection.

And now what has happened to you? Some of the ancestors
are not pleased. They fear for you; some fear for themselves.
They would tell you not to be messy and bold. Don't take us down
with you, they say. But listen to me. We oldest ones remember: The dying
was worth it, every pain. We were chosen to bring something new
into the world. They had to keep us from singing. They had to keep us
from singing.

MEMORY

Views from a Pond:
Dirk the Idealist
Ian Huebert

MAURICE MIERAU

Amish Wedding Hymn

The martyr Hans Haslibach will not recant.
At his death three signs will prove his innocence:

> *As his head is severed from his body it leaps into his hat*

> *The sun turns red*

> *The town pump flows blood*

The martyr Hans Haslibach will not recant
as you now sing for 32 stanzas
standing up in wooden churches on hard pews
at weddings.

KRISTEN MATHIES

Alchemy for Survival[1]

(i)

Dutch Mennonites have the instrument
that held the tongue of Maeyken Wens as she burned.
Let me visit the room in Amsterdam
(not a whole museum, not an exhibition) where the screw is kept
in a modest, unassuming drawer lined with worn cloth,
a buckled drawer which won't slide out smoothly
no matter how slowly you pull it.

Let me visit the room in St. Catharines
where my grandmother is kept
in a modest, unassuming manner,
the rich fabric of her life a worn cloth now,
without the memory that kept it plush all these years
and the life which kept weaving additional length.
Stories that rolled out eloquently buckle
now, won't slide smoothly
no matter how gently you pull on them.
Let me visit the room in St. Catharines
so I can ask the woman who lives there
what she's done with my grandmother.

The woman has used a tongue screw
to keep my grandmother quieter than she's ever been.

---

1   Ed: Mathies wrote the first portion of this poem in 2002 about a composite character in-
    spired by the experiences of some seniors. The second half, written in 2010, more directly
    connects to her grandmother, Lina Ida Heinrich Wohlgemuth (1912–2002). Blended
    together, they demonstrate the interplay of time and memory in the writing process.

My grandmother was not so loud but she talked to me.
Stood next to me in church and sang with the rest of the congregation,
rubbed my back when my child-self tired of the preaching,
debated with me as we grew older then told me lovingly that
I just liked to argue.
She won't get into long chats with me anymore.
She's busy arguing with herself about where she went.

(ii)

Let me visit the room in St. Catharines
where my Grandma lives
a modest, unassuming life,
the rich fabric of her memory a little worn now.
Less time at ninety-one for her to weave additional length.
Let me visit the room in St. Catharines
so I can ask my Grandma
if there's anything else she wants to tell me.

Lina never called it suffering
to live without a husband, forced into the German army
then death in a prisoner of war camp six months after his family fled.
She didn't complain
about running with small sons and smaller daughter
ahead of armies toward Atlantic passage and refugee life in Canada.
No fiery martyr's death, none of Maeyken's screams for passage to God
and refusal to recant.
Instead the slow burn of missing Heinrich,
what fifty-six years of marriage might have been, instead of six.
Some gracious alchemy
kept Lina from bitterness as she grew stronger,
metal liquefied and formed again by slow-burning flame
melting any bones that didn't break.
My Grandma remade in an unexpected form.

Soon Maeyken and Lina face to face.
See my hands and side? See where the flames
roasted my feet
buckled my legs
burst my heart
licked at my fingers splayed out for God to grasp?
Understand how God's grip pulled me up.
My scars are supple enough for me to grasp your hands, my ears
can hold all you told none but God since last you saw your husband.
See that the taste of metal is gone from your mouth, see that
your tongue is freed.

Jesus Wasn't No Mennonite

Peter did not know when his Grandfather Martin died. He only knew that Grandfather was gone when he got home from school that Monday, walking the one mile south from the two-room school at Cearfoss, walking in the same dreamy slouch that irritated his twelve-year-old sister, walking into the kitchen not knowing that the fine old man was dead. Another stroke, his mother said. *The third stroke struck: strike one, strike two, strike three. He struck out. Strike, stroke, stricken.* The words skipped in Peter's mind, and he was powerless to make them lie down with respect. *Lie, low, lowing, the cattle are lowing, low in the grave he lay lowing.* He was powerless; it was pitiful.

That was Monday. Today was Wednesday. March winds washed down the bright skies over the farmlands. It was not cold, it was not warm. It came in like a lion and went out like a lamb, so what was it halfway through the month? The pigeons over old Middlekauff's barn wheeled into the bright air and their wings flashed messages.

"Would you hurry up, Pete!"

His sister, Susan, groused at him again. He did not know that he had stopped walking to look at the pigeons spraying up lovely into the clean air over Middlekauff's barnyard full of steer-muck.

"Don't you want to see the body!"

"Grandfather's?"

"Who else! Mama said it'd be there when we get home from school today."

It? It would be there? Did one not say *he?* He would be there. His spirit is asleep in Jesus, Mama had said on Monday. This is only his body, she said. So, Peter thought, fighting down the sudden wild cheer; he did not die by fire, or at the stake, or on the wheel, or at papists' hands—not mirrored a martyr. He only slept. And this is only his body; it is not him, not Grandpa Martin anymore? Just his body, like his gold pocket watch, his fine black hat, his teeth he took out every night to soak in an old shaving mug. He stepped out of himself like he did his high-top shoes, and set the body aside. Could Grandpa see his own body lying there in the casket, like one might look out from the bed and see his trousers and shirt hung on a chair back?

"The viewing's tonight. Uncle Sem and Aunt Elsie's coming for supper."

"Will Benjy come too?"

"Of course. But you can't play." Ahead, Susan stopped and turned to him. "This is a solemn occasion," she said. "Don't you go horsing around upstairs in your room with Benjy, knocking about overhead, over the parlor full of weeping people and Grandfather Martin laying dead there in his casket. You hear?"

For an answer Peter walked by his sister and asserted himself by crashing his lunch box into her knuckles.

"Ouch! that hurt, Peter Martin!"

Then they were running, but he knew she would not chase him far. Ahead, on the road now a vehicle came toward them. She would not want anyone to see her chasing a little brother. But he went on running, his sister's threats coming muffled and high-pitched in anger. The rush of the passing truck swallowed up the words and for a moment Peter was free of her tyranny. He knew without looking up that it was Holsinger's meat truck passing. Loaded with a fresh carcass from the Hagerstown slaughterhouse, the truck whined unhappily, familiarly in his ears. It too carried a dead body. Did the farmer also say of his steer: it is only *its* body? His spirit is at rest with—well, what? Thinking: with Jesus! *But that was steer-crazy or was it stir-crazy? Steer clear of stir-crazy steers.* The silly words slipped about in his mind. He was helpless before words. Grandfather Martin liked big words: *Excommunication, transubstantiation, incarnation, accusation, fornication.* Menno Simons' words: *For no other foundation can no man lay than that is laid, which is Jesus Christ* (1 Cor 3:11).[1] And martyrs' words: *stake* and *fire, the wheel and the sword, the screaming for Jesus.*

Uncle Owen, his father's older brother was drinking coffee at the kitchen table when Peter came through the door. He closed the door against the high March skies and his sister. His mother came forward quietly, smiling down and taking his book satchel and lunch-bucket.

"First you must wash your hands," she said.

One washed to approach a dead body? Even the dead body of a fine old man whom he visited every afternoon fresh and grubby from school, when Grandfather was alive? But now he must wash—?

Old Uncle Owen was saying: "Well, I think that he was kinda—"

"It's only *his* body," Peter said aloud. "Why wash?"

The uncle stopped talking, and Peter was aware that everyone was looking

---

1   KJV.

at him. But he went on washing his hands, making it a small ceremony at the bowl in the corner of the kitchen, not favoring any of them by looking up.

"Hurry up, Pete." Susan now stood waiting to wash.

"They were great friends," his father said to Uncle Owen. "He taught the boy many things. Many things from the Bible—"

"And from the *Bloody Theatre*," Susan said.

"Now, Susan, you be quiet," their father said.

"—always checked on Peter's Bible memory verses for Sunday school."

"Yes," his mother said. "And Peter always knew them."

Peter dried his hands on the rough towel. Turning from the bowl, he risked a glance at his Uncle Owen. A half-eaten piece of lemon meringue pie lay by the yellow coffee cup. A fat red hand, arrested, waited, held the empty fork halfway between plate and mouth. Uncle Owen began to swallow, no doubt getting ready again to give his mind on child-rearing. He went on looking at his nephew for a moment. His little black eyes blinked, shutting so slowly his nephew wondered if the old uncle would doze off before he spoke or finished his pie. The face was fat, round and pink, without a wrinkle, amazing for his seventy years. Wire-rimmed reading glasses reared upon a fat bulb of a nose. Behind the polished lens the eyes shut and opened again, doll-like.

"Yes," his mother sighed. "Peter will miss Grandfather Martin. They made each other such good company."

Uncle Owen turned back to his pie. Some cog turned in the thickly thatched head and lowered the hand holding the fork. Then he spoke:

"I wouldn't have let no child of mine be too much with him. Particularly not these past months. He was—"

Peter watched his uncle's fat little mouth nibbling at words, working his lips like the gold fish in the aquarium; he was surprised that the words didn't come out inside little bubbles like the characters in the Little Orphan Annie funny strip, little fishlike bubbles through his fish lips.

"Oh, and why not?" his mother said.

"Young boys after school should be out at the barn and not be in here . . ."

The boy's father raised his eyebrows above his glasses, wrinkling his forehead into great white creases. He sat quite still, drawing powerfully to himself some current eddying recklessly about the room, then spoke firmly to his older brother. "Peter has chores. Mind you, we look after things."

"Would you like another piece of pie before you go, Owen?" his mother said. "Here, let me heat up your coffee." She moved away to the cook stove.

"No, no. I've quite enough."

"But why do you think it wasn't good for Peter to be with his grandfather so much?" His mother stood with the blue-flecked enamel coffee pot.

"I'm surprised you ask—"

"I didn't," his father said. He had lowered his eyebrows and the wrinkles in the forehead were gone. But his eyes in the framed glasses were wide with a warning.

"I'm surprised, Lydia, that you asked." Ignoring his younger brother, Uncle Owen went on. He drew out his important notions by pausing to drink a mouthful of coffee. *Busy old fool*, Peter thought, borrowing his mother's words. *Fussy old maid*, borrowing his father's. "A child this age is tender and so impressionable and might hear things he's liable to. . . ."

"Never mind that, Owen," his father said. "We did our best by Lydia's father. He wouldn't stay with her other sisters or brothers."

Peter felt himself fill with dread, listening to the old voices going on levelly, coldly about him. He stood quietly behind his mother in a flat strip of sunlight and studied the dark brick patterns and colors of the linoleum. He listened to Susan drying her hands.

"Come, children," their mother said. "You've got a moment alone with Grandfather before supper." She moved to the stove with the coffee pot.

"Well, I must go out and help Theodore milk." His father stood up and walked past Uncle Owen at the table. "You're welcome to stay for supper. Sem and Elsie will be here and some of their younger children."

Uncle Owen rolled up from his chair. "No, thank you. I'll just be off."

"You be here for the viewing." His father spoke from the doorway to the wash house where his barn jackets hung. Peter listened to his father's words and knew they were not a query; they were a command. Something dark came up in his throat.

"I'm just going home to dress up," Uncle Owen said.

His mother led Peter and Susan through the hallway to the parlor. The polished door with its wavy painted grain stood open to warm up the room for the evening's viewing. The room was suffused with an ash-rose light falling through the stained glass borders of the tall windows. The carpet beneath his feet quieted his tread across the room. And it was quiet as death, waiting with its dead. So death is quiet, Peter was thinking, quieter than sleep. He is asleep in Jesus. Yes, his young spirit said. Yes, that was just fine, that an old man dead is only asleep in Jesus. But is a child, even a good but noisy boy, dead, also asleep? He did not think he would like that long sleep, even with Jesus. Might the dead child be at play with Jesus? He should like that—it had to be that, he consoled himself. He saw that the heavy mauve chair was moved and the double doors to the sitting room were open. The coffin was long and black and half of the lid was lifted, lined with puffed white silk which gathered up the ash-rose light. It was a wing lifted to fly the coffined body to heaven; it was a shimmering seraphim hovering over the ark of the coffin. His was no fire at the stake. No stoning. Just sleeping with Jesus. *Jesus loves me this I know . . .*

"It was a blessing the old man could go," his mother was saying.

She had provided for her son a low stool by the coffin. Peter stood on it and looked at his Grandfather Martin. *It is only his body,* he said to himself. There the body lay, solemn and slight and strange—yet familiar. Grandfather looked as if he were napping, the square face a little slack in sleep, the brown splotches on the cheek more gray now, the nostrils very black. Merely a black shadow, not black from fire soot and ashes and a martyr's clubbing of the face.

Peter looked at his Grandfather Martin and did not cry. He had stood by his bed many times while the old man slept in the long afternoons; it was all quite familiar. But strange, too. The face wore the gold wire glasses and the body the black suit with its high pointed collars. He looked dressed and ready for church, if only he held his wide black hat in his hands. *But Jesus didn't wear a black hat. Jesus wasn't no Mennonite.* One did not lie down wearing his glasses and his Sunday suit for a long sleep with Jesus. But something more was wrong. Peter stood looking at the square face. It was something so slight his eye could not find it deliberately. So he looked away quickly to let his eye catch it at a glance. But he could not take in the mistake. He flicked his eyes away again, again glanced back. His mother lay her hand on his shoulder and spoke his name.

"You must go do your chores."

In the bedroom that he shared with his brother Theodore, a dozen years older, Peter changed into his old clothes and shoes. Going out into the evening, he felt the chill in the air, saw the dusty rose of the sun setting on the heart-shaped hills. The evening sky was the color of the morning sky those winter days he carried hot Postum and dry toast to his grandfather. The old man did not eat breakfast with Peter's family, although he rose promptly at six. And promptly at seven his mother let Peter carry on a small round tray the cup of hot Postum and a plate of toast.

"What do you do for an hour?" he had once asked Grandfather Martin.

"It takes me a long time to shave now."

"It smells good—like lilac."

Grandfather Martin ran a finger wet with the lilac cologne on Peter's lip under his nose. He had done it every day for the year he had come to live with Peter's family. And Peter was smelling it now as he stood in the hog pen and ran water into their trough full of mash. The hogs looked soft and blurry in the deep shadows of the pen. Their tan hides were pink, the browns lavender, the spotted and white were rose and pearl. The failing evening light would have suffused them with an uncommon beauty before his eyes, but he could hear their squeals and grunts; their pig-like manners at the trough recalled to Peter that they were only hogs. But Peter did not smell them; the nostrils of his memory filled with the lilac cologne. Thinking: *so, I will always smell it, even while the old man sleeps with Jesus*. Even though he would never again shave and himself never again come into the room carrying the roasted smell of Postum. So that too was eternity—the lingering odor of lilac. Though the fine old man went away forever, yet, forever a grandson would remember the odor of a lilac shaving lotion.

"And then I brush my hair fifty strokes so—"

A sudden white wing of knowledge brushed Peter's mind. He stood dead still by the hog trough, waiting until his mind traveled back to the coffin, to his dead grandfather's face. So it was the white wing of hair—and then he knew what was wrong about the old face.

Peter went about his evening chores with a mind boiling with a child's rich confusion and plottings while his hands handled their familiar chores. In the chicken house, lifting the white eggs of the Leghorns, he remember the white peppermints and pink chalky lozenges his grandfather kept in a small brown paper bag in the top drawer of his bureau. The name of the pink lozenges had confused him, Peter remembered. His grandfather had called them wintergreens.

"But they're pink," he had protested.

"Yes. So?"

"They're not green."

"No, they're not green. So?"

"Why call something pink wintergreen?"

"Oh, yes, I see!" the grandfather laughed. "It is the name of a flavor—wintergreen."

The explanation had not satisfied Peter, so that on another day when he said to the old man, "Could I have a winterpink?" it was the grandfather who now was confused.

"Winterpink? What's that?"

"I've given a new name to the wintergreens. I call them winterpinks!"

The grandfather laughed and said something foolish about his grandson being a young Adam, naming the candies as they passed before him. And then there were the Sen-Sens—tiny, bitter, black licorice seeds, tiny as mice turds, but his mother would not allow the word: she called their droppings "mice seeds" when she found them in the pantry. Once he was tricked by the old man when he begged for just one piece of candy.

"Just one piece, Peter?"

"Yes."

"You'll be content with just one, Peter?"

"Yes."

Grandfather Martin had reached a finger and a thumb into his vest pocket and then held them out pinched together to Peter's hand. The boy held up his palm and waited for the sharp peppermint or chalky winterpink. Instead, into his hand fell a little black thing so small he thought it a dirty seed, brought mistakenly from his grandfather's pocket.

"A Sen-Sen," the old man said, smiling, a bit of spittle on his lips. "They're good." His grandfather's eyes twinkled behind their polished glass. "You said— just one, Peter." He reached into another pocket and pulled out a tiny yellow metal box with blue printing on it. His thick old fingers slid the lid to a tiny hole through which he tapped out another tiny black seed.

Peter held the tiny seed for a moment and thought of mice turds and tasted betrayal, his mouth already filling with its own saliva for a winterpink.

"It's licorice—licorice Sen-Sens," the grandfather said.

"It looks like a mouse turd," Peter said.

"Yes! Yes!" the old man laughed and shook a second and a third seed into his grandson's hand. That wing of white hair lifted gently with the grandfather's shoulders shaking with laughter.

Peter put them on his tongue, and they were bitter, and later, it was always a good joke between them—the bitter joke of Sen-Sens.

In the pen beyond the cow stable where his brother and father milked the Holsteins, Peter spread out the sweet alfalfa for the calves; he patted their noses quickly before they shook their heads and blew snot on his hands. The alfalfa had lost its green color when freshly cut, but its perfume still lay on the little dry leaves. It was as sweet a grass as the lush stuff by the mouth of the wet-weather spring in the old orchard.

Suddenly, Peter stood very still in the dim light. He often did that, listening for mice. But now he was watching himself at the coffin, seeing what else he must do, quickly, before the uncles and aunts and the good folk from church came to see his dead grandfather. He went out of the barn, carrying himself carefully, less he spill away the sudden joy visiting him.

In his unheated bedroom again, Peter leafed through his packet of old drawings, then he found a clean sheet of paper. Still in his barn jacket, smelling of lime and silage, he stood by the nightstand to draw his grandfather a last picture. It was the last scene, Peter imagined, that his grandfather looked out on before he died. The tall south bedroom window with its border of tiny squares of colored glass framed his picture. His colored pencils made some panes pink, some green, some lavender and blue. In the wide, clear window, Peter drew the old apple orchard, the trees black and bare in winter; on one side rose the tall stalks and prickly leaves of the yucca, its waxy white flowers dried now. The split-rail fence lay across the middle like a horizontal window-sash. Drifts of snow softened the branches, the rails, the stalks. Colored pencils lay blue and lavender shadows in the snow drifts. Finally, with brown pencils he drew himself sitting in the deep window and looking out. Then he was finished. Yet, he lingered, thinking maybe his grandfather would also like a drawing of a martyr in the mirror, pictures in that thick book from which he read to his grandson so often. But Peter shook off the notion. He was indeed finished.

He turned on the light by Theodore's side of the bed and looked more closely at his drawing. And he saw that it was good. There was no time left; he must hurry. Peter picked up his brother's comb, and with the drawing in hand, he went quietly down the carpeted hall stairs and into the parlor. The room was gray now, the ash-rose light gone. His grandfather's form was very dark on the white silk. Peter climbed on the stool. With Theodore's comb, he lifted the thin white wing of his grandfather's hair and lay it across to the other side of the balding scalp. Peter looked at the face. Now everything was ready. He slid his drawing far down to the foot of the coffin, under the half of lid that was closed. If Jesus did not find it first, Grandfather would, on the resurrection; he did not quite know how these things worked. This death. This being only asleep with Jesus. The resurrection. *This foul flesh putting on the incorruptible.* But Peter was full of a dreadful grace: when the old man awoke in heaven he would find his grandson's drawing of the family orchard, the last earthly thing he had seen. And seeing it, he would remember the land, the good earth, the grandson, and he might, with some clean pride, show the drawing to Jesus and say: "This is Peter's. He is a good boy."

"Peter! Peter!"

His sister's voice came to him, distantly, through closed doors. She was calling up the kitchen stairs to the boys' bedroom. Peter went out of the parlor to his supper. Uncles and aunts and his favorite cousin, Benjy, had arrived.

He did not horse around with Benjy in the room above the parlor full of relatives. He stood between his father and mother by the grandfather's coffin and listened to the words for the fine old man mumbled above his head: "The Lord is good . . . You did what was right by your Papa . . . It must have been hard to care for him . . . It is a blessing . . . A full life. . . ." Peter looked out from his parents at Benjy suffering alone on a couch. The cousin had wanted to play quietly in the room upstairs, but Peter wanted to hear these words about the grandfather. "He didn't suffer . . . The Lord will reward you . . . He looks quite resigned . . . It was a blessing. . . ." The old voices went on and on over his head, as the relatives and many from the church came and went "to pay our respects," they said.

The women kissed his mother; they all wore their best black bonnets tied on with shiny black ribbons; and they did not take them off as they stood about. Some of them made quick dabs at their moist eyes; others blew their noses respectfully. The men greeted his father with the holy kiss of peace. They did not weep as they looked in the coffin and turned away, their black hats in their thick fingers. It was not altogether a sad thing for an old man to be struck down a third time, speechless with a stroke, Peter consoled himself, standing under his parents' elbows and looking up at these dark-clad church folk.

Then all the distant relatives and people from the church went away, and it was only Uncle Sem and Aunt Elsie, Aunt Veronica and Aunt Fannie, two old unmarried sisters who lived together in a yellow house in Maugansville, and Uncle Henry and Aunt Mary. And, of course, old Uncle Owen, the family's fat bachelor.

Now the women took off their bonnets and coats and all of them ate strange pies and cakes from the stock of food which had arrived as gifts of consolation during the past two days.

Benjy wanted to go up to the room and play with the barn and wooden cows and rubber horses, but Peter still wanted to hear words. All evening he caught snatches of words about a man he did not know, about his own grandfather. So that too was his Grandfather Martin, he was thinking. Everyone who looked on the old man saw a different man. *So, one would need a thousand eyes—well maybe five hundred—to see him*, Peter said to himself, *but they could not know him as a grandson did.*

"Ever since Mama's death," Aunt Veronica was saying, "a year ago this very month—"

". . . and he'd been acting mopey." Her sister, his Aunty Fannie, finished most sentences begun by the elder maiden aunt.

"Do you think he knew . . . that his time was . . ."

"Some do have a premonition, it seems. That's what I hold," Uncle Henry said.

"It does not matter; one must be ready at any moment to meet his Maker." That was from his Uncle Sem who looked about at his siblings as though someone might challenge this bit of settled orthodoxy.

"Old Middlekauff's wife found him wandering. . . ."

Aunt Mary cleared her full throat and said pointedly to her husband: "Little pitchers have big ears."

"Why don't you take Benjy upstairs and show him your drawings, Peter?" His mother spoke to him from across the table. Peter was running his finger around and around a little blue square in the patterned oil cloth. He was wondering why one said *around and around* if he followed a square; could one also say he went *asquare and asquare*?

"Did you look to see what he was reading in his Bible when he died?" Uncle Sem asked.

"Yes," his father said. "The Song of Solomon."

"That won't do," Uncle Owen flared out. "Nothing there for a funeral service."

"Ask Peter where Grandfather was reading in *The Bloody Theatre*," his sister said.

Peter knew that he was being observed, but he went on tracing the edge of the blue figure in the oil cloth. He would not betray the old man. The last story in the *Martyrs Mirror* was a familiar one he had asked for many times. He had traced out the picture of Leonhard Keyser who, bound in a cart on the way to his execution by fire, reached down and plucked a flower. He liked the word *pluck*; until then he thought of the word only with barnyard fowl, plucking their feathers after scalding them in the big metal bucket by the chopping block at the woodshed. *He plucked the flower*, old Leonhard Keyser plucked the flower and offered it with a challenge to his tormentor: "If you can burn me and this flower. . . ." He plucked dandelions and held them, muttering Leonhard Keyser's dare, but the dandelion seemed too common. He looked at all the flowers in his mother's flower beds; considered the geranium, the snapdragons, sweet williams, coral belles, bleeding hearts, delphiniums, foxgloves—rejected them all—the canna, the rose, the portulaca, the columbine. All were unworthy to taunt his tormentor. He saw himself going bound in his red Radio Flyer wagon without a flower for taunting until he heard from his grandfather's own lips: "consider the lilies of the field. Are they not. . . ?" Yes, they were. But then he was tormented; going for the cows all summer he looked for lilies-of-the-field along the lane, in the meadow, in the cut hayfields. Peter could find nothing that looked like the drawing of lilies in the *Westminster Bible Dictionary*, so he—

"What do you mean, Susan, *The Bloody Theatre*?"

"Oh, she means the *Martyrs Mirror*." His mother spoke with a contented little sigh. "He did like that book."

"Who?"

"Why both," she said. "They both liked those stories. They were such good company for each other."

"As I said before and say so again—" It was Uncle Owen's pig-whistling voice going on. The noisy old fool. "That's not a book for a child—beheadings and burnings at the stake and—"

"And the pictures, Chris, think of the pictures!" Aunt Fannie said. Peter heard her false teeth click and her mouth snap shut quickly. He smiled a little.

"It never hurt none of us," his father said. "We all read in the *Martyrs Mirror* on those long Sunday afternoons."

"Oh, those Sunday afternoons in winter, sitting with nothing but that book or *The Complete Writings of Menno Simons*!"

"You had the Bible story book." Uncle Owen cut off Aunt Veronica's whimpering flight.

"I'd like to have seen your face, Chris." Uncle Henry was teasing Peter's father, forgetting already the solemnity of their gathering. "When you found him in the outhouse, wearing his—"

"For shame, Hen, have a little respect for your dead Papa!"

"For your honorable Papa!"

"I meant no disrespect." Uncle Henry sat up and blustered at his older sisters. "I like Papa—he did many funny things."

"Yes, you were his pet!"

"Now, Veronica." Aunt Fanny leaned over to her sister. Peter shot them a glance. They could have been twins, draped in aprons and capes of the same dull black stuff. He saw that his father was smiling a little as he looked on his maiden sisters sitting heavily in their kitchen chairs.

"His mind was a little affected then," his father explained, "after that second stroke."

"Queer, plain queer he was, if you ask me," Uncle Owen said. "That's why I said you wouldn't want no child to be around him much. He might say something—something to give a child wrong ideas."

"They made each other good company, they did," his mother said again.

"Couldn't find him anywhere, could you, Chris?" Uncle Henry nudged his father to tell the story again. "You looked high and low—what made you think of the old outhouse?"

"Little pitchers have big ears," Aunt Mary declared again.

"So he was sitting there on the toilet hole in his good suit and wearing his Sunday black hat . . ." Uncle Henry went on, ignoring his wife.

"Hen, you've heard all this," Uncle Sem said.

"How did he say it then, Chris—?"

"Jesus ain't never wore no black hat." His brother Theodore blurted it out, his voice fighting the edge of a full laugh.

"Shame, Theodore! For shame!" The maiden aunts cried together and twisted in their chairs; their fat little hands fluttered about their capes like small birds looking for places to perch.

Uncle Henry lay back in his chair and chuckled quietly to himself, satisfied.

Uncle Owen grumbled: "You see what I mean? You see, Chris? Even the child knows." The old uncle looked at Peter his nephew and blinked his eyes, doll-like, but Peter slid his eyes away from the tiresome old tub of guts. He looked at his brother. Theodore winked at him.

Peter lay a long time in the double bed he shared with Theodore, and he could not sleep. He was angry with Uncle Owen for calling him a child. He went to school now, didn't he? He could read and write, couldn't he? In his dark bedroom, he imagined he saw again the square face of his dead grandfather. The thin gray lips moved and Peter understood that they were trying to say something. He felt his chest stop breathing, his heart widen and go out to the image as he listened, straining to hear what the fine old man was saying.

With a smile and a little spittle, the lips moved; the murmuring voice was telling a story from the *Martyrs Mirror*, the story of Anneken van den Hove, imprisoned for two years and seven months and suffered much temptation from the priests, the monks, and the Jesuits who sought to make her apostatize from the Anabaptist faith. "Nay," she cried out, "through the grace of God I have apostatized from your Babylonian mother, the Roman church, to the true church of Christ!" And the Friar cursed and cried: "Do you call our holy Roman church the whore of Babylon? And do you call your hellish, devilish sect of Anabaptists the true church of Christ? Who the devil taught you this, your accursed Menno Simons, I suppose?" And the young maiden cried: "Nay, it is not necessary that Menno Simons should have taught us as something new that the Babylonian whore signifies the Roman church. The Apostle John teaches us enough in his book of Revelations."[2] So she remained steadfast in her faith in the Lord Jesus Christ, her Bridegroom. Then her tormentors told Anneken to prepare herself to die.

As Peter listened to the gray lips moist with spittle and the square jaws go on, he felt something was wrong with the story, yet he lay quietly by Theodore asleep, and in his mind he went on listening.

"And the next morning about eight o'clock, Peter, they took the young maiden named Anneken half a mile outside the city of Brussels where the justice of the court and the Jesuits had dug a pit. But going by a pond covered with thin ice, Anneken broke lose and fled over the ice. One of the Anabaptist-catchers with the monks hotly pursued her. She got across the pond with considerable peril. The Anabaptist-catcher following her broke through the ice. When Anneken perceived that the Anabaptist-catcher was in danger of losing his life, she quickly turned back and aided him in getting out and thus saved his life. The Anabaptist-catcher wanted to let her go, but the Jesuits sternly called to him to remember his oath and the pay. So they went on to the dug pit, having captured the young girl."

Peter knew then that his grandfather, confused, had jumbled several stories together with the telling of Dirk Willems' saving his captor's life. "And then fearlessly, the young girl undressed herself and lay down naked in the grave to shame the priests, that looking on her virginal white body they would turn away with shame. But did they, Peter? They did not! Instead, they quickly threw big clods of earth upon her body, up to her throat, all the time promising to stop and take her out of the pit if she would recant her Anabaptism. Did she recant, Peter? She would not hearken to them; it was all in vain, Peter! So they cursed her and threw sod upon her face and filled her mouth with dirt to stop her praising her Bridegroom Jesus. And when they had thrown more soil upon her body, they stamped with their feet upon it to kill her. Oh, Peter, Peter, my

---

2   Ed: This interchange comes from the disputation between Jacob de Keersgieter and Friar Cornelis in 1569, as related on pages 774-75 of the *Martyrs Mirror*.

dear grandson Peter," the old man's voice went on, now gently, gently, "you must come to the faith and adhere to it like this young girl, the Christian faith of your Anabaptist Mennonite forefathers. It is the most faithful to the teachings of Christ of all sects of the Reformation. Yet . . ."

Then the old man was laughing softly to himself in his grandson's dark bedroom. And at the sound of that laughter, Peter was falling back through the last months before his grandfather's second stroke when they had sat in the gray light of a winter Sunday afternoon and he had heard his grandfather tell stories from Menno Simon's life and the *Martyrs Mirror* and of his own great-great-great-grandfather who lived at a place in Pennsylvania called Hammer Creek and had a mill and the red-coat soldiers stole his horses and carried off large quantities of grain and flour. And on a second raid they took his great-great-great-grandmother's pewter dishes and spoons, and she threw her apron over her head so as not to see them take an oven full of freshly baked bread and pies. So Peter heard stories of Mennonites and Anabaptists and Jesuits all that long afternoon, listening to the fine voice going on, thinking about his own Hammer Creek people in the *Martyrs Mirror* and wondering why there were no drawings of red-coats and stolen bread in the big book, imaging one day he himself would draw them for the book. Until laughing softly to himself, the old man came back, Peter could see by the eyes, from a far, far place, possibly from Hammer Creek, possibly from the Netherlands, to the room, to their two chairs drawn up to the window of weak winter light.

"But Jesus wasn't no Mennonite, Peter." The old voice was laughing softly. "No, Jesus never wore no black hat . . . . I often wonder what Jesus would've looked like in my black hat."

It was no shock to Peter to hear those words then. He knew for a truth, from the pictures in his Bible story book that Jesus wore only long purple and white robes and went about without a black hat healing lepers and raising the dead. He did not know why it should have shocked his two old aunties to hear Theodore quote their old father. So Peter smiled in the darkness, and sleep came up over him with the stillness of his dead grandfather. Peter settled against the dead-in-sleep body of his brother Theodore. Now smiling in his own sleep, Peter wondered how he should paint a Martyr in the Mirror? But that was the future, and it could wait.

DAVID WALTNER-TOEWS

Tante Tina and Little Haenschen: How Rudy Wiebe Saved the Communists

Listen Little Haenschen, one time in the Molotschna when
the Revolution was—
the picture on the table there, by the window
on the doily, see? My mother is there,
but she already dead was.
There Red soldiers were and White soldiers
and the Machnovites who were a black flag waving
and the Mennonites in the *Selbstschutz*,
who just hello waved with Wilma Thiessen's laundry,
they not fighting were,
only self defending by shooting and
very fast running and then being shot.
Always Mutti has soup gemade
for everyone, no matter what colour.

Rudy Wiebe was one time the kitchen rug out-shaking
for my mother; he visiting was
and something for his soup he needed to do.
Mutti wasn't soup for nothing giving.
But the Reds they are seeing him waving and thinking
he is with the *Selbstchutz*, so Tolstoy
himself is coming and after Rudy running.

                                    Tolstoy? You mean Trotsky?

Ja, the Kommunist, that one, through the barn
and over the river chasing. He is wanting
Rudy Kommunist to be making or to shoot.

But it is April and in the Dnieper River has a hole cracked
in it like the old toilet seat behind the house,
slippery and cold just like that,
so Trotsky is through falling.
Plumps just like that. Nick has once almost been
in slipping like that even.

In the river?

In the outhouse.
Then Rudy the cries hears Help! Help me comrade!
and is turning and him helping
from the hole.

This is just like in the Mennonite Martyrs book
Felix Manz or someone.

We have soup from Felix the cat made
after the Revolution. But that is a different story.
And after they are to Mutti's
for soup coming.

I think in the Martyrs book
the fleeing Mennonite is hauled up before the Catholics,
or was it Lutherans? And drowned,
hung into the icy water by his feet.
Or maybe burned
in a street full of shoppers.
That sounds like a German thing,
doesn't it? How *did* they kill,
usually? His mouth gagged? How will
you sing now? they laughed.

But he hollered through the rags.

Some early version of *Ich weiss einen Strom.*[1]

This, after dragging the pursuer to a warm inn.

That's the *Englische*[2] for you. Not even singing

moves them.[3]

Listen, *bursch.* I am about Russia talking.

Are you not history knowing?

Then Trotsky is to Mexico

going, because there are so many Mennonites

and he is the soup so much liking and at home

to be feeling. He has there I think a Petkau girl married.

Trotsky?

Tolstoy. Listen *mal*, there is more.

More important.

So many soldiers to feed

my mother is in the evening down lying

and in the morning she is not up-getting.

My Uncle Fritz is looking.

The Lord has come for Mutti, he is saying

but I have already

for the picture taker paid,

because Nick and I will be to Canada going

and everyone else is behind staying

so we a picture are needing. But Mutti with the Lord is.

Was ist zu tun?[4]

We are the navy dress on her pulling

and the Sunday hat with the flowers

---

1   *Ich weiss einen Strom* —literally, "I know a stream," but in English titled "Oh have you
     not heard," or "The Beautiful Stream," is a hymn that was composed in the nineteenth
     century and has since become (in German) something of a Mennonite standard.
2   *Englische* is used here as a generic term for all non-Mennonites.
3   The story is actually attached to Dutch Anabaptist Dirk Willems, who saved his pur-
     suers from an icy grave. The man he saved immediately arrested him; he was burned
     at the stake on May 6, 1569.
4   What's to be done?

on her planting,
and Nick and me are her upholding
so now we the picture have,
all my life to remember.

                                        Your mother is dead
                                            in this picture?

A good picture, *Ja?*

                                        She doesn't look dead.

So ist das Leben.[5]
I am wondering now
what has to Rudy Wiebe happened?

---

5   That's life.

JEAN JANZEN

Triptych: After Ghent

1564, and they are pulling Mayke[1]
from the castle's dungeon, up
the winding stone steps, dragging
her chains. The wheels groan
toward the stake where she will
be burned, toward the watching crowd
where her small son stands.
She reaches out and places
a pear in his hand.

•

Just across the river in Van Eyck's
triptych, Eve is looking at Adam.
Her arm will reach across the middle panel,
will brush against the lamb
who shivers on the throne.
The centuries are kneeling, watching.
The apple is fresh and glazed with oil.

•

Now I stand in the archives
holding Mayke's pear,
a brown oval, light as ash.
I hold the strength

---

1   Maeyken Boosers.

of her last glance—
her son's pale face,
the stopped river.
And I hold the tree,
its blossoms flaring
around her feet.

Jean Janzen

After the Martyrs Exhibit

The way the sparrows sing
in the bushes, you would think
that no one could torture another,
especially this hour before dinner
as evening spreads its silk cloth.
We had seen the copper plates
under display lights, each line
etched to evoke remembrance
acid for my conscience.
Rolled ink, the press on paper,
and there she stands,
her skirt flaming, mouth singing.

We dip hummus and swallow,
talk easily as evening folds.
Sliced bamboo driven under fingernails.
The jeering. The betrayal of dawn.
I never said I could do it.

remember our generations
remember when we burned
& where we buried
remember the windmills caught
the sun each morning held
back the flood once more
remember the sky blue burning
over the steppes white
unto winter remember
the woman's soft cry the child's
coming pink & new
the man black with harvest
his pale forehead hatless
in the evening the kerosene
lamp lighting home remember
the new carrots the new beets
the sunflowers the summer
pale with heat remember waking
remember the bride walking
before the congregation
her love an ache in the blood
remember that remember
the guile the sex in the feather
bed warm the snow outside blowing
cold remember the old woman's
hands the spots the tender skin
the needing wanting remember
the one face only that you

long for the grains of corn
dropped in the earth the children
remember the child's crying
by the green tree the kiss
that makes all things well
the clanging cowbells the low
german tongue the love that forgives
remember

ENEMIES

Views from a Pond:
Dirk—Cat and Mouse
Ian Huebert

Salt

Leonard Bernkop refused to recant, refused absolutely
to indulge the flesh. He was fried in Salzburg

on a slow fire. *Turn me around* he said.
My side nearest the fire is roasted: the other

remains undone.
He was quoting St. Lawrence, an early saint

barbarians grilled in Rome on a gridiron.
A saint Bernkop's executioners revered,

whose death they regretted.
Whose murderers they'd gladly burn alive.

Leonard Bernkop
Salzburg, 1542

JOANNE EPP

The Baker's Dog[1]

The dog knew it first: strangers at the door.
But Augustijn was working, sleeves and trousers rolled.
Augustijn was up to his elbows in dough,
adding flour, folding the sticky mass
over itself, pressing the heels of his hands
down and down. He put his shoulders into it,
Augustijn did. Leaned his weight on the dough,
hummed to the heavy rhythm: fold, push down,
turn.

He reached for more flour; the dog barked:
footsteps at the door. Augustijn saw,
turned, ran, but no use—
the bailiff seized him, put him in jail

and as he was a man who was much beloved,
it greatly grieved the bailiff's wife, who said
to her husband, "O you murderer,
what have you done!"

      but all in vain
the bread dough rose
till it overflowed the trough.
The bailiff's man kicked the dog.

---

1   Lines in italics are from the *Martyrs Mirror* story of Augustijn the baker, burned to
    death around 1556.

Recanting

Felistis for her execution tied
a snow-white apron around her waist.
She was always a good woman:

served the jailer's wife any way she could
up until the burning, cleaning pots, setting the table,
keeping the fire alive in the kitchen. Humble enough
she volunteered to take the stinking garbage out.
But won't you run away? the jailer's wife
asked. Felisitis searched
the unexamined corners of her heart.
Convicted
she admitted: knowledge
of the body's frailty, fear, unbridled desire
to keep on breathing. To behold the sun.

Compelled to withdraw the offer Felistis remained
faultless to the end.

Felistis Jans, surnamed Resinx
Amsterdam, 1553

Menno Simons Sighs and Leans Back in His Seat

smiling,
as the lights
come on in the
Groningen
Cinema after a
double feature.
"That was great,"
Menno said to
himself, swallowing
the final kernels
of popcorn,
"my favourite
movies, a
comedy and a
western."
Bounty hunters
seeking
Anabaptists
rarely bugged
unforgiving
movie fans,
so Menno
frequently
sought a few
hours of peace

and safety
at the cinema.
And what more
does any
Anabaptist need,
Menno thinks,
besides a
good laugh
and a
fast horse.

David Augsburger

Excerpts from "Menno Simons' Birthday Tales"[1]

Menno Memory #2

"It's the sheriff," cried Anton from the barn door. "Sing, everyone, sing."

The congregation, suddenly on its feet to block the view of the minister, broke into song with the most familiar psalm, *"Aus tiefer Not screi ich zu dir"* ("Out of the depth to thee I cry"). Only those near the front—the women sat in the center while the men stood shoulder-to-shoulder as protection around the outside—could see the drama which would become synonymous with the name of their minister. In his haste to leap from the impromptu platform—an upended hogshead of molasses—he had kicked in the end and sank to his knees in the sticky stuff. He was caught by the good sweet glue of Dutch blackstrap as, in a moment, his feet would be fettered by the chains of the law.

Except for the courage and wit of Dutch women, Menno would have been led away laying a gooey trail. Two seized his arms and lifted him free, then looked in dismay at his boots and leggings. Quickly one sister stripped the molasses from his trousers as her hands circled his ankles, and a second took a great mouthful from his shoes. In a trice, he was licked clean as a kitten and disappeared through the stable amid the Friesian milk cows.

"What sort of ritual is this?" the sheriff demanded as he burst through the packed crowd of singers to see the sticky-faced women and open barrels.

"When we have no bread or wine, we simply have to make do," said one.

"This, too, is a feast of love," said a second.

"May all your children be cursed with a sweet tooth," the sheriff said.

"May it be so," they all replied.

And it is so.

---

1   1996 was the 500th anniversary year of Menno Simons' birth. Ausburger introduced his eight Menno Memories: "Folktales, historical vignettes, and biographical fragments about the venerated priest-turned-Anabaptist elder have grown, been told, and then re-told for years. Here is some of what has been adrift, and some more recent additions."

Menno Memory #3

The coach was full, I tell you. There was only room for one more so I put Gertrude inside and I climbed up with the driver.

The driver? I knew him well. I had baptized his first child, little Joost, when I was the village priest in Pingjum, and I had baptized him at Leeuwarden in the dike behind Classen's mill a decade later. So we talked through the night about many things.

At the border, instead of the usual wave from Sergeant Terpstra, there was a lowered pike and six archduke's servants at law.

"Is Menno the Heretic in this coach?" they asked.

Ulrich looked at me, shrugged his shoulders, and said "Footman, find out who the passengers are." I climbed down slowly, and opened the carriage.

"Is Menno the Heretic in here?" I asked. "The archduke's men are searching for him. Is he here?"

"No," shouted the passengers, one by one. The torch light of the captain of the guards flickered across their faces.

"They say he's not here," I said, closing the door.

Back in my seat beside Ulrich, I nudged him with my elbow. "I think we can go," I whispered.

He nodded to the guard, and we creaked away in the muddy tracks, the squeak of the stretching leather traces like music in our ears.

Menno Memory #8[2]

"Out of all the memories of a lifetime, it's strange how an odd moment sticks with you," says Gertrude to her friends as they grieve together.

"We were lying on our backs between the rows of cabbages, and Menno and I kept silent until the last of the sheriff's men had gone. Then, chuckling, we sat up and surveyed the field. When the warning cry had gone up from the men watching the barn door, we had to run for our lives through the stables. The barn was packed with worshipers, so we had more than enough time to steal beyond the house and hide ourselves in the kitchen garden before the police could push through the crowd.

"'When it is time for me to die,' Menno said, 'you must bury me here, in a cabbage patch.' I thought of it while hiding here, looking at the stars overhead

---

2 Ed: Augsburger notes in retrospect that Gertrude Simons actually died before her husband, so a bit of poetic license is taken here. Menno Simons was indeed buried in his garden.

and hearing the police searching the barn and the haystacks. Lying among the cabbage heads is the place for long thoughts.

"'Where else could you be buried?' I asked him. 'No church yard will be open to a heretic.' We smiled at each other. Being fugitives together can be good for a marriage.

"'I've work to do, but I'll be back to the cabbage patch some day,' said Menno.

"Now there he is, lying between the rows again. No police can find him there, steal his body, and burn it in town. He is hidden for one last time. And none of our people will eat our beloved cabbage soup without giving thanks for Menno, too."

Close Call

Uniformed and well-armed bullies surrounded the car. Here, where his well-known piety and reliance on higher powers should have sustained him, M the cripple was secretly ashamed that he could only maintain his calm by an act of vanity, the desire not to act in any way other than what would be expected of the notorious M. His pale companions seemed relieved as he stepped out of the car to face the brute police. No doubt they anticipated a miracle, or at least heroic defiance and death. But M was terrified and feared his bowels would loosen. He was too frightened to speak, which gave him the appearance of dignified silence. The chief officer, looking stupid and mean, approached him where he stood by the door of the car. "Is M the cripple in that car?" M had to fight both tears and a giggle. "No, on my honor, no he's not." The officer looked suspiciously within and repeated his question. M leaned on his good leg, trying to appear casual. Satisfied by the answers of the trembling riders, the officer left. M the cripple sighed. He could feel his piety returning.

Eric Rensberger

M the Murderer

That man locked in an argument with his wife, the young girl screaming at her parents, the youth looking enviously at his friend's lover—how could they not understand they were murderers? M the cripple knew how many people he had killed, mentally, and he felt the murders hanging from his curved shoulders like ragged clothing. His famous refusal of violence was the natural result of his understanding of his murderousness. He held conversation with other killers every day, and none of them seemed to comprehend that he was in on the secret. A nation, a world of butchers, he thought to himself, and I, by giving away my apron, my sledgehammer, and my long sharp knife, have become the least-known one, the most secretive. . . .

JULIA SPICHER KASDORF AND RUDY WIEBE, TRANSLATORS

The 78ᵗʰ Song
from the *Ausbund*[1]

In the tune of the Tholer Song

1.
Beloved knights of Christ!
Behold our Captain here.
When you are called to war
expect a bitter fight;
enemies will surround you:
World, Flesh, Sin, Satan, Death.
Leap to your Captain's side;
he will destroy them all
and save you from your pain.

---

1   *Ausbund* Song #78 was written by Christof Baumann, who also wrote #76, 77,
    and 80. Nothing is known about his life, except that he was long imprisoned in
    Landshut, Bavaria, and likely died a martyr there; he may well have helped compile
    the first part of the *Ausbund* that is, before 1565. He is one of the most gifted poets
    of the collection, and the first syllables of the eight stanzas of #78 reveal a personal
    acrostic:

    Christ/P[B]au/Man/Gefangen/Zu/Gottes/Preis/Amen:
    Christ[of] Baumann imprisoned for God's praise, Amen.

    The image of the Christian as knight/heroic warrior is occasionally used in *Ausbund*
    songs, but in this one is extended throughout; it is doubtless based on Paul's imagery in
    2 Timothy 2:3 and Ephesians 6:11-17. The tune is a "Wach Auf"—"Wake Up" melody
    like those sung by night watchmen at daybreak. For sixteenth-century people, largely
    illiterate, these memorable songs of the Christian life may well have been as significant
    as any biblical text.

2.

In the colors of our band,
Paul has wrapped a shield,
helmet, armor, gorget—
a sword is also there—
always be armed with these
for the inevitable event
when the enemy of a thousand deceits
will deploy envy and malice
to attack the gentle Christians.

3.

Stand by the little banner
that is proclaimed to us.
Do not let yourself be driven
from the Captain Jesus Christ.
If you would inherit with him
the glorious crown and joy,
earn triumph and victory,
you must also die with him,
endure affliction and grief.

4.

Christ the Captain
was imprisoned and beaten,
tormented like everyone
who follows in his way.
Great pain is now upon us
everywhere on this earth,
and those who long for Christ
are hunted with shackles and chains
through almost every land.

5.

For them, we won't forsake
the true knight's honor.
We'll cut off the enemy's streets
until we take them all.
Strangulation and stabbing
will come, brutal tyranny.
Our Captain will avenge us,
shatter his enemy's might;
he stands by his little flock.

6.

Beloved knights of God,
be manly in the fight.
The furious storm
will last but a little time.
Only remain firm
and faithful unto death;
do not let yourself be driven back—
whether you are men or women—
have confidence in God.

7.

We give him praise and honor,
his alone is the glory.
While we have life,
help us, O God my Lord!
Respond to our lament,
look upon your children:
we are imprisoned and tortured,
banished from every land—
My God! Attend to us!

8.
Amen, it will come to pass
that in the blink of an eye
we will see God's power
demonstrated soon, when he
reveals the world's malice,
including its arrogance,
which now rages so violently—
My God! Protect us,
keep us in your care.

Amen.

Translated from the Ausbund *1720/1750.*

the martyr's escape

how can we forgive, when the
fable has no moral, this tale
from a slave in silken
chains? today you might be
a babe among beasts, a novice
befriended by thieves, little lamb,
who made thee? you slip
past the guards, child
in sheep's clothing, no passport required
of the meek and mild, and a rickety
ramp into the slaughterhouse. or

you might lower your horns, charge
through the gates, gore
the sentries clenching
butcher knifes. you snort
blood, bull in an army's
china shop. we
face each other on the slippery floor
of the abattoir.
neither of us understands.
or could you be

common as a housefly,
buzz over dungheaps, make
for the crack in the window,
wait for the breeze? unfold

transparent wings, and
fly? past a soldier's clumsy slap,
past beasts queued
for slaughter. into
multifaceted light, ride the wind, beyond
webs glittering with lust.

AMY CALKINS

Dirk Willems, Asperen, 1569

—copper plate etching, Jan Luyken

Death row rations made you thin enough to
bounce off ice, guided like Rahab's spies by
a rag rope out the palace window, dropping
tenderly to run across moat water.

The guard threw down his lunch in pursuit, gaining
across the skeletal flatness of a
Dutch landscape, his thighs anxious to interrupt
your unheralded heretic rapture.

You skated across the patchy pond-glass of
the Hondegat, the slowly defrosting
only road to liberty, wind threatening
your tentative grip—unchained soul on ice.

The pursuer's lunch jostled too heavy,
snapping the surface, rippling and crunching
ice arcs around his submerging bulk—his "help!"
ricochets now like death on the still air.

Turning back onto the wounded ice, you skirt
the hole, suck a last free breath, and retrieve
your captor, dragging him to shore like a hooked
fish, knowing he's swallowed your hand whole.

MAURICE MIERAU

Revenge Stories

Oh merciful Father, Thou knowest that we do not desire revenge.
—Romans 12:19

1 The Bridge

Since he refused to die in his lord's private army
his lord's priests took him
to the bridge outside town.

(This was where he had the first
vision, when the devil stepped out
of his spaceship and gave him the weapon.)

They tied his hands and dumped
him in the river. He said
"no one shall pass over this bridge again!"

(In the second vision he learned
how to touch the exploding switch
in his mind that activated the bomb.)

That evening a violent
flood washed away
The bridge.

(Then others had the vision, a bridge
to another world.)[1]

---

1   Martin the Painter, d. 1531.

2 Nose for a Head

when the executioner struck off the man's head something flew
off his face so he put up his hands

(no one saw what it was or why he put his hands up but some
said they saw a black hen he tried whisking away and

others said it was a demon with shears
dancing and glinting in the sun) but everybody soon saw

the executioner's nose drop off which was
definitely God.[2]

3 Gospel Song

> *Tempted and tried, we're oft made to wonder*
> *why it should be thus all the day long,*
> *while there are others*
> *living about us, never molested though in the wrong.*
> — "Farther Along"

In AD 1529 George Bauman was arrested
in Banschlet, for his faith and his eagerness to die.

After application of the rack, assorted torture and a lie
Bauman recanted twice in church.

On his way to church for the third time
he had a vision of a peacock with 500 feathers

---

2   Philip of Langenlonsheim, d. 1529.

beckoning to him, untying the priest's tethers
calling from the gates of heaven.

So Bauman did not recant, but confessed
his faith, defied the priests and revoked

their creed, while the extorters choked
on their elegant gruel.

He sang on his way to the death place,
happy, and when his shoes stuck in the village mud

he sang like the last bird left after the flood,
he kicked off his shoes and ran for courage, for joy.

Then he was beheaded with a heavy sword
and the nobleman and all the priests who judged him

came to ends just as grim
dying miserably and in pain as Jesu Christ is our Lord Amen.

Julia Spicher Kasdorf

Catholics

In third grade all the girls got confirmed
and had their ears pierced. They flaunted
those dingy threads that hung from the lobes,
telling how the ice stung, how the cartilage crunched
when the needle broke through, how knots
in the thread had to be pulled through the holes,
one each day, like a prayer on the rosary.

At recess I turned the rope
while Michelle skipped and spun and counted to ten,
and a scapular leapt from the neck of her dress.
She dangled that pale pink ribbon,
a picture of the Blessed Mother on one end
and the Sacred Heart on the other,
saying, "This is my protection, front and back."
That was when I called them Catholic
and said, "Your people killed my people;
your priests threw a man into a river,
tied in a sack with a dog, a cat, a rooster, a snake,
think how they scratched and bit going down,
think how they drowned. Your priests
burned holes in the tongues of our preachers,
and put pacifists naked in cages
to starve and rot while the birds
pecked off their flesh."[1]

---

1 Ed.: Kasdorf writes, "Not only is the business with the drowned animals an erroneous
conflation of the *Martyrs Mirror* and *The Musicians of Breman*, but the bit about pacifists
'naked in cages' is also an error, strictly speaking—assuming, as I do, that it's a reference to

Michelle and Vicki and Lisa just looked at me,
the jump rope slack as a snake
at our feet. But in my memory
I want these girls with fine bones and dark eyes
to speak up:
> those priests were not me,
> those martyrs weren't you,
> and we have our martyr stories, too.
I want to take their slim girl-bodies into my arms
and tell them I said it only because
I wanted to wear a small, oval medal
I could pull from my T-shirt to kiss
before tests. I wanted a white communion dress,
and to pray with you
to your beautiful Blessed Mother in blue.

—*for Julia Lisella*

Muenster, where folks were anything but peaceful. So, more evidence that memory, especially as it comes from a childhood rich in imagination, is not to be trusted."
The *Martyrs Mirror* celebrates the execution of the early Christian Ulpian in AD 304, near Tyre, by a method not unlike that imagined by the young Julia. He was "wrapped stark naked, together with a dog and an adder, in the fresh hide of an ox or a cow and thus thrown into the sea."

Baptized Again

> *We . . . renew the previous imperial law . . . that . . . every Anabaptist*
> *and rebaptized man and woman of the age of reason shall be condemned*
> *and brought from natural life into death by fire, sword, and the like. . . .*
> —Imperial Mandate, April 23, 1529[1]

The words leap off the page, so familiar, yet it's as though I have never read them
before. It is only one book among the many resting on my table: a Bible surrounded by volumes of stories and songs, memories and dreams. These stories are
haunting my sleep and filling my waking moments with the weighty tension of
connecting to something far greater than the rhythms of everyday life.

Tears run down my cheeks as I imagine a woman standing defenseless on a
grassy field, baptismal water streaming down her face, watching as armed men
approach to take her away. I hear her voice softly, almost inaudibly, echoing the
words of the martyr Paul:

> *But whatever was to my profit*
> *I now consider loss*
> *For the sake of Christ.*
> *What is more,*
> *I consider everything a loss*
> *Compared to the surpassing greatness*
> *Of knowing*
> *Christ Jesus my Lord,*
> *For whose sake*
> *I have lost all things.*

∽

The castle was dark and the stones were rough and cold. The walls could not keep out
the bitter wind of reformation hatred. Inside, the prison contained dozens of the people

---

1   As quoted in Arnold C. Snyder, *Anabaptist History and Theology: Revised Student
    Edition*, (Kitchener, ON: Pandora Press, 1997), 3.

harshly called "Anabaptists" ("rebaptizers"). They were hungry, sick, dirty, and in excruciating pain. A man was tied to a rack with his arms and legs extended. As his captors turned the crank, ropes pulled his extremities apart, slowly tearing him to pieces. Others, maybe three or four, probably more, hung from their arms, their legs weighted by heavy balls. They were all men, of course. The women were tortured in more humane ways—like having their fingernails removed. All the while, the prisoners were offered escape. "Repent! Reject your faith. Deny your baptism." When they refused, the torture increased. The captors accused them. "You are of the devil!" They demanded, "Who are your leaders? Where are the others hiding to worship?" The prisoners no longer remained silent. They looked their captors in the eye and began to speak to them of God's love, mercy, and forgiveness. The guards became infuriated and the torture continued.

In Switzerland, hundreds of people gathered in May 2003 for a conference called "Heal Our Land."[2] Swiss Reformed pastors mixed with American Mennonites and Amish families who were in full dress, bonnets, and beards. Together the people wept, grieving what had been lost. The Swiss Reformed stood, bowed with the burden of guilt that had hung over their people for generations. One Mennonite woman took the stage and faced them openly, losing her battle with tears, her voice shaking. "We have been impacted by the persecution years as sins and wounding trickled down from generation to generation. . . . It is time to let our hearts feel the loss we have experienced as a people group, and to recognize that we have been traumatized."

The Swiss Reformed took their Mennonite and Amish guests to the prison. Together, they stood where atrocities were committed. The metal and wood of torture instruments sat abandoned in the room, a forgotten testimony to a people's strength and faithfulness. Now protected by the rough stone walls, their descendants mourned and forgave.

Down in the courtyard below them, a group of students from a Mennonite college were taking a routine tour of the prison, oblivious to what was happening above. They were unaware that a rift had been healed and their future would be free because of that reconciliation. They didn't know that centuries of pain and guilt were flowing away.

---

2   For a more complete account of the 2003 reconciliation event, see Rusty and Janet Richard's video "It's Time" (available on YouTube and linked through www.martyrbook.com) and Pastor Charlie Ness's "Our Painful Past" in *Glimpses,* no. 201 (Christianity Today International, 2006).

The water sparkled and flowed under the bridge, dancing around rocks and sticks, completely oblivious to the death that lay in its depths. Felix Manz observed it calmly. He watched as the soldiers fastened a weight to his bound feet. A deep sadness filled his eyes as he turned to face the crowd.

I consider them rubbish,
That I may gain Christ
And be found in him.

As I bury my head in my hands, I wonder: Was she like me? Was she tall and thin? Did she come home to a five-year-old's laughter? Did she sing to herself as she washed the dishes? What gave her strength to stand against an army of accusers?

The Anabaptists had a bad reputation—they couldn't hold their tongues. Even when they stood in the midst of the fire, instead of crying out in pain, they would preach to those who watched, sharing their faith—and singing. They encouraged fellow believers to stand firm in their faith, and they begged those who didn't believe to turn to Jesus before it was too late. "Only love," they said. "Love for God and love for man." The authorities grew frustrated at how many people converted from the Roman Catholic, Lutheran, and Swiss Reformed Churches to the Anabaptist faith because of these fireside concerts. Many times they cut out their prisoners' tongues or clamped them with tongue screws before the execution so that the Anabaptists couldn't witness to those around them.

Even so, the movement grew. The more the radicals were persecuted, the more they gained converts. In prison, men and women wrote songs which were smuggled out and printed on leaflets. Hundreds of these songs were written, each one striving to spread the faith that these people believed with all of their hearts.

He . . . makes them rejoice
And strengthens them when in need
They commit all their matters
Solely to God,
They are like sheep for slaughter

Brought unto death,
Carried out by man's weapons,
Regarded as a prey
Having no secure place
Where man lets them abide,
Because of the Word of God
They will be continually hated,
They cry out and nearly weep,
The world rejoices therein
And does vehemently deny
The voice of the innocent.[3]

Dirk Willems was in prison for so long that he wasted away to skin and bones. Amazingly, one day he managed to escape his cell in the old castle by climbing down the wall using a rope made from strips of cloth. He needed only to cross the frozen pond and he would be safely away. Willems easily ran over the water, barely making an imprint on the ice. He was almost to the other side when he heard a crack behind him. He turned to see the guard who was pursuing him fall into the freezing water. Without a second thought, Willems turned around and raced back to where the man was drowning. Falling to his stomach, he reached in and pulled the man to safety.

Following orders, the guard immediately detained him and returned him to his cell. Dirk Willems never saw freedom again—within the year he was burned at the stake.

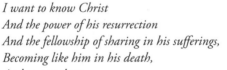

I want to know Christ
And the power of his resurrection
And the fellowship of sharing in his sufferings,
Becoming like him in his death,
And so, somehow,
To attain to the resurrection
From the dead.

---

3   The martyr hymn is referred to as "another song of suffering" in the Anabaptist hymnal, the *Ausbund* (No. 19, stanzas 9-10, c. 1552). Its author is unknown. It was translated from German to English by the Ohio Amish Library in 1998.

Who am I? I live in a nation where I am free to meet with others to worship as I wish, a reality that many of us still struggle to accept. How do we know that persecution is not waiting around the corner? We have been worn down, scarred, and frightened into submission. We are a rejected people who often don't have the courage to speak the truth at our kitchen tables, much less in the fire. We are no longer called radicals but, instead, "the quiet in the land" as we avoid confrontation and isolate ourselves in our own little community. I see the woman's strength and determination and realize—I don't deserve the label I carry as her descendant. Did she die in vain?

On the stage, a Swiss Reformed pastor stood alone to address the gathered worshippers. He shared his recent struggles with his church's teachings and his frantic searches to find the truth. He acknowledged that he had been rebaptizing adults in secret. His voice shook with emotion as he stated, "We were wrong. You were right. . . . Will you stand with us when we are thrown out of our churches for becoming Anabaptists?"

He and his black-robed colleagues knelt on the floor before the entire delegation of Amish men, women, and children. Following the example of Christ, the pastors showed their humility by washing the Anabaptists' feet. When they finished, an Amish bishop rose and embraced the man before him. They wept on one another's shoulders and their tears cleansed away years of fear, hate, and rejection.

The time had come to celebrate. The music pounded out as the assembly erupted into dancing. Even the Amish threw their hands into the air and joined their brothers and sisters in a time of jubilation: freedom at last.[4]

---

4   Since 2003, the reconciliation work has been ongoing: In 2004, the Swiss dedicated a plaque along the Limmat River where Felix Manz was drowned (press release from Mennonite World Conference: http://www.mwc-cmm.org/News/MWC/040709rls1.html; in 2005 Swiss Reformed leaders came to the U.S. for reconciliation meetings in Pennsylvania; in 2009, a delegation of American Mennonite leaders met with German Mennonites about possible repentance for Anabaptist involvement in the tragedy of Münster.

No Apologies

Oh, Jan Gerrits,
>Your missive to the Lutheran Preacher
>Addressed as a "beloved friend"
>Challenged his "unreasonable or willful stupidity"
>>In regard to baptism.
For this you became ashes.

Dear sister, Maeyken de Kort,
>Your presence where the
>one sought was not found,
>angered desperate captors
>>distracted by your joy.
For this you were pierced.

And merry Maeyken Boosers,
>You could no more keep from
>singing praise to Jesus
>than the warblers in Spring
>>shouting hallelujah.
For this, you too burned.

What more can I say of Cecilia or Elizabeth,
>tortured for the light your executioners could not bear.[1]
Or of Tijs, the cripple, and Beerentge, the infirm
>whose prison cell bred such holy communion
>your hearts became one.
In a single sack, you were slung into a castle moat.[2]

---

1   Cecilia Jeronymus; Elizabeth, d. 1549.
2   d. 1553 in Leeuwaerden.

You were imprisoned, beheaded, racked and weighted,
screwed, burned, strangled and drowned.
Speaking Scripture to Power,
you refused to sacrifice your young
to the Pope or to Luther.

My heart bleeds for you,
my sisters and brothers,
but only for you.
As for me,
I married a Lutheran!

JOHN L. RUTH

Lecture for a Limited Audience[1]

Preacher Christian Halterman, of the Salford Mennonite congregation,
Wrote, in 1782,
On Easter Sunday, no less:
"There are two kinds of people in the world."

Two centuries later, as I preach in the same congregation,
I remember how, as I studied in the university,
A philosopher told me such thinking was embarrassingly too simple.
So did an anthropologist, several types of psychologists,
A sociologist, a historian, and a theologian.
Also a European writer who came through and said
(Being quoted complete with accent for the next half a month),
"The executioner is the bond of the community of man."

A friend at a party did agree there were two kinds of people,
For about thirty seconds, but then amended it to three:
Bad men, liberated men, and women.
There might be—it was conceptually possible—
Some bad women, too,
But you couldn't be sure which ones they were,
Because they had all been so immemorially victimized
That for the next while, at least,
Moral categories were not useful in this case.

---

1   Ed: Published in *Mennonite Life* in 1983, earlier read in a convocation at Bethel
    College. While much has changed in the world—for instance, we're no longer wait-
    ing for Pakistan to get the bomb—the sentiments remain startlingly relevant.

Talking about "two kinds of people,"
My friends told me, was potentially dangerous:
A Cain-and-Abel type of dichotomy:
And we need as few oversimplifications as we can get
For the next century or so,
Or at least until we can get the computer fully humanoid.
It's necessary to realize, they said,
If you expect to be taken seriously in today's global milieu,
That there are *innumerable* types of people.

Having experienced this stimulating intellectual interchange,
It tickled me to remember how much gall old Christian Halterman had.
You've got to live in a small township like Upper or Lower Salford,
To believe what he did, or believe that some people can believe it.
As Shakespeare once wrote:
"Home-keeping youth have ever home-bred wits."

There are two kinds of people, this preacher said.

Now Christian had an ancestor, Hans Halteman,
Oh, about a great-great-grandfather,
Who was arrested in Switzerland, under the sign of the Bernese Bear,
Which was branded onto the back of his friend Henry Funck,
Who was then expelled into neighboring Burgundy
With pus running down his back,
Because he wouldn't go to communion in the right church,
Wouldn't get his babies baptized,
And wouldn't fight for his country.
(His people also insisted they would tell the truth without an oath.)
His expulsion was done at the recommendation of some convinced clergymen.
The only valuable export Switzerland had then was soldiers,
And when you refused to respect the military system,
You were unraveling the texture of Christian society.

The difference between kinds of people
That made a difference to Hans Halteman—
Christian's great-great-grandfather—
Was that there was a kind of fellow Christian of his
Who claimed a God-given responsibility
To apply red-hot iron to his friend Henry's back.
Maybe that's where those Haltemans and Funcks got their habit of
      oversimplification.
They would have been sorely tempted to believe
(In the heat of the process)
That either they were a different kind of people than those other Christians,
Or that they were believing in two different Gods.
Being a monotheist, certainly, Hans must have thought—
Well, you draw the conclusions.
It would have been very confusing for Hans,
And of course quite painful for Henry.

I trust Henry had prayed, "Father, forgive them,"
As he felt the kiss of the iron,
But could you blame him, or Hans's descendant Christian, preacher at Salford,
Hearing, or reading about this in the *Martyrs Mirror*,
For concluding that there *were* two kinds of people:
(1) Those who believe in a God who says you can kill
If you're morally certain it's necessary,
And have checked with a bishop first if there was enough time,
And (2) those who believe in One who says,
"Thou shalt not kill, and there's no fine print to that"?

Two kinds of people, not psychologically, but theologically.

What I seem to be trying to say is: it's a fact
That there are people in the world who will use a sword
On human flesh,
Or an M-16 or an Enola Gay,

If there are good enough reasons,
And then there are people who won't do such things for any reason,

That second category does exist.

I've never seen a systematic history of it from Crowell or Macmillan's
(Well, yes I have, but it was a history of pacifism.
Christian Halterman, the farmer-preacher, never heard about pacifism.
He didn't say there were two kinds of philosophies,
Or two kinds of ethics.
In his parochial way, he said there were two kinds of people.)
I can't remember any documentaries on the phenomenon as such,
Not even on PBS.
And you know, they could do something like that, even on commercial TV.
A few good-looking actors, some helicopters and a haystack or bedroom scene—
You can make any theme interesting.
I even saw the Holocaust done that way once.
You could have a name narrator,
And use Joan Baez's voice on the music track.

As little as I read about this phenomenon in the *New York Times*,
I do pick up, in odd pages, evidence that in every war
(And sometimes it's not even a war, just some kind of polarization)
The strange species, the second kind of people, appears,
In of course statistically insignificant percentages.

They just won't fight.
Sometimes they'll even carry guns, but won't shoot,
Or they'll shoot, but never hit anything.
Stonewall Jackson complained about people like that around Harrisonburg, Virginia.
In World War I, one man used to go "over the top," day after day, in France,
With his rifle held flat against his chest.
He shook hands, once, with a German soldier.

He knew only two German words—*Mann* and *Liebe.*
He said them both, and the German smiled before walking away.

On the streets of Tashkent, I talked with a Russian,
In the 50th year of our comrade Lenin,
Who told me that though he served in the Soviet Army,
He would have died before killing anyone else, even an enemy.
He was a Baptist. Think about that,
Some of you liberals who think you own Peace.

This species, I insist, exists internationally.

Now I don't necessarily mean the people you always see on marches.
At the Washington Moratorium in 1969 I met a lot of anti-types.
One young gang with a flag was chanting:
"Six-seven-eight, smash the state!"
"You're planning," I yelled, "to bring in peace that way?"
"That's where it's at, man!" one of them hollered back.
And marched on like any Prussian.

So I found my Falcon and drove home to Lower Salford,
And there I read again this crude sermon by Christian Halterman,
My predecessor in the Salford pulpit,
Who had the gall to say there were all of two kinds of people in the world.

Now just how ignorant, though, is that?

I mean, there are some people who categorically won't kill,
And the rest of them will.
It's what you might call binary.
It's a funny line to draw, I suppose,
Because there are Christians on both sides of it,
And Buddhists, I imagine, and atheists, and even Republicans.

Certainly, there were masses of Christians who went on the Crusades,
When the *Papa* of the Church said you could enjoy killing,
But I'll wager there were a few who wouldn't have gone
Even if you'd threatened to kill them,
Or if *Papa* would have damned them to hell for cowardice.

(I wonder what would happen today, if an American evangelist announced·
A "Crusade for Christ" in, say, Saudi Arabia.)

I once saw an arresting cartoon:
A victorious Crusader enhorsed—the holy cross on his banner—
Had a paynim down on his back on the ground.
As the point of the Christian's lance quivered over the pagan's nose,
The latter gazed upward with sincere attention.
"Tell me," he begged, "about this Christianity of yours.
I'm terribly interested."

As I said, there are two kinds of Christians
(And, I often hope, two kinds of Muslims, etc.—
If you are out there, please write me before Pakistan gets the Bomb),
And I don't mean Fundamentalists and Modernists.
The dividing line I'm talking about runs right through both their ranks.
Most of them, when a war heats up,
Either say that the Sermon on the Mount must after all be seen as an ideal,
Or, if they hold to Scriptural Innerrancy,
That it doesn't completely apply yet:
What it is is a glimpse we can have of the beautiful Kingdom that some day,
If we take Jesus as our personal Savior now, and are born again,
We'll inherit;
Where it will actually be natural to live like the Beatitudes
(Loving your enemy will be academic; there won't be any.
All evil will be removed by Divine Fiat).
In the meantime we must be wiser than serpents,
And as harmless as is consistent with common sense.

So both Fundamentalists and Modernists, on this point, are in the same church.
They both carry rifles on both sides of all the wars.

What I'm saying is that there are millions of this kind of Christian,
But that there are also a few like Christian Halterman, the other kind of people,
Who say you have to live by the Sermon on the Mount
And accept any consequences.
Luther called them *Schwärmer,* fanatics,
People who think the Kingdom of Heaven is at hand, already in time:
A species of naïveté, often rural.

Now, as a student of world reality,
I find that every ethnic group claims folk wisdom on this matter,
And has short-story writers.

Many of them seem to feel that if they could just share their secret,
Play their zithers, sing their song,
Do their dance on the world stage:
It might charm us all into World Peace.
When somebody from one of the ethnic groups does something good,
And the media ask them how they did it,
They often say, "Well, I guess it's because I'm a, an _____,"
And then they name their group.
Others, who feel no ethnicity,
Explain that they were following out their correct ideology.
Some say it was their sex.
And some, of course, give all the credit to the Lord,
Right on Phil Donahue.

Some people feel that it's the poets who will bring in peace.
Schiller wrote, and Beethoven heard music for, *"Alle Menschen werden Brüder."*
They sing this all over the world, in concert halls,
And for the moment, apparently, feel as moved by it as if they believed it.

The confusing thing is that in the crunch,
Ethnics, ideologues, believers and poets
Seem to rest their case as much on their bullets
As on their songs, their ideology or their Lord.
And all those groups have both kinds of people in them:
The kind that can use a weapon on other people,
And the few that absolutely can't.
(Catholics handle this in part by calling the latter saints,
Which allows them to be viewed as spiritual freaks,
Beautiful but not normative.)

It's funny, it seems that all the ethnic groups
(I should know—I'm Pennsylvania Dutch when it helps),
If they get a crack at cultural ascendancy,
Directly extrapolate from this to divine favor,
Or at least to historic destiny, or something,
And then to keep this status, they do what Jesus himself wouldn't—
Rig threat-displays to keep boundaries sacred:
"Stay on your side of that line, friend,
Or I'll be forced to,
Reluctantly, after due deliberation, anticipatory expiation, legislation,
Or prayer, as the case may be,
Fry your hide.
(Nothing personal: it's simple deference to Nature's First Great Law
Of self-preservation.)"

Now the small percentage of the other kind of people
(Too small to show on most graphs)
Refuses to be serious about these sacredest boundaries.
Conscientious, ethical Gypsies, you might call them,
With cousins on all continents.
They dream that they have property that moths can't eat,
And that thieves have no motive for stealing.

When the recruiters' posters go up, and the bands march,
The politicians and generals,
Thinking, as they do, of the greatest good for the greatest number,
Simply can't depend on this type of people.

The Pentagon, of course, is safe, as is the Kremlin:
There aren't enough of these people
To compromise the viability of the international order.
There are probably not enough of them, in any significant county,
To elect, in a fair vote, the dog-catcher.

But they do exist.
To use a phrase of Immanuel Velikovsky's,
These people amount to "more than zero."

Now then,
In addition to the people who are glad to have an excuse to kill,
And the people who are willing to kill if they have to
(Which are both subdivisions of an admittedly asymmetric category),
There exists this other species,
Who are willing to die if they have to,
But who can never,
By the Army, the Navy, the Marines, the Air Corps,
The local high school band,
The Pope, or Commissar,
Their priest or minister or rabbi or psychology,
Or Satan himself,
Be made willing to kill.

A phenomenon is a phenomenon.
Christian Halterman was on to something.
There are definitely two kinds of people.

HEIRS

Views from a Pond:
Dirk the Farmer
Ian Huebert

Sarah Klassen

Street Scene

Anneken offers her body, blood, breath
a warm sacrifice, her beautiful young son
Isaiah—to anyone who'll take him home.

A decent baker holds out
his snow-white arms. His wife protests
six children are more than enough

in these hard times. Anneken composes her last
testament: leaves her son wisdom
to be his mother, fear of God for a father

and the overflowing cup
of her suffering. She leaves the baker a full sack
of money. The boy grew up to be a brewer, became

mayor of Rotterdam. Never claimed his mother's faith.
They tried to drown it with her body
which had born and fed

Isaiah. See how the rope binds her
to the jailer's wrist, the fibers twisted
rough as justice. Shoved from arm to arm

look
how that innocent child
smiles.

Anneken Jans[1]
Rotterdam, 1539

---

1   Also Anna of Rotterdam.

Becca J. R. Lachman

No Stoplight in This Tourist Town

Those who are not among us bring
their cameras and their children. They leave
what's heavy on their hearts for a morning, a day.

Those who are not among us bring ready
billfolds, pay for bentwood rockers and log cabin
quilts. So easy to buy
an hour of quiet. It is not surprising
on Sunday mornings to see a car with windows open

stopped where the road dips between Salem and
Sonnenberg. God is a cappella
on the seventh day. Hymn crosses
hymn between these two churches, and music carries
off centuries of feuding (This the visitors
don't know; it is rarely talked of now—how coffins
were plucked like red beets in the middle
of the night, away from the mother church.)

What does our martyr family think as we
sit back, barter our quiet to the world, pretend
that we are holy, different? *Six friends ended their lives in*
great joy, and those that saw them burn went and
penned a hymn, the first letter of each verse
replacing the names of the dead.

Do *we* feel warm when breathing deep to offer up
our harmony? Do we think of them
as verses change? And what *would* they say, after
watching us join the frontlines, deadlines, the weight
of such wealth: *Burn us, bake us, drown us,*
world—yet in the end, make us yours?

Ross L. Bender

Writing for Mennos or Not

The thought has fascinated me from time to time that there were probably more Anabaptists who recanted under torture than not in Reformation times, and the question that follows is whether they were not as heroic in their own pathetic way as those staunch and stern believers who went to the stake or the river fiercely refusing to yield to their interrogators and staunchly proclaiming the nonresistant Anabaptist faith. The idealized Anabaptist martyr went to his or her death singing a hymn or preaching to the executioners, assuming his or her tongue had not yet been torn out or his or her mind driven around the bend by the horror of it all. The science of torture has advanced with the times so nowadays I understand they can bring you back from the refuge of insanity with drugs or electricity, but I always imagine, when I gaze into the mirror of the martyrs, that the first smoking caress of the red hot tongs on my flesh would send my mind straight to the moon and sort of nip the catechetical give-and-take with the inquisitor right in the bud. On the other hand, I can also imagine that it wouldn't have taken much more than a little visit from the local constabulary to loosen my lips. I can hear it—the knock on the door, the splintering of the wood as it's kicked in—"I'll talk! I'll talk! Yes, I can give you names! All the names you want! Graber—he baptizes adults in the duckpond at midnight! Detweiler! Yoder! Schwarzendruber!"

As a people who revere the founding martyrs, hang really horrifying caricatures of the Anabaptist heroes in seminary lounges, and are always ready to buy a new edition or treatment of the *Martyrs Mirror,* Mennonites are trapped in an abominable psychic pretzel. While there is a rather outré theory going around that Mennonites are all screwed up in the style of abused children due to the founding Anabaptists' experience of torture and abuse being handed down through the generations, I would submit that the problem is much simpler. There is simply too much of a cognitive dissonance between the experience of, say, Felix Manz and your average family in Franconia Conference in the year of our Lord 1997. This is true in a way that it is not for followers of Luther or Calvin. Lutherans have a plausible religious hero. Although certainly extraordinary in the strength of his defiance of Rome, Luther was, after all, a very earthy, believable human being and could in no way be seen as superhuman or supernatural.

In their 1990 collection of excerpts from the *Martyrs Mirror* entitled *Mirror of the Martyrs,* John Oyer and Robert Kreider briefly review the history of the big book and find that it has always served a didactic purpose for Mennonites: "story as a means of renewal and restoration. We come to the presence of the *Martyrs Mirror,* and these selections from it, with thanksgiving for storytelling and with expectation that in the recovery of a martyr memory, a weary and uncertain people can renew their strength and vision."[1] Now this is fascinating—"a weary and uncertain people." Do they mean the Mennonites? The North American Mennonites? The average family in Franconia in 1997? This is certainly an interesting perspective. To the best of my knowledge, the only thing uncertain about life in Franconia is whether or not we're going to buy the second BMW. While it may be true that Mennos need renewal, I think far better descriptors would be "sleek" and "wealthy" rather than "weary" and "uncertain."

The point here, if there is a point, is that the Mennonite narrative does in fact have a point and a good didactic purpose. The martyrs have not died in vain. Their story will renew and restore us. This is one of the one-dimensional Mennonite narratives and has inspired a certain genre of hagiography—"Conrad Grebel, Son of Zurich"; "Pilgrim Aflame"; the movie "The Radicals."

The difficulty is that Mennonites have great trouble perceiving the multi-dimensionality of their psychic situation. The juxtaposition of the average Franconia family with some particularly nasty piece of torture from the sixteenth century induces a sort of muted neurosis. Consider some of the elements in this emotional milkshake: venerable Anabaptist saint barbecued to a crisp; a homeless dying and rising god who preached the power of powerlessness and that the rich would be consigned to hell; one BMW; considerable financial assets but you couldn't really call me rich especially compared to those Wampler-Longacres down the road; a profound sense of humility; a profound sense of pride in my spiritual heritage.

The Mennonite story is not a narrative but a sort of consensual hallucination. Look in the mirror, take some Dramamine, and call me in the morning.

1   John S. Oyer and Robert S. Kreider. *Mirror of the Martyrs: stories of courage, inspiringly retold, of 16th century Anabaptists who gave their lives for their faith* (Intercourse, PA: Good Books, 1990), 15.

Please Sarah, Do Not Laugh

My eyes scan the bookshelf. She is not hard to find. Between water-stained covers, she carries her treasure, but at 173 years old, her spine is broken and every brush fells orange flakes of leathery skin. Her name, *Martyrs Mirror*, is barely readable. A rubber band encircles her girth. She reminds me of the 90-year-old biblical character Sarah—sitting in withered wonderment between barrenness and fertility. Oh, she has been with child countless times, but can this worn woman yet again fulfill the fancy of her creators? Can this matriarch of martyrdom give birth to another youthful Origen who ran into the streets to give the ultimate sacrifice? Can she still conjure the spirit of Truyken Boens, "daughter of Wilhelm Boens of Antwerp," who went a second time under the waters of baptism only to be burned at the stake?

I reach for her. To hold her is to cherish the hopes and memories of parents who would have found no greater honor than to be recorded in her pages. Martyrdom was God's highest calling; the second best, in our Mennonite family, was the mission field. My parents chose the latter and glorified the former, and this book was at home with us. She was formed from the bloodied dust of martyrdom to "multiply and replenish the earth." Her mission was to seed the passions of future generations who would willingly "subject their young members to His yoke."[1]

I reverently leaf through the pages. Her lap is a story land of faith. One narrative in particular stirs my soul. The subtitle reads: "Jacob Dirks, and his two sons, Andrew Jacobs and Jan Jacobs, A.D., 1568." I have two sons. One carries the middle name of Andrew. My boys are in their thirties, but they never age beyond "my beloved." Mr. Jacobs and his boys "fell into the paws of the wolves at Antwerp." They drew a guilty charge simply for being Mennonite. All three were to meet death by fire. They were tied to the stake. Andrew's bride-to-be watched and wept. Just before the piles were ignited, Jacob Dirks asked his children: "How do you feel, my dear sons?" The tenderness of the tragedy grabs me. My eyes moisten. Those words—those boys—could be mine. I can see their

---

1   Page xiii of Leaman's 1837 first English translation.

faces. What a terrible, sweet moment of perplexity and pride. The executioner strangled each of them and their drooping bodies were burned, "thus sealing the truth with their blood." Though frightened by the thought of martyrdom, my fragile faith is momentarily emboldened. I am born again. I tell her that I will be strong like them. I will forsake all for Jesus. She bursts forth with victorious song. Unlike Sarah, this elder knows that age need not close the womb.

But does she lift her voice too soon on my behalf? So many proved to be faithful to the end with no regard for what that end might be. Could I do the same? Do I hold heaven's joy so dear? Would I really be a Germanicus of AD 170, who stood flint-faced before the wild beasts? Does not the midnight cry of the bobcat frighten me? Might I be shamed by the likes of Hans Simeraver who was "imprisoned for the divine truth and ultimately shared the fate of John the Baptist? I am so much closer to Pilate's heady question of "What is truth?" than to Hans' unwavering heart.

Perhaps, if my options were open, I would plead for the quick and painless—the guillotine over the rack: just do it. It would be dangerous to prolong the decision of this doubter. Sarah might laugh again. I find no greater gain or glory in torture. I see no need for me to say with Jan Wouters upon his whipping, "O flesh, methought, you must now suffer." Dare I whisper in the executioner's ear, "You can damn me for heresy, but don't drag me, dunk me, or slowly do me in"? It's foolish for me to think that I would have any say.

Oh, I too easily vacillate. I peek through the door with a chilling reluctance. Is death merely an exit or is it an exodus into a new life? The Apostle Paul writes of a sublime eternity that "no eye has seen, nor ear heard, nor human heart conceived" (1 Cor 2:9). I like this, but I don't know this. Do I, like Abraham, fully believe in a promised land that far exceeds the wonder of warm lips, clasped hands, and the familiar love I have known on this side of the Jordan?

John writes the book of Revelation during Domitian's rampage of persecution (AD 96). He attempts to encourage his people. John envisions a peaceful paradise where the tears of the believers will be wiped dry by God himself (Rev 21:4). "Yes, yes," I say, "I long for the solace of heaven's kindness." But the moment is quickly shattered. I read on and find that those who are "cowardly and faithless" will be cast into "the lake that burns with fire and sulfur" (Rev 21:8). The pungency of such vengeance repulses me. Should my fear of the God I am supposed to love move me to martyrdom? I want to recant for the sake of all sinners. I want to be Moses who challenges God when the Almighty refuses to forgive the idol worshippers. God wants to kill them, but Moses has the tenacity to declare that if God does that, then "blot me out of your book that you have written" (Exod 32:32). In both cases, the

Tongue Screws and Testimonies_

protests of the patriarchs were meant to save many lives. Will my audacious pleas rescue anyone from perishing?

Would so much questioning sustain me in the face of prolonged suffering? An open book, a blank page, and Sarah watches intently. What will the records show? Would I say: "I recant" or, like Martin Luther, "here I stand, I can do no other"?

Please, Sarah, do not laugh.

Darren Byler

The Gorilla in the Mirror

I read Dorcas Hoover's book *Awaiting the Dawn* late one night when I was ten years old. It was a story about guerillas and Mennonites in Guatemala. The main character in the true story, Tall and Strong John Troyer, was killed by shadowy Marxist rebels because he wouldn't fall. He wouldn't fall because he was so strong in faith and he was praying aloud as though in a trance. As I remember it, it took eight bullets to knock him down. The "lesser" missionary in the story survived by playing possum after a bullet to his shoulder.

Lying awake for hours, I mulled over the story, the incomprehensible evil of it all—gorilla vs. Mennonite—and finally stumbled into Mom and Dad's room as the long night finally began to break apart in shades of red. Between sobs I told Mom all about it: evil men, machetes, guns, slaughtering, missionaries. Mom walked me back to my bed mumbling that everything was going to be okay.

The first whiff of the gorilla story had snuck up on me a few months earlier when I overheard my Dad discussing it with an electrician from Keim Electric downstairs in the furnace room. Paul the Electrician mentioned that he knew some current missionaries in Guatemala and wondered if my Dad knew anything about John Troyer, "the guy who was killed by gorillas" back in 1984. Since I had never heard of missionaries being killed by apes, I asked Dad about it as soon as Paul was out of earshot. Why would a gorilla kill a man? And, in particular, why a man with the same last name as my Dad's Beachy-Amish breakfast buddy David; a man in a plain suit without buttons, and a beard without a moustache? Dad said a guerilla was a kind of soldier.

I grew up believing my family and community were pretty special: we were part of an embattled minority set apart to God. We weren't as plain as our Amish neighbors, who I learned as a five-year-old to greet with the little rhyme "Vo bist du, Ole Cu" (How are you, Old Cow), but we were clearly the next thing to it. No TV. No T-shirts. My mom, while driving against traffic in a Wal-Mart parking lot one day, was told by a fellow driver, gesturing with his middle finger, that she should go back to driving horse and buggy.

The Swartzentruber Amish boys I hung out with told me important stories about Paul Bunyan and Babe the Blue Ox rather than the horrors of gorilla killings and the weight of social hatred. Though they had a German *Martyrs Mirror* next to their heavy German Family Bible in an otherwise bare whitewashed cabinet in the living room of their farmhouse, it didn't seem as though they looked at it too often. Sam Gingerich, the oldest of the Swartzentruber Amish boys (my third cousin once removed), told me he was going away to fight in the army as soon as he turned 18. He told me to keep an eye out for helicopters or they might take me away too.

My Dad kept his copy of the *Martyrs Mirror* in his study next to stacks of back issues of *Church History* magazine and miscellaneous sermon notes. I didn't read it as much as look at the macabre illustrations of stake-burnings, live-flayings, and upside-down crucifixions. It was plain enough that Mennonites were the direct descendants of the true church—the etchings of 17 centuries of continuous torture made that clear. Countless turns around the *Behalt* ("To Remember") mural at the Amish and Mennonite Heritage Center in Berlin, Ohio, gave color in these black and white prints. Our history was red, dark red; we had lived through hell and survived, always survived. Our story was not so much a struggle with the earth, with hunger and poverty, but a struggle with midnight terrorists who forced us away from the Truth and persecuted us until one by one we fell. We struggled not with regular people in our Red State, those who wanted small government and strong limits to social welfare, but sinister men with fancy suits and immodest women from big cities who wanted us to fight in their armies or at the very least participate in their progress. They wanted to take our children away from their families in order to brainwash them with liberal agendas. The gruesome etchings in that book showed me that Tall and Strong George Blaurock was a hero just like John Troyer who fell before dawn. They showed me it was better to die with Christ than to compromise with the World.

Since our Mennonite church was a special church that made visitors feel awkward with all the holy kissing, segregated seating for men and women, and kneeling to pray with your nose pressed into benches that smelled like wood and warm bodies, we didn't get to know too many Worldly Christians. Every once in a while one family would bring over some tourists from their Amish Country Campground, whom we viewed with a mixture of ambivalence and smugness. As a gesture toward community outreach, our church had a rotating system where a family was assigned to serve as Host and Hostess each Sunday and as a consequence we some-times happened to have some of these visitors in our home. Invariably, it seemed, there was at least one woman with "cut hair" involved. They would murmur over our food and would want an ontological explanation of what made Mennonites special, we would tell them about the not baptizing babies, the not fighting, the covering the head, and they would say (as though they hadn't heard us at all), "We're not that much different from you. We're Southern Baptists."

In college I wrote an essay on the experiences of local Amish during World War II. I was fascinated by stories of Amish conscientious objectors to war who were grabbed by men from town. They held those Amish men down and cut off their beards and tried to steal their souls through shame. I had to read about that in old newspaper clippings, because no one talks about that anymore. I thought "Didn't outsiders understand that Amish just wanted to be left alone and that this was their right as Americans?" While this might be what Amish wanted, I learned in a summer missions trip to Southeast Asia that our calling as Mennonites was even more estranging; not only were we to "focus on the family," but we were meant to "go unto all nations and preach the gospel" Truth. We had been told to beg for persecution by living for heaven and bringing people there with us.

In graduate school I learned from Frederick Nietzsche and Max Weber that suffering produced a sort of *ressentiment* in people. For these scholars, this men-tality made people appreciate their suffering as a way of being made special in God's eyes. True believers thought that by staggering through the pain of this world they would pass a physical test from a terrible God and their patience would be rewarded with paradise on the other side of the bloody veil. This sort of thinking makes liberation theology seem like Godless communism and preach-ers of end-times apocrypha seem like latter-day prophets who deserve tax breaks. A reified tome historicizing this process might tempt believers to think they are responsible to maintain an exclusive remnant of suffering ascetics. Outside on the stone steps of the lecture hall I discussed this understanding of suffering with a Bosnian imam and a Pakistani Muslim. It seemed clear to them that Muslims have been the object of persecution as long as there has been a Muslim minor-ity in the world. Muslims in Bosnia, Muslims in China, Muslims in India have always been hated by Christians, communists, and Hindus. "It has something to do with their perceptions of a final, complete Revelation received by Prophet Muhammad, peace be upon him," they said. In their thinking, non-Muslims re-sent the totalizing message and the smugness that accompanies exclusive reliance on Islam. It is only when a group compromises with a dominant cultural system that its religious idiosyncrasies can be tolerated and persecution abates.

When I got married a few years ago to a beautiful Burkholder girl who is my seventh cousin, a life-long friend of mine gave me my own copy of the *Martyrs Mirror* as a wedding present. He said, "If anyone can appreciate what this is worth, I think you can." Then he apologized for getting some coffee on the cover during the long car trip to the wedding. I told him not to worry; those sober old books seem to collect all kinds of junk and I would rather see it be treated as just another book and not as an infallible sacred object. My wife always thought the scariest thing about her family's *Martyrs Mirror* was the dead fly pressed between the front pages.

The part of the *Martyrs Mirror* I've decided to take home are the stories of regular people standing up for what they believe and living out of their convictions. I think of this ability as fostering a conscientious society without a plan outside of the local community and the strong partial truths it cultivates. It is this sort of speaking into the void that I will honor and teach to my children. I want them to understand the powerful perceived memories Mennonites have etched into their book of the dead. I want them to understand why these tragic stories are powerful and how they can be transmuted into our present world— giving our past a future. But most of all, I want them to understand that I will not sacrifice them, my children, for this heavy legacy of heroic death. I will tell them that we are all equal in dying and it is living that matters and fills the world with light. I want them to know that I hope to be a minor hero at best and a reluctant traitor at worst. They need to understand that I've worn the gorilla suit myself for small roles in oppression (don't they always seem small?) behind the front lines and at times turned my cheek out of weakness and insularity. These are important old Mennonite stories too.

Maybe someday I'll sober up and settle down enough to keep our *Martyrs Mirror* in a closet for use as a hammer since as Chekhov noted "Every happy man should have an unhappy man in his closet, with a hammer, to remind him that not everyone is happy." But for now our edition is in a storage box in the basement garage of a Mennonite bishop in Ohio. It's lost in a warren of Chinese histories and moldering papers on narratives of cultural conflict among Turkic Muslims—which I've adopted as my field of study. The singular weight of that heavy Anabaptist book is beginning to lessen a bit in all those stacks of other books and ways of remembering the story of the world, and it's becoming harder and harder to distinguish between the gorilla and the martyr in the mirror.

DAVID WRIGHT

A New Mennonite Responds to Julia Kasdorf

This is why we cannot leave the beliefs
or what else could we be?
—Julia Kasdorf, from "Mennonites"

As best I can tell, most of our quilts here were inherited,
or bought at relief sales, spread on guest beds,
displayed on polished oak racks. Not much borscht,
few shoofly pies at potlucks—instead it's
hummus, free range chicken, carob brownies.
No bacon-laced bean casserole. Someone
steamed soy beans last Sunday, right in the pods.

Maundy Thursday we wash each other's hands.
It is optional, so I stay seated,
beside a Lutheran woman, Harvard
theologian, and we wish together
for liturgy because we cannot play
the name game. Neither can my agnostic
Quaker friend. We drink coffee on Mondays
to talk politics instead. Between fields,
one of our farmers, ex-Amish and an Otto
brother, teaches medieval Catholic
thinkers whose names I can never recall.

So many new and remade and restless
and not-quite Mennonites, driving Volvos
and minivans. We park ourselves in pews

next to women and men who know better
what real Mennonites really are, at least
have usually been, who tolerate us
when we do not know (or want to) the so
many stories we should. Some seem amused,
some even grieved, others simply angry
that our martyr stories come in children's
sermons where Dirk rescues and is killed right
next to Rosa Parks and Ruby Bridges,
where Luther himself nails necessary
correctives on Wittenberg's door.

                             We sing,
though, a solid four parts; the hymns here have
a sturdy bottom (though I need the book
on 606).[1] And we make our way through
less solid but sweet guitar-sent songs
your great uncles would never recognize.
Our preacher never swoons. He's biblical,
careful, and knows the university
crowd listens each week. Once, he prayed, "May God
bless your mind's wanderings." Which go now to
China Buffet, where two tables away
a woman wears heavy head covering
and pale green dress as she eats with her son.

---

1   Ed: "606" refers to a version of the doxology known variously as "The Mennonite
Anthem," "The Anthem," and "118" (in *Hymnal: A Worship Book*); to some Mennonite
groups it is as strong an emblem of identity as the *Martyrs Mirror*. According to Anna
Groff in the March 18, 2008, issue of *The Mennonite*, the hymn vaulted into popularity
at a General Conference convention in Turner, Oregon, under the auspices of Mary Oyer
during the summer of 1969. That particular weekend in August was a pivotal moment for
another counter-cultural movement, too. I'm offering a prize to anyone who will compare
the GC proceedings and the Woodstock performance lineup to tell me what that other
bunch was singing when 606 was first sung by a mob of Mennonites. Terms of competition: Prize only to the first respondent, bragging rights to all. Document sources and account for time zone differences. This may not be legal in your state.

I say to Becky, "Should we tell her?" "What?"
"That we're Mennonites too?" Becky smiles, licks
sugar from her fingers, the residue
of deep fried dough passing here for ethnic
dessert. "Maybe we could tell her we're new
at it?" God bless our wandering, indeed.

JAMES LOWRY

A Meditation on Dirk Willems
Upon a Visit to a Dutch Village

Dirk Willems, whose story was given briefly in the preceding section on non-resistance, lived in Asperen in the province of South Holland. Once, my three teenage sons and I were traveling in Europe, and we had an opportunity to visit the village of Asperen on a pleasant August day.

We arrived on Saturday morning and, unfortunately, got Jan van Leerdam, a school teacher and local history expert, out of bed rather early. He graciously agreed to meet us later at the large village church and give us a tour. Jan's family name derives from the village of Leerdam, which is nearby. The village of Leerdam comes up in the story of Dirk's execution.

Jan, a large man in his thirties, slightly balding, did know a great deal about local history, as it turned out. He explained the very large Reformed church in detail. It had been built of brick in 1471, as a Roman Catholic church, and was already there when Dirk Willems was living in Asperen.

Later the church had burned, destroying the roof and wooden parts, but the very massive tower at one end of the church had remained untouched by the flames. The church was rebuilt. But it was the tower, which had not needed rebuilding, that interested us. It is thought that after Dirk's arrest by the thief catcher, he was imprisoned in this same tower.

Jan van Leerdam said that Dirk had earlier been imprisoned in the Lord's castle, no longer standing, but he had escaped, was recaptured, and then placed in the church tower for safer keeping. Although I asked repeatedly, van Leerdam said that he knew of no source of information about Dirk Willems other than the *Martyrs' Mirror*.[1] The above information, which he gave us beyond what

---

1 The story of Dirk Willems did not appear in any of the editions of *Het Offer des Heeren*. Pieter Jans Twisck introduced the account of Dirk Willems into the martyr book of 1617. On page 742 of the *Martyrs' Mirror* appears an exact copy of the sentence of Dirk Willems and a note at the bottom says the document was copied in 1606. Kühler remarks that already by this year the Old Friesians were collecting material for their enlarged martyr book, which appeared in 1617. *Geschiedenis van de Doopsgezinden in Nederland: Tweede Deel 1600-1735: Eerste Helft* by W. J. Kühler (Haarlem: H. D. Tjeenk Willink & Zoon N.V., 1940), 99.

the *Martyrs' Mirror*[2] says, is local tradition, or, I suspect, may derive from a Dutch novel, which includes a fictionalized story of Dirk as a subplot.[3]

Jan van Leerdam guided us through the empty lower room of the tower to a door at the side, the door to the stairs. We opened the door and were confronted with a narrow, turning brick stairway, which wound around a narrow center column of brick. We climbed in the very narrow space, always turning and brushing against the walls that crowded in against us, 56 steps to the second level, then another 27 steps to the third level, where the old church bell hung. The hour was approaching, and so we waited to hear the bell ring eleven o'clock. It was quite loud, but not loud enough to be unpleasant.

We climbed another 27 turning steps to the next level, where prisoners had been kept. The room was stripped of any objects from earlier days, except for a set of wooden stocks with enough holes for three prisoners. How could a prisoner have slept in this room right above the bells? How ironic to use a church tower for a prison!

We climbed two more flights of stairs, and then a ladder, to a trapdoor, which was heavy enough to make our rather youthful guide strain to push it up. Out we climbed onto the platform at the top of the tower, about 180 feet above the ground.

From here we had a cool, windy, and slightly frightening view of the church roof below us, the crowded cemetery, the village of Asperen, and the Hondengat,[4] the long pond across whose breaking ice Dirk once fled for his life, and a street called Dirk Willemszstraat. Again, how ironic, the village where Dirk was not considered fit to remain alive now has a street named for him!

Also in the distance we could see a lake that now covers the spot where it is thought that Dirk was burned alive. On the windy top of the tower, Jan van Leerdam explained the origin of the lake this way. Once, during a flood, the dam next to the regular place of execution broke, and the water escaped in a mighty gush and washed out a hole in the sandy soil, which became a pond. This happened a second time, making the pond into a lake. More recently, sand has been dredged out of the bottom of the lake for use elsewhere, making the spot where Dirk was burned now

---

2   Ed: Lowry belongs to a school of thought that prefers *Martyrs' Mirror* over *Martyrs Mirror*. Lowry's style is consistent with the *Mennonite Encyclopedia* and the work of Harold S. Bender.

3   *De geuzenjongens van Asperen* (The Beggar Boys of Asperen) by A. H. Arnoldussen (1946; Veenendaal, the Netherlands: Uitgeverij Kool B.V., 1983), 75-86.

4   The Hondengat is connected by a canal to the Linge River.

rather deep. The former place of execution is a short distance from Asperen in the direction of Leerdam.

On the day of execution, the wind was blowing quite strongly, as it was on the day of our visit. The *Martyrs' Mirror* tells us that the wind carried the fire away from the upper part of Dirk's body, so delaying his death. He cried many times in the fire, "O my Lord, my God!" The wind carried his voice to the neighboring village of Leerdam, where they heard him cry out more than seventy times. Seventy times! Peter asked Jesus if he should forgive one who sinned against him seven times, and Jesus said not seven times, "But, until seventy times seven" (Matt 18:21-22 KJV). Dirk forgave his enemies many times.

Let's look at his story again carefully.

The *Martyrs' Mirror* tells us that the authorities seized Dirk Willems in his native village, Asperen, in 1569. They blamed him for being rebaptized in his late teens in Rotterdam, a large city nearly thirty miles to the west. They also blamed him for allowing secret meetings to be held at his house in Asperen, meetings for preaching and for baptisms.

The *Martyrs' Mirror* does not give more details about his earlier life, but it does tell about his final arrest.

Dirk was hotly pursued by a thief catcher, followed by an official called the burgomaster and perhaps others at a more leisurely pace. Dirk came to an expanse of water covered with the cracking ice of early spring. He hesitated a moment and then dashed across, followed by the thief catcher. Dirk made it across.

But the thief catcher was breaking through the cracked ice and hesitating. He would never get across. Dirk stood on firm ground on the far shore. It would take the others a long time to go around the end of the ice covered waters. Dirk had gained much time. He could easily escape.

Now the thief catcher was down in the freezing water, threshing around, grasping at the breaking edges of the ice, calling for help.

But Dirk was across and safe on the other side, like the Israelites fleeing their Egyptian enemies at the Red Sea. Dirk had crossed the Red Sea. Dirk was free. Had not the Israelites stood on the opposite shore and watched the overthrow of the Pharaoh and his armies in the midst of the sea? Had not the Israelites watched the waters of the sea cover the Egyptians? Had they not taken up a song of praise to God for the overthrow of their enemies, now drowning in the midst of the sea? Had not Moses said,

> I will sing unto the Lord, for he hath triumphed gloriously:
> the horse and his rider hath he thrown into the sea . . .

The enemy said, I will pursue, I will overtake . . .
my hand shall destroy them.
Thou didst blow with thy wind, the sea covered them:
they sank as lead in the mighty waters.
Who is like unto thee, O Lord . . .
who is like thee, glorious in holiness,
fearful in praises, doing wonders?
(Exod 15:1, 9-11 KJV)

But Jesus said, "Love your enemies." How? How could Dirk love his enemies? Jesus said, "Do good to them that hate you, and pray for them which despitefully use you, and persecute you" (Matt 5:44 KJV). The thief catcher had just been despitefully using Dirk. Should Dirk do good to him?

Was not the thief catcher a wolf? Christians are as sheep among wolves. Should a sheep save the life of a wolf, pull him out of the water, save his life? Dirk himself might be drowned in that numbing, icy water. The springtime ice was rotten, cracking, and treacherous. The thief catcher might resist, grab Dirk in his panic, drag them both down. Should two be drowned, when at most only one need be?

But Jesus said, "Love." And Jesus also said, "Greater love hath no man than this, that a man lay down his life for his friends" (John 15:13 KJV). But the thief catcher was a wolf, not his friend. Let the other wolves save him. Let the burgo-master and the helpers standing on the opposite shore save him. Wolves can save the lives of wolves, and sheep the lives of sheep.

No one in Dirk's church would ever criticize him for running on. Dirk would never be called into account by the church for not saving the thief catcher. It would never be a matter of church discipline. The story might even be told as a judgment of God on the persecutor, as such stories had been told before and were found also in the New Testament. God did rightly punish sin and justly carry out judgment. But the thief catcher was not yet dead. God had not yet judged him.

If Dirk tried to save his life, it was quite possible he might succeed. Dirk might not be drowned, but he might be captured and burned. Dirk well knew what was going on. The authorities were capturing Anabaptists and executing them at the stake. Dirk knew of some who had been burned alive in recent months. The authorities made sure that everyone found out.

Was not there a Scripture about being burned? "Though I give my body to be burned. . . ." Yes, there is such a Scripture, but what is the rest of it? "Though I give my body to be burned, and have not charity, it profiteth me nothing" (1 Cor 13:3 KJV).

Jesus said, "Love."

Should a sheep love a wolf, save the life of a devouring, ravening wolf? The wolf is a wolf, but the wolf is also a lost sheep, a helpless lamb floundering in the water. This is one of the great mysteries of nonresistance: enemies and wolves at the same time are lost souls and straying sheep.

Dirk should love his enemies as God had loved him: He had loved Dirk while he was still His enemy, living in sin and serving the god of this world; He had given His Son to die for Dirk's sins.

In a flash Dirk turned back. He pulled the thief catcher out of the water. The *Martyrs' Mirror* says he did it "quickly," probably with very little deliberation, simply as an expression of his Christian character.

Not many Anabaptists had the opportunity Dirk had—to love the enemy so actively, to do good so strikingly. Dirk did this act of obedience for Jesus and for all of us. Not many of us will ever have the opportunity to love our enemies so dramatically and in such a costly way. But we do have occasions in a much smaller ways to do good to them who despitefully use us.

Dirk stoops on the ice to save his enemy's life. The cold, slippery, breaking ice where Dirk kneels to pull the enemy out is a holy place. For it is one matter to worship God with our words and songs, but it is a far greater matter to worship God with our deeds.

To conclude the story, the thief catcher, after he had been pulled out of the water, wanted to let Dirk go. But the hard-hearted burgomaster and the others, standing safely the whole time on the other shore, shouted that he must arrest Dirk. They said that he had sworn an oath to fulfill his office, and if he broke his oath, he faced a fearful punishment. Reluctantly the thief catcher brought Dirk back.

Dirk was found guilty and sentenced to burn at the stake. As we said before, Dirk suffered greatly in his death. Peter says, "For this is thankworthy, if a man for conscience toward God endure grief, suffering wrongfully" (1 Pet 2:19 KJV).

The word *thankworthy* causes us to pause for thought. Why *thankworthy?* Jesus told his disciples in a parable that those who have obeyed God will be greeted with the words, "Well done, thou good and faithful servant" (Matt 25:21 KJV).

Such an expression of commendation from God is an enormous reward.[5]

---

5 Joseph Liechty has a lengthier article on Dirk, but from a different viewpoint in *Mennonite Life* (Sept. 1990), 8-23. Some of the ideas for the use of Scripture here come from that article. David Luthy tells of the growing use of the story of Dirk Willems in "Dirk Willems: His Noble Deed Lives On," *Family Life* (Feb. 1995): 19-22.

Churches, Cathedrals, and Caves

Three Excerpts

The evening we arrived in Zurich by train it was already 7 p.m.; we were tired and hungry, but determined to see the place where, perhaps more than any other, the Anabaptist movement began. No one knows exactly which upstairs room on the Neustadtgasse Felix Manz and Conrad Grebel and George Blaurock gathered in, with eleven others, to perform the first adult rebaptisms on January 21, 1525. We do know that Manz, the illegitimate son of a priest, lived there with his mother under the protection of his father, who was canon of the Grossmünster church just before Ulrich Zwingli.

A block from the spot on the Limmat River where Manz was put to death by drowning on January 5, 1527—the first Anabaptist martyr—we got a sandwich and a salad at an overpriced, pretentious yuppie café. Today the Neustadtgasse and the streets around it are lined with restaurants, bars, sex shops, and tattoo parlors, and on pleasant summer evenings the area teems with young people. It's lively, polyglot, only a little tacky. One end of the Wasserkirche was given over to an exhibition of conceptual art. At the other, the famous Zwingli statue—he holds a Bible in one hand, a sword in the other—was boxed in completely with sheets of white plywood. A clatch of scruffy youths huddled on the steps, beating guitars and hanging out, while six police officers stood by, watching and muttering gravely to each other. Not sure what we were missing, exhausted from a long day's touring, we caught the train back to our hotel.

The next morning we left Zurich and drove north and east, through a series of smaller and smaller towns and villages. Hinwil, Ringwil, Bäretswil, Wappenswil—then a tiny sign marked "Täuferhöhle." We parked and followed a steep path up through a horse pasture, across two tiny streams. At last we found a set of logs laid in to form rough steps. Above them, with a spray of water coming down across its entrance, was the cave where Anabaptists of the villages around met to sing and pray during the years when they were forbidden to gather or to marry or to spread their peculiar version of the Gospel, when they were thrown in jail, sold as galley slaves, drowned in rivers, burned in public squares. In 1641, a little over a century after Manz and Grebel and Blaurock first met, the last of these Anabaptists fled for the Palatinate and Holland. The low-ceilinged cave remains—it might fit a hundred crowded tight. Its muddy floor had been strewn with straw, and char and ashes from a recent campfire lay in a corner.

The day was wet. We sat for a bit on the bench at the entrance and looked out through the veil of water. There was a clear view down into the valley, but I found myself thinking that if pursuers came, there would be nowhere higher or more remote to go. This green little valley, this cave with its rough bench and muddy straw, seemed far off in space and time from bustly, up-to-the moment Zurich—but we were less than two hours away. Four hundred years ago the journey would have been longer, but not long enough to keep anyone safe from determined authorities. You have to be in the world—where else? The path to your secret retreat has to run through somebody's pasture, cross someone's creek. The geography of Europe, and increasingly of the whole crowded world, allows for only so much distance between the great cathedrals and the most obscure caves.

The *Martyrs Mirror* is an odd text to find at the heart of a sect. Its heroes, almost without exception, are respectful of the authorities but insist that nonconformity and nonresistance are the true way of Jesus, and that their tormentors—earnest Christians though they may be—are deeply mistaken. Their arguments, testimonies, sufferings, and deaths are given in earnest and often gruesome detail. The combination of zeal and humility, along with the intensity of human drama, create a haunting, disturbing, elusive effect that contemporary Mennonites still struggle to explain or come to terms with. One of the best-known stories concerns Dirk Willems, who was imprisoned in Asperen, Holland in 1569. In midwinter he escaped in the classic manner—knotting rags to make a rope, descending from a window, and fleeing across an ice-covered pond. When a pursuer, not thinned by prison rations, fell through the ice, Willems turned back to rescue his enemy. He was recaptured and returned to his cell; when he refused to recant his beliefs, despite his good deed, he was burned at the stake. Anabaptists have been trying to puzzle out the practical implications of *that* example ever since.

In my own childhood I learned martyr stories in my turn, though I also turned to science fiction, sports, and TV shows for less austere edification and entertainment. Many years later I tried to capture one of those early moments in a poem, which offers its own take on the Dirk Willems story.

Ancient Themes #14: The Martyrs & the Child
-for di

this is really pretty cool isnt it
leaving it all out but the letters wow
it'll confuse my mom & piss off my teachers
so bad i always wanted to be bad or at least
i thought i was bad anyway i cant forget
those sunday school teachers
bernice for example my moms 1st cousin
there we all were in the church basement
i was 10 years old maybe & shes asking
if we are ready to die like the martyrs
get our tongues screwed & fingers splintered
get burned up like firewood to heat
the hearts of those left behind well
thats some question when youre 10
in the middle of america in 1962
already scared of dying aglow
with radiation never mind with zeal
for the lord so there i sat gulping
& stalling with only those flimsy
beige curtains between our class
& the others with only a floor & a ceiling
& several miles of sky between me
& god leaning down to listen
& then my cousin connie who later went
wild & beautiful said she would do it
she would die for jesus yes she would
& bernice seemed pleased & forgot to ask
the rest of us & so i blundered on
into the rest of my life sweating out
the nuke tests & the bullies & the wondrous
heedless girls treading the tender grass

of my stupid young heart & i was surely
not so much worse for being forced
into uneasy contemplation of the fiery
heroes of old of the godless commies
& whether indeed i was ready to go up
in pain & splendor for jesus for believers
baptism for dirk willems turning back
half crazed with love for his pursuer
half full of pious shit surely clear
full of some weird lust to leave
this world & head out on the ice not
the canal not the lake no the true crazy
buckling thin ocean of ice jesus laid down
behind on his way out of town follow me
follow me well are you coming or not

If the martyr-heroes are hardly conventional, consider that the villains include, at least by extension, most of the rest of the world—especially those Christian authorities, Catholic and Protestant, who sent their victims to the stake or
the river. If you grew up with such tales shaping your view of the world and of
human society, as I did, you might also find it hard to be easy in the world even
when your own persecutions were limited to an occasional, trivial remark. You
might find it difficult to be entirely comfortable with the Catholics or Lutherans or agnostics who outnumbered you everywhere, even while you worked and
played and studied with them. You might find yourself wondering who was really
on your side, even as you were going about most of your days with very little to
distinguish you from every other ordinary American. You might always carry a
faint sense of reserve, a suspicion of "the world," a thread of conviction that you
were somehow not *supposed* to belong.

~

Like many of my people, I find myself conflicted about my tradition—drawn to
the hidden churches and the quiet circles that meet outside the great halls of the
majority, loving the old stories of sacrifice and fidelity, yet baffled and depressed
by the hard, stubborn will to power that seems so often to triumph over love and

generosity among us. Three hundred years later the particulars have changed, but Mennonites are still hurling accusations of apostasy and arrogance at each other. The two largest Mennonite groups, having agreed nearly a decade ago to merge, have seen the process thrown into disarray by a bitter debate over whether practicing homosexuals can be admitted as members. Congregations and church leaders with liberal views have been disciplined, while groups of conservative churches have threated to leave if discipline is not enforced even more strictly. Meanwhile, the Amish continue to grow in numbers and to keep most of their many young people in the fold, although they also have struggled to contend with modern society and with the impact of tourism, cell phones, and cocaine on their communities.

Underlying nearly every one of these issues, I think, is the problem of "the world," and of the relationship between that world and a body of believers which is expected to be somehow both *in* and not *of* it. Where do I belong, if at all, in such a tradition? It is mine by blood—one direct ancestor, Hans Gut, sided with Jacob Amann in 1693, while his brother Jakob Gut wrote some of the most temperate letters on the other side. Through three grandparents I can trace my family lines far back, through Mennonite to Amish, from Illinois and Ohio to Alsace or the Palatinate or Hesse, and from there to Switzerland. For the past three generations my ancestors have been marrying across the lines of the two main Mennonite groups mentioned above, and I have spent nearly all of my adult life first attending and then working for Mennonite colleges.

In the postmodern world such a pedigree by itself is neither necessary nor sufficient to keep me, even uneasily, within the faith of my fathers and mothers. No tenet of Anabaptism is more basic than its voluntarism—even the most uncompromising church leaders have always maintained that this church was only for those who earnestly desired to join it. Many do leave the Mennonite church—some for more liberal churches or for the broad buzzing world that is America today, where religion can easily become just another lifestyle choice, and some for more charismatic or evangelical churches. During most of my twenties I would have said, if anyone asked, that I was an ethnic Mennonite but not much of a believer. Yet in my late forties I find myself still in the midst of the church, for reasons I have difficulty explaining to myself, let alone to anyone else.

Anabaptists have been coming to the New World for centuries; some were among the first white settlers of Pennsylvania and Virginia. My own people stayed longer in Europe, most coming in the mid-nineteenth century—a heritage still regarded as suspect by some of the descendants of the first settlers. Nonetheless,

Europe has been only a hazy montage of mountains, martyrs, and hymns to me and to most other American Mennonites, one filled with strong but murky emotional overtones. The myths and stories are powerful, but inevitably they are incomplete.

Throughout my life I have felt drawn, irregularly but repeatedly, to learn the stories of the martyrs, of the prisons and thumbscrews and fires, the Amish Division and Münster and all the rest. But nothing I had learned quite prepared me for the austere clarity of the hidden churches, or the damp earth and rock of the Täuferhöhle, or the beautiful and still flourishing estates in the Palatinate from which my Stalter ancestors left for America. When I saw Monbijou and Kirschbacherhof, resplendent in the sunshine, I wondered why anyone would have left such places. When I looked south from the village of Gunten over gorgeous Lake Thun and the Alps rising into the afternoon haze on the other side, I tried to imagine how that distant von Gunten from whom my name comes had felt as he turned his back on the village and headed north.

Likewise, nothing I had learned prepared me at all to step from a narrow staircase into the Upper Chapel of Sainte-Chapelle, with Vivaldi reverberating off the stones and glass and with the sudden blaze of what seemed to be a whole sky lined with brilliant, multicolored, vibrant light, as though the stars had suddenly gone Technicolor. *So this is the world*, I found myself thinking as I groped my way to a chair: this place of grandeur and delight, where men had labored with enormous craft and care to put into shape and light the stories of the whole, holy, fallen world, all the way from creation to apocalypse. This is the world, where such resources and knowledge can be gathered and directed into something that will echo for centuries without diminishing, that is still as tangible and spectacular as on the day the last scaffold was removed.

And here I was, come not even to worship but only to look, driven less by piety than by my hunger for beauty—a hunger that knew well the difference between a small, functional back room painted gray and this spectacularly transformed space, one as dense with beauty and meaning as any human creation I had ever encountered. My people fled as far and as fast as they could from the grandeur of the great cathedrals, convinced that their beauty was inseparable from their corruption. Now I moved among them and marveled.

Toil and Grace

Grandma said a lazy Mennonite
doesn't understand his Bible.
Praying can be done while working.

Remnants remain
and my generation still believes,
even while growing richer
and moving to cities,
even though no one dies for the faith
like Dirk Willems or Anneken Hendriks.
We like to think we inherited
those stiff stubborn beliefs,
banished from Zurich and Landau,
fleeing to Philadelphia,
finding farms in Waterloo.

Surely Jesus was joking,
his parable of the vineyard workers,
that the less than industrious
will get into heaven.
He began life as a carpenter,
worked miracles on Sundays,
walked miles, taught multitudes,
looked after his mom while being crucified.

I lay block for old Charlie's foundation,
take Mrs. Gingrich Sunday dinners
mixing mortar, kneading bread.

How else would I know if the baptism took?
We love with our hands,
rebuilding after hurricanes,
piecing quilts for refugees.
We work till we are too tired to sin
(but we sin anyway.)

Sunday mornings we gather to sing
loud, unaccompanied
our hands quiet and still for this hour,
our voices so sure of grace.

DALLAS WIEBE

The Anabaptist Radiance

We are marching, marching upward
  into the afterglow of our ancestors.
We are marching into the light
  that streams from their words.
We are marching into the radiance
  of Bible-ridden revolution.
They gathered secretly to reaffirm
  that all was not well in the world.
They met in homes and barns to verify
  that they could change religion.
They died in flames and on gallows
  to witness for their souls.
They came down the Rhine River
  like misguided migratory fowl.
They sneaked into the Palatinate and Holland
  like unwanted relatives.
They hid among the bourgeoisie of the North Sea
  until even Rembrandt painted their portraits.
Now they are marching on in us,
  the progeny of their abuse,
  the pale glow of their suffering.
They are marching on in us in our squabbling,
  in our schisms,
  in our refusals of each other,
  in our refusals of the world,
  and in our persistent, religious democracy.
They are marching on in us to tell the world
  that we have choices,

that we can all worship
according to our own beliefs.
They are marching to say
that if there is no free will
then nothing matters.
The radiance of the Anabaptists
still shines out in our lives
when we say to those about us,
"Not us, friends. Not us."

Artist Statement

Within the Mennonite faith, religious icons have always been held at arm's length, dating back to the iconoclasm of the sixteenth century and exemplified in the Mennonite tradition of simple living. The image of Dirk Willems strikes a certain chord concerning Anabaptist core beliefs. Defacing the image may be seen as a conflict with what it represents. Conversely, however, defacing the image suppresses the dogmatic safeness that traditions accrue over time. The defaming is an acknowledgment of iconoclasm: by not making these variations, the original image may thus be seen as all the more sacred. By breaking the order, the drawings that follow seek not to defame the image in a negative way, nor worship the image by leaving it alone; instead, they provide a new function for the image by adapting existing vocabulary, acknowledging the historical context while simultaneously creating a new present context.

While not an engraving like the original, the pen and ink drawings provide a good representation of the Luyken technique while at the same time employing technology that was available at the time the originals were created. This integrity of materials acts as a vehicle for meaning, showing an existential decision-making process at work where every aspect is taken into consideration, including the frames in which the drawings are housed: They are faux-wood grained, a nod to the traditional Mennonite furniture, where elegant veneers were painted over more economic building materials such as pine. The variation of situations proves arbitrary; the deduction of possibilities concerning Dirk Willems gives the viewer full reign to interpret and devise more. As there are several variations presented, the images can be seen individually or sequentially, the latter providing space in between the physical manifestations, where the mind has plenty of room to roam.[1]

With the "Views from a Pond" series, the old is the new and the new plays the intended roles of the old. It is not sacred. It should not be exalted but rather looked at, plain and simple.

—Ian Huebert

---

1   From "Views from a Pond: The Dirk Willems Variations," *Pacific Journal*, 4 (2009): 5-6.

Author Biographies

David Augsburger (1938) is professor of pastoral care and counseling at Fuller Theological Seminary. Augsburger has written twenty-five books on pastoral counseling, marriage, conflict, and human relations. Augsburger taught at seminaries in Chicago, Indiana, and Pennsylvania and served as radio spokesperson for the Mennonite Churches. His productions won ten awards for creative religious broadcasting and a more important honor, during the Vietnam war: his sermons on nonviolence caused the cancellation of The Mennonite Hour on over twenty stations. His feature articles have appeared in more than 100 different periodicals. Augsburger is an ordained minister of the Mennonite Church and a diplomate of the American Association of Pastoral Counselors.

Ross L. Bender (1951) was born in Ontario and currently lives in Philadelphia, Pennsylvania. He received a BA in history from Goshen College in 1971 and a PhD in Premodern Japanese History and Religion from Columbia University in 1980. Bender is an independent scholar specializing in eighth-century Japanese history.

Di Brandt (1952) is an award-winning poet, essayist, novelist, playwright, and librettist. Her poetry has been adapted for video, television, music recordings, dance, installation, and sculpture. She has given poetry readings and lectures around the world. Her most recent poetry collection is *Walking to Mojacar* (Turnstone 2010). Her recent opera, *Emily, the Way You Are*, with composer Jana Skarecky, premiered in Ontario in 2008, with Ramona Carmelly and the Talisker Players, conducted by Gary Kulesha.

Darren Byler (1982) is the son of Mennonites from the Midwest. Byler is currently studying the cultures and geographies of Turkic Muslim groups in Northwest China. Strangely, he's drawn to the markets and narrow streets of dusty oasis towns where men with long beards and women in headscarves gather in separate clusters to disseminate the news. When not in China, he lives in Seattle with his wife and contemplates the beautiful air of the American Northwest. (MA Asian Studies, Columbia University.)

Amy Calkins (1982) is a stay-at-home mother and a part-time freelance copy-editor (she found a way to make her Grove City College English degree pay the bills). Her poems have been published in the anthology *Becoming Fire: Spiritual Writings From Rising Generations* and in *Relief: A Christian Literary Expression.* They are also forthcoming in *Radix Magazine*. She, her husband, Mark, and their three young children live in Rochester, New York. These days, culinary experimentation has become one of Calkins' favorite creative outlets. In her spare moments, she enjoys reading and praying.

Todd Davis (1965) teaches creative writing, environmental studies, and American literature at Penn State University's Altoona College. He is the author of three books of poems: *The Least of These* (Michigan State University Press, 2010), *Some Heaven*, and *Ripe*, as well as co-editor of *Making Poems* (State University of New York Press, 2010). His poems have been nominated for the Pushcart Prize, have won the Gwendolyn Brooks Poetry Prize, and have appeared in such journals and magazines as *Iowa Review, Shenandoah, Sou'wester, Gettysburg Review, Indiana Review, West Branch, River Styx, Green Mountains Review,* and *Poetry East.*

Cheryl Denise (1965), native of Elmira, Ontario, is the author of the poetry collection *I Saw God Dancing.* She and her husband, Mike Miller, live in an intentional community, Shepherds Field, near Philippi, West Virginia. She is currently producing an audio recording of poems and has a forthcoming collection, *What's in the Blood*, scheduled for publication by Cascadia Publishing House.

Diane Driedger (1960) is a poet, writer, academic, and author of the poetry collection *The Mennonite Madonna.* Her poetry has appeared in literary journals and anthologies in Canada, the U.S., and Trinidad and Tobago. Her latest book, co-edited with Michelle Owen, is *Dissonant Disabilities: Women with Chronic Illnesses Explore Their Lives.*

Omar Eby (1935) is professor emeritus of English at Eastern Mennonite University, where he taught English literature and writing for 28 years. Eby lives with his wife, Anna Kathryn, in the Shenandoah Valley of Virginia. He was born near Hagerstown, Maryland, and taught for six years in Somalia, Tanzania, and Zambia. Eby has published books of fiction, biography, and personal experience.

Joanne Epp (1963) grew up in Rosthern and Lanigan, Saskatchewan. She graduated from Canadian Mennonite Bible College in the 1980s and worked with MCC in the '90s. Her poetry has appeared in *CV2, Other Voices,* and other Canadian literary magazines. Joanne lives with her husband and two sons in Winnipeg, Manitoba, where she serves as assistant organist at St. Margaret's Anglican Church and is working on her first book of poems.

Debra Gingerich (1968) grew up in upstate New York near the Lewis County Mennonite community of her birth. She has since lived in Lancaster and Philadelphia, Pennsylvania, before moving to Sarasota, Florida, where she works as a Web communications and publications manager. She completed her undergraduate studies at Eastern Mennonite University and received an MFA in writing from Vermont College. Her poems and essays have appeared in *Mochila Review, MARGIE: The American Journal of Poetry, Whiskey Island Magazine, The Writer's Chronicle,* and others. Her first collection of poems, *Where We Start,* was published by Cascadia Publishing House.

Jeff Gundy (1962) Gundy's poetry collections include *Spoken Among the Trees, Deerflies, Rhapsody with Dark Matter,* and *Flatlands.* His prose books include *Walker in the Fog: On Mennonite Writing, Scattering Point: The World in a Mennonite Eye,* and *A Community of Memory.* His poems and essays appear in many journals and magazines, including *Georgia Review, The Sun, The Christian Century, Mennonite Quarterly Review, Image, Shenandoah,* and *Rhubarb.* A 2008 Fulbright Lecturer at the University of Salzburg, he teaches at Bluffton University.

Chad Gusler (1970) graduated in 2007 from Seattle Pacific University's MFA program. He has a BS in Biblical Studies and Theology from Eastern Mennonite College and an MA in religion from Eastern Mennonite University, where he currently teaches.

Ann Hostetler (1954) is a professor of English at Goshen College in Goshen, Indiana, where she teaches literature and creative writing. She is the author of *Empty Room with Light: Poems* and editor of *A Cappella: Mennonite Voices in Poetry.* Her essays and poems have appeared in many journals including *PMLA, The American Scholar, The Valparaiso Poetry Review,* and anthologies such as *Common Wealth: Contemporary Poets on Pennsylvania, Are You Experienced? Baby Boom Poets at Midlife,* and *Making Poems: Forty Poems with Commentary by the Poets.* She is the website editor of the Center for Mennonite Writing at www.mennonitewriting.org.

Sheri Hostetler (1962) is pastor of First Mennonite Church of San Francisco. She is also a poet, a gardener, a wife to Jerome, and mother to Patrick. She grew up in Holmes County, Ohio.

Ian Huebert (1983) was born in Nebraska. His illustrations have appeared in *McSweeney's*, the *Believer*, and the *San Francisco Chronicle*. He draws the *Pornographic Barn Owl*, a comic strip posted every Thursday on the *Rumpus*, an online literary magazine. His artwork has been featured in numerous group and solo shows in the San Francisco Bay Area and elsewhere. More of his work can be seen at www.themilkmachine.com. He lives in San Francisco.

Jean Janzen (1933) was born in Saskatchewan and raised in the midwestern U.S. Since 1961 she has lived in California, where she graduated from Fresno Pacific University and California State University, Fresno. She has five collections of poetry and a book of essays based on the Menno Simons lectures she gave at Bethel College. Her poems have appeared in *Poetry, Gettysburg Review, Image, The Christian Century, Prairie Schooner*, and many other journals and anthologies. Janzen received a creative writing fellowship from the National Endowment for the Arts in 1995. She taught poetry writing at Fresno Pacific University and Eastern Mennonite University. Her latest collection of poems is *Paper House* from Good Books.

Rhoda Janzen (1963) Janzen's poems have appeared in *Poetry, Yale Review, Gettysburg Review, Southern Review,* and others. She has authored a poetry collection, *Babel's Stair*, and a memoir, *Mennonite in a Little Black Dress* (Holt, 2009). Janzen teaches English and creative writing at Hope College in Holland, Michigan.

Andrew Jenner (1982) works as a freelance journalist and writer. He is a graduate of Eastern Mennonite University and holds an MFA in creative nonfiction writing from Goucher College. The essay in this collection is adapted from the introduction to his graduate thesis—an unpublished book-length manuscript attempting to answer the question, "Are you a Mennonite?" He and his wife, Rachel, live in Harrisonburg, Virginia.

Anna Maria Johnson (1979) Johnson's stories and essays have been published in *Ruminate Magazine, DreamSeeker Magazine, The Mennonite*, and aired on public radio. Her monthly column appears in *The North Fork Journal* and *The Shenandoah*

Journal. She is currently pursuing an MFA in creative writing at Vermont College of Fine Arts. Johnson writes, gardens, and makes art along the North Fork of the Shenandoah River with photographer Steven David Johnson, their two daughters, a dog, a cat, and an enormous sheep.

Julia Spicher Kasdorf (1962) Kasdorf's third poetry collection, *Poetry in America* (University of Pittsburgh Press) is forthcoming in 2012. Of her other collections, *Eve's Striptease* was named one of *Library Journal's* Top 20 Best Poetry Books of 1998, and *Sleeping Preacher* won the Agnes Lynch Starrett Poetry Prize and the Great Lakes College's Association Award for New Writing. She also published a collection of essays, *The Body and the Book: Writing from a Mennonite Life*, and a biography, *Fixing Tradition: Joseph W. Yoder, Amish American*. An associate professor of English and women's studies at Pennsylvania State University, she teaches in the MFA program in creative writing.

Sarah Klassen (1932) lives, reads, and writes in Winnipeg. Her most recent books are *A Feast of Longing* and *A Curious Beatitude*. Honors include the Canadian Author's Association Poetry Award, the National Magazine Gold Award for poetry, and the High Plains Fiction Award. Klassen has taught high school English in Winnipeg and English language and literature at LCC International University in Lithuania. She is involved as mentor, teacher, and editor in the Winnipeg writing community and is a member of the River East Mennonite Brethren Church.

Stephanie Krehbiel (1976) is a PhD student in American Studies at the University of Kansas. Her dissertation research is an ethnographic study of the experiences of LGBTQ Mennonites and Mennonite attitudes concerning sexuality issues. She has master's degrees in flute performance and ethnomusicology from Michigan State University and has published and presented work on the politics of Mennonite congregational singing and on her experiences as a church musician. In her spare time, she is a runner and an avid reader of kids' fantasy novels. She lives in Lawrence, Kansas, with her husband, Eric.

Becca J. R. Lachman (1980) grew up in the Amish/Swiss Mennonite village of Kidron, Ohio. *The Apple Speaks,* her first book of poetry, is forthcoming from Cascadia Publishing House. Lachman's chapbook "Songs from the Springhouse" won the 2004 Florence Kahn Memorial Award from the National Federation of State

Poetry Societies, and her original musicals have been produced at college, community, and dinner theaters. She is a composer/lyricist for the Lorenz Corporation's Heritage Press and teaches English at Ohio University.

Mel Leaman (1950) is an associate professor of religion at Lincoln University in Pennsylvania. He was raised in the Mennonite tradition. Following graduation from Taylor University in 1972, he taught school and then served six years as a director of Christian Education and Youth at a United Methodist church in Maitland, Florida. It was during this time that he joined the UMC and eventually served as a pastor in Ohio and Pennsylvania for 18 years. He received a DMin in marriage and family from Eastern Baptist Theological Seminary in 1990. Mel has been at Lincoln University since 2000.

James Lowry (1934), member of the Washington County, Maryland and Franklin County, Pennsylvania, Mennonite Church, is married and has five married children. He has worked as a teacher, librarian, and writer.

Robert Martens (1949) grew up in the Russian Mennonite village of Yarrow, British Columbia, where he experienced the heaven and hell of the ethnic community. He encountered the bafflingly individualistic "outside world" at Simon Fraser University during the rather Anabaptist years of student protest. Robert has co-edited and co-written several regional histories, as well as an anthology of Mennonite British Columbian literature, *Half in the Sun*. A sense of outraged *Gelassenheit*, if that is not an oxymoron, motivates his writing of poetry.

Kristen Mathies (1972) lives and writes in Kitchener, Ontario, and has lived in Blantyre, Elmira, Mbabane, Chicago, and New York City. She teaches English as a Second Language and creative writing to high school students. Previously, she worked with an NGO at the United Nations, and her graduate degrees are in English literature and peace studies. Lately her favourite reads are Arundhati Roy, Barbara Kingsolver, Chimamanda Ngozi Adichie, and Vincent Lam. Her four-year-old nephew Stefan is always one of her favourite people, as was her grandmother Lina Ida Heinrich Wohlgemuth, who appears in part two of the poem "Alchemy for Survival."

Maurice Mierau (1962) lives in Winnipeg, Canada, where he works as a writer and editor. His most recent book, *Fear Not*, won the 2009 ReLit Award for poetry.

A previous book of poems, *Ending with Music*, appeared in 2002. He served as writer in residence for the Winnipeg public library in 2009–10.

Rachel Beth Miller Moreland (1975) lives in central Ohio where she and her husband are raising three young sons. A graduate of Goshen College, she has worked as a newspaper reporter, a writer for Mennonite Central Committee, and a freelance writer. She is the author of the *Simply in Season Leader's Study Guide*.

Jeremy Nafziger (1969) lives in Weyers Cave, Virginia. He writes software manuals and does freelance writing. He was a newspaper reporter and received a yearlong writing fellowship from The Milton Center. He is a graduate of EMU and earned a master's degree (in linguistics) from George Mason University. Jeremy and his wife, Michael Ann, have four children.

Jesse Nathan (1983) is the author of *Dinner*. He grew up outside of Moundridge, Kansas, and lives now in San Francisco. He is an editor at *McSweeney's*.

Barbara Nickel (1966) Nickel's collection of poetry, *Domain*, was listed in *Quill & Quire's* Best Books of 2007. *The Gladys Elegies* won the Pat Lowther Memorial Award. Her work has appeared in *Notre Dame Review, Prairie Schooner, Poetry Ireland Review, The Malahat Review, The New Canon: An Anthology of Canadian Poetry, The Walrus*, and others, and she is a winner of *The Malahat Review* Long Poem Prize. Barbara also writes books for children; her novel *Hannah Waters and the Daughter of Johann Sebastian Bach* was shortlisted for the Governor General's Award and won the BC Book Prize. She lives and writes in Yarrow, British Columbia.

Leonard Nolt (1948) is a writer, poet, book and film reviewer, and photographer whose work has been published in *Rhubarb, cold-drill, Mennonite Life, Boise Weekly, American Geographic*, and other publications. Some of his work can be found on his blog at www.leonardnolt.blogspot.com. He's a graduate of Lancaster Mennonite High School, Amarillo College, and Boise State University. Leonard is a charter member and on the leadership team at Hyde Park Mennonite Fellowship in Boise, Idaho, where he lives with his wife and grandson.

Jessica Penner (1978) grew up in Kansas, attended Eastern Mennonite University, and then moved to New York City, where she passed out peace fliers with Catholic activists, worked at an afterschool program, briefly sold academic biblical software, graduated from Sarah Lawrence College with an MFA in creative writing, and taught English for Speakers of Other Languages. She has published work online with *Lost Writers* and *Void Magazine* and won an honorable mention in an *Open City* contest for her short fiction. Three essays appear in *Ghost Writers*. She now lives in the Shenandoah Valley of Virginia.

Audrey Poetker-Thiessen (1962) is the author of three poetry collections: *i sing for my dead in german*; *standing all the night through* (nominated for the McNally Robinson Manitoba Book of the Year Award, 1992), and *Making Strange to Yourself*. As translator together with her husband, Jack Thiessen, she has forthcoming from the University of North Dakota, *The Russian Germans under the Double Eagle and the Soviet Star*, Bernd G. Längin's pictoral history, *Die Rußlanddeutschen unter Doppeladler under Sowjetstern* (Weltbild Verlag). She lives in rural Manitoba.

Emily Ralph (1983) is a worship pastor, website designer, and radio personality with a passion for Jesus, the Church, and sharing hope with a broken world with creativity and enthusiasm. Emily has spent the past decade researching and sharing her Anabaptist musical heritage through song, story, and teaching. She loves to be active, and if you come across her during one of her rare free times, you'll most likely find her playing with her family, walking her dog, or eating ice cream.

Byron Rempel (1962) Ten days after Byron Rempel was born, Marilyn Monroe sang "Happy Birthday, Mr. President" to John F. Kennedy. Believing this performance was really meant for him forever instilled delusions of grandeur in a boy otherwise meant for a future as a drifter and ne'er-do-well. A mid-career shift toward tanning and surf culture ended abruptly after an unfortunate snowshoe incident, which was when Rempel reluctantly took up the pen. He has been paying the price ever since.

Eric Rensberger (1950) was born in Elkhart County, Indiana, on a small farm. The entire world of his earliest years was dominated by Mennonite and Amish families. He thought they were the majority of Americans. Rensberger discovered modern poetry through an anthology his mother used for a class she had taken as a young woman studying at Goshen College.

John L. Ruth (1930), born on a Mennonite farm in Eastern Pennsylvania, was ordained a minister at the age of twenty. After taking a PhD in English literature at Harvard, he taught for 14 years at Eastern University and Universität Hamburg in Germany, while continuing to serve in the ministry. In 1975 he accepted a call from Franconia Mennonite Conference leaders to write on themes of Mennonite heritage. Among his titles are film documentaries on the Amish and Hutterites, a biography of Conrad Grebel, a text for the *Martyrs Mirror Oratorio* by Alice Parker, and two conference histories.

Esther Stenson (1951) The life journey of Esther Yoder Stenson, Harrisonburg, Virginia, extends from an Amish Mennonite home in Stuarts Draft, Virginia, to El Salvador, to China (where she met her husband), and back to Harrisonburg, Virginia. She is the author of a book of poems entitled *Miracle Temple* (Cascadia, 2009). Currently, she teaches literature and composition at James Madison University.

Joseph Stoll (1935) is an Old Order Amish minister, writer, and editor.

David Waltner-Toews (1948) is professor in the Department of Population Medicine at the University of Guelph and founding president of Veterinarians without Borders/Vétérinaires sans Frontières—Canada (www.vwb-vsf.ca). He is an author on about 100 peer-reviewed papers and texts on ecosystem approaches to health and sustainability, and he has published half a dozen books of poetry; a collection of recipes and dramatic monologues, *The Complete Tante Tina*; an award-winning collection of short stories, *One Foot in Heaven*; a murder mystery, *Fear of Landing*; and three books of popular science, including *The Chickens Fight Back* and *Food, Sex and Salmonella*.

Annie E. Wenger-Nabigon (1951) was born to Mennonite missionaries in 1951 in the Ozark Mountains and now lives in Sudbury, Ontario. She graduated from Goshen College, received an MSW from the University of Michigan, and is currently completing an interdisciplinary PhD in Human Studies at Laurentian University while serving as a concurrent disorders specialist with a mental wellness team pilot project in ten First Nation communities. She was a poetry finalist in the Press 53 Open Awards Contest 2008, and her work appears in *Fission: A Collection of New Canadian Poetry*. She and her husband, Herbert, have four adult children and two grandchildren.

Dallas Wiebe (1930–2008) Born in Newton, Kansas, Dallas received his doctorate from the University of Michigan and was a professor in the Department of English at the University of Cincinnati. He was founder and editor of *Cincinnati Poetry Review* and founder of the Cincinnati Writers' Project. His books include *The Kansas Poems, On the Cross, Monument: On Aging and Dying, Skyblue the Badass, Our Asian Journey, The Transparent Eye-Ball, Going to the Mountain, Skyblue's Essays, The Vox Populi Street Stories*; his short stories appeared in numerous journals. Among many honors, he received the Aga Khan Fiction Award from *Paris Review* (1978), a Pushcart Prize (1979), the Post-Corbett Award for Literature (1984), the Governors Award (1998), and an Individual Artist Fellowship (1999) from the Ohio Arts Council.

Rudy Wiebe (1934) is widely published internationally and winner of numerous awards, including two Canada Governor General's Awards for Fiction. Wiebe is the author of nine novels, four short-story collections, and ten non-fiction books. His latest publications include a novel of the historical Mennonite diaspora *Sweeter Than All the World*; the children's book *Hidden Buffalo* based on a Cree creation legend; *Of This Earth: A Mennonite Boyhood in the Boreal Forest*; and the biography *Big Bear* in the Extraordinary Canadians series. His *Collected Stories, 1955–2010* will be published in 2010 by University of Alberta Press. He lives with his wife, Tena, in Edmonton, Alberta.

David Wright (1966) Wright's most recent collection of poems is *A Liturgy for Stones*. His work has appeared in *Image, Artful Dodge, The Christian Century*, and *A Cappella: Mennonite Voices in Poetry*, among many others. He lives with his family in Champaign, Illinois.

Credits

Index of Martyrs and Witnesses

Page numbers of the martyr accounts in the *Martyrs Mirror* appear in parentheses.

The editor

Kirsten Eve Beachy teaches creative writing and journalism at Eastern Mennonite University in Harrisonburg, Virginia. With her husband, Jason Alderfer, she raises Muscovy ducks, backyard chickens, and honeybees in Briery Branch, Virginia. With roots in Paoli, Indiana, she received degrees in Philosophy and Theology and Theater from Eastern Mennonite University and an MFA in creative writing from West Virginia University. She covenants with Shalom Mennonite Church in Harrisonburg and often attends Philippi (West Virginia) Mennonite Church in spirit.

Beachy's stories and essays appear in literary journals, including *Shenandoah, The Tusculum Review, Relief: a Quarterly Chrisitian Expression, Rhubarb,* and *Dreamseeker.* Her shortest fiction can be found in Norton's anthology of *Hint Fiction.* She is a contributing editor to *The Tusculum Review.* For more information on her current projects, reach her author website through www.martyrbook. com.